The Enterprise Engineering Series

Enterprise Engineering is an emerging discipline for coping with the challenges (agility, adaptability, etc.) and the opportunities (new markets, new technologies, etc.) faced by contemporary enterprises, including commercial, nonprofit and governmental institutions. It is based on the paradigm that such enterprises are purposefully designed systems, and thus they can be redesigned in a systematic and controlled way. Such enterprise engineering projects typically involve architecture, design, and implementation aspects.

The Enterprise Engineering series thus explores a design-oriented approach that combines the information systems sciences and organization sciences into a new field characterized by rigorous theories and effective practices. Books in this series should critically engage the enterprise engineering paradigm, by providing sound evidence that either underpins it or that challenges its current version. To this end, two branches are distinguished: Foundations, containing theoretical elaborations and their practical applications, and Explorations, covering various approaches and experiences in the field of enterprise engineering. With this unique combination of theory and practice, the books in this series are aimed at both academic students and advanced professionals.

Jan De Winter

Concise Guide to Enterprise Transformation

A Systemic Approach to Changing Social Systems

Springer

Jan De Winter
DWT Consulting bv
Pellenberg Belgium

ISSN 1867-8920 ISSN 1867-8939 (electronic)
The Enterprise Engineering Series
ISBN 978-3-032-29930-7 ISBN 978-3-032-29931-4 (eBook)
https://doi.org/10.1007/978-3-032-29931-4

This Springer imprint is published by the registered company Springer Nature Switzerland AG
The registered company address is: Gewerbestrasse 11, 6330 Cham, Switzerland

The road not taken

Two roads diverged in a yellow wood,
And sorry I could not travel both
And be one traveller, long I stood
And looked down one as far as I could
To where it was in the undergrowth;

Then took the other, as just as fair,
And having perhaps the better claim,
Because it was grassy and wanted wear;
Though as for that the passing there
Had worn them really about the same,

And both that morning equally lay
In leaves no step had trodden black.
Oh, I kept the first for another day!
Yet knowing how way leads on to way,
I doubted if I should ever come back.

I shall be telling this with a sigh
Somewhere ages and ages hence:
Two roads diverged in a wood, and I-
I took the one less travelled by,
And that has made all the difference.

Robert Frost,
(San Francisco - California, 26 March 1874 - Boston - Massachusetts, 29 January 1963)

Foreword

While transformation is an intimate, deeply personal journey, it is also a universal force that shapes organisations, systems, and ultimately our lives. Only few individuals embody the essence of transformation as profoundly as Jan De Winter, the author of *Concise Guide to Enterprise Transformation*. Like a craftsman refining a masterpiece over decades, Jan's career reflects a dedication to change – change that is sustainable, meaningful, and, above all, human-centred.

Born in Mechelen in 1963, Jan's journey began in the dynamic field of organisational psychology at KU Leuven, where he earned his Master's degree in 1988. His thesis under the supervision of late Professor Willy Lens laid the foundation for his lifelong interest in motivation and organisational behaviour. Yet Jan's career has never been a straightforward path – his professional story reflects the very principles of transformation he espouses. "Two roads diverged in a yellow wood," Robert Frost wrote – and Jan has consistently chosen the road less travelled, shaping the unique perspective that permeates this book.

Jan's early career was marked by a period of exploration and growth. Starting as an HR assistant at Bank Card Company, he immersed himself in the complex interplay of people, processes, and strategy. His tenure as HR Manager at Wolters Kluwer Belgium in the late 1990s was transformative, as he led critical initiatives such as the implementation of integrated HR systems and the digitalisation of knowledge dissemination – long before such transformations became commonplace.

A pivotal moment in Jan's career came when he encountered Appreciative Inquiry (AI) through Dr. Ronald Fry, whose influence profoundly shaped his approach to change. Dr. Fry's philosophy emphasising strengths, possibilities, and co-creation, soon became a cornerstone of his work. Whether guiding organisations through mergers or helping create networked collaborations like "Antwerp Against Poverty", Jan's application of AI has always been rooted in fostering mutual respect among those involved and shared vision among all stakeholders.

Equally transformative was his engagement with Enterprise Engineering methodologies during his studies at Antwerp Management School and subsequent professional certifications. He became a champion of integrating technical rigor with organisational creativity, particularly through modelling techniques like Design and Engineering Methodology for Organisations (DEMO). Jan recognised that true transformation lies in the symbiosis of structure and spirit – where technology serves people, not the other way around.

Over decades, Jan has worked with a diverse array of organisations – from digital transformation for the largest Belgian retailers to the nuanced challenges of centralising the Antwerp Local Police. Each project reflects his ability to harmonise technical expertise with human empathy. As he often says, “If it doesn’t work in the workplace, it doesn’t work”.

But Jan’s professional life has not been without its challenges. In 2023, his personal journey took an unexpected and arduous turn. A severe illness led to months of hospitalisation and a long rehabilitation journey. Yet, even during his most trying times, Jan’s commitment to transformation – both personal and professional – remained unwavering. It was during his recovery that the framework for *A Concise Guide to Enterprise Transformation* took shape. This book, a synthesis of decades of experience and introspection, is as much a testament to resilience as it is to expertise.

What makes Jan’s work extraordinary is that it is grounded in reality. He understands that transformation is not an abstract concept or a lofty ideal; instead, it is a lived experience. It is the manager grappling with a new system, the employee adjusting to a redefined role, and the team striving for shared goals despite differing perspectives. Transformation, via Jan’s methods, becomes a collaborative art – an enterprise of the heart as well as the mind.

This book is more than a guide to navigating change; it is an invitation to reimagine how we engage with the world. Through rich examples and practical frameworks, Jan empowers readers to see transformation not as an obstacle but as an opportunity. He challenges us to embrace complexity with curiosity, to approach obstacles with a spirit of co-creation, and to build systems that reflect our highest aspirations.

For those embarking on their own journeys of enterprise transformation, this book offers not only tools and insights but also a source of inspiration. It reflects Jan’s belief in the power of human potential, his respect for the intricacies of systems, and his unwavering optimism that positive change is always possible.

To know Jan De Winter is to understand that transformation is not just his work; it is his way of being. This book is his legacy – a gift to all who seek to make a difference in their organisations and in the lives of others. As you turn these pages, may you find the courage to take the road less travelled and discover the profound difference it can make.

Pellenberg, July 2026

Acknowledgements

This book is the outcome of a long intellectual journey shaped by dialogue, practice, and reflection. I am deeply indebted to several scholars whose work and personal guidance have influenced my thinking.

I would like to express my sincere gratitude to Jan Dietz, Jan Hoogervorst, and Hans Mulder for their foundational contributions to Enterprise Engineering and for the inspiration they have provided over the years. I am equally grateful to René Bouwen, Ronald Fry, David Cooperrider, and Gervase Bushe, whose work in Appreciative Inquiry and dialogical organisation development broadened my understanding of change as a generative, conversational process.

Much of the methodology presented here was refined through consulting practice. I am deeply grateful for the many consulting assignments that allowed me to develop, test, and refine the methodology presented in this book. Numerous clients entrusted me with complex transformation challenges at moments when parts of the approach were still emerging and not yet fully stabilised. Their openness and confidence provided the experiential foundation upon which this work rests.

In particular, I wish to thank the management team and collaborators of the National Geographic Institute of Belgium for their trust and their willingness to allow their transformation journey to be documented and reflected upon in this volume. My special appreciation goes to Wim Ploegaerts for co-executing the NGI case and for his sustained intellectual partnership.

My sincere thanks also go to Michelle Rodrigues for her careful reading, constructive corrections, and valuable suggestions that significantly improved the clarity and coherence of the manuscript.

My appreciation extends to Hans Hoegaerts for the illustrations that enrich the narrative, and to Dieter Proost for developing the demo modeller that enabled the visualisation of the conceptual models presented in this book.

On a personal note, I thank my sons, Hendrik and Thomas, for their patience and encouragement throughout this process.

I am deeply grateful to the medical professionals who cared for me during a period of severe illness, and in particular to Wim Laleman, whose expertise, dedication, and perseverance were decisive in my recovery.

Finally, and above all, I thank my wife, Ann. Her unwavering support, her strength during difficult times, and her determination when circumstances seemed uncertain have sustained me far beyond the writing of this book. She encouraged the doctors to continue seeking solutions when it mattered most, and she allowed me the time and space to pursue this intellectual endeavour with focus and discipline. This book would not exist without her.

If this book emphasises that enterprises are social systems sustained by relationships, dialogue, and mutual support, it is because my own life and work have been shaped in precisely that way.

Table of Contents

Abbreviations

Remark of the author.
This book is more about Appreciative Inquiry than it is about Artificial Intelligence.
'AI' will be used as the abbreviation of Appreciative Inquiry.
Artificial Intelligence will not be abbreviated in this book.

ADKAR	Awareness, Desire, Knowledge, Ability, Reinforcement
AI	Appreciative Inquiry
AOC	Area of Concern
API	Application Programming Interface
BAFO	Best And Final Offer
BANI	Brittle, Anxious, Non-linear, Incomprehensible
BIA	Business Impact Analysis
BPR	Business Process Reengineering
CI/CD	Continuous Integration/Continuous Deployment
CM	Construction Model (DEMO)
DATD	Detailed Actor Transaction Diagram (DEMO)
DEMO	Design and Engineering Methodology for Organizations
DOD	Dialogical Organisational Development
EE	Enterprise Engineering
GATD	Global Actor Transaction Diagram
GIS	Geographic Information System
GPS	Global Positioning System
ITGI	Inventaire TopoGéographique/TopoGeografische Inventaris
NGI	National Geographic Institute
NS	Normalized Systems
NSX	Normalized Systems Institute
OD	Organisational Development
PID	Project Initiation Document
PMBOK	Project Management Body of Knowledge
PMI	Project Management Institute
PMO	Project Management Office
POC	Proof of Concept
PRC	Payroll Consultant
PRINCE2	Project in Controlled Environments (version 2)
RACI	Responsible, Accountable, Consulted, Informed
RFI	Request for Information
RFP	Request for Proposal

ROI	Return on Investment
SSE	Social Secretary for Enterprises
STARS	Situation, Task, Approach, Result, Success
SWOT	Strength, Weaknesses, Opportunities, Threats
VUCA	Volatility, Uncertainty, Complexity, Ambiguity

Illustrations

Chapter I: Understanding Social Systems

Imagine walking into a bustling factory, where machines hum, workers collaborate, and products roll off the assembly line with clockwork precision. Now imagine the same factory as a living organism - a one that grows, transforms, and adapts seamlessly to meet the ever-changing demands of its environment. This metaphor helps illuminate the essence of systems theory – how complex entities operate, evolve, and ultimately flourish.

A quick glance at Wikipedia (2025) reveals a dizzying array of variations of 'systems theory', each tailored to a different scientific discipline. Yet, in this book, we will focus on two key definitions most relevant to understanding enterprise transformation: one rooted in Enterprise Engineering (EE) and the other in Organisational Development (OD). Together, these perspectives provide the tools to reimagine enterprises not as static constructs, but rather as dynamic systems built to achieve specific purposes, capable of transformation.

Let us begin with a foundational idea: an enterprise is a system. It is deliberately designed to achieve a purpose, whether that's delivering goods, providing services, or creating value for stakeholders. Every decision – from how it interacts with suppliers to how it delivers to customers – shapes its function and structure. However, unlike purely technical systems, enterprises rely on people, and where there are people, complexity follows. This social dimension adds layers of nuance, making enterprises what we might call social systems.

In the chapters ahead, we will delve deeper into the fundamental concepts of systems theory and social systems. But first, let us establish a shared understanding of what makes a system function.

Systems Theory

To transform enterprises effectively, we need to understand the anatomy of systems. Think of it as learning the rules of the game before stepping onto the field. We will start with the definition of a system stemming from a structural-functionalist point of view:

- **Composition:** The parts that make up the system.
- **Environment:** The surroundings of the system and its interactions with other actors in these surroundings.
- **Structure:** The way the parts work together within the system and interact with elements in the environment.
- **Production:** The goods and services provided by the system to the environment.

J. De Winter, *Concise Guide to Enterprise Transformation*,
The Enterprise Engineering Series, https://doi.org/10.1007/978-3-032-29931-4_1

Figure 1. A social system embedded in its environment

Consider a confectionery company that decides to offer personalised T-shirts as an example. The system's composition includes printing machines, design software, logistics for delivery, and employees. Its environment involves customers uploading designs and suppliers handling and shipping the goods. The structure consists of intricate interactions between the employees, printing and plotting machines, design software, and the website. Finally, the production goal is to deliver high-quality personalised T-shirts.

In the field of EE, an enterprise is regarded as a goal-oriented, deliberately designed social system, which implies that any enterprise transformation requires a degree of redesign or re-engineering. In the following paragraphs, we provide a summary of the implications of this philosophical foundation.

While there are several definitions of a 'system', the most relevant for this book aligns with systems engineering. According to Hitchins (2009), engineered systems are combinations of technology and people created to achieve goals valuable to stakeholders. Central to this definition is the system's goal-orientated nature which is also true of enterprises.

Difficulties defining living and/or social systems

The above definition of engineered systems stems from a structural-functionalist view of a system. Structural functionalism sees society as a complex, stable whole of interdependent parts that work together to ensure order, balance and stability. This view of society has been dominant in our society since the 16th century. When applied to an enterprise, we also refer to this as the mechanistic viewpoint. Because this view of society has been dominant in our thinking for so long, we will also find traces of this view in books, education and certainly also in companies. In this book, we will refer to a viewpoint other than the mechanistic one. This is necessary in order to be able to explain other developments within companies. After all, there are other options than a top-down approach.

In the light of what we want to achieve in this book – defining a systemic approach to develop and improve social systems – it is of prime importance to formulate a definition that incorporates more aspects of a system than the definition based on the mechanistic viewpoint.
First, we think about the social aspects of an enterprise. The human actor plays a pivotal role in the creation, evolution and management of an enterprise. When we talk about humans in an organisation, it is important to also consider aspects related to society.

A second aspect that is important in defining a system is the capacity for emergent change. We believe that an enterprise does not evolve only through top-down decisions, but it also dynamically changes as insights emerge from within the system.

A third aspect that is important is strongly related to the concept of emerging change. It is about what is called a living system. A living system develops continuously, often through iterations, in response to changes in its environment. These changes emerge from the interaction of internal elements of the system with this environment. It is a specific form of what we see as emergence from within the system.

As mentioned by Philippe Bailleur in his blog on the link between Lean and Living Systems (2021), "*If experimentation, learning and mutation can unfold on a large and small scale, you end up with an organisation that grows with the changes in the market and society, naturally, from within*".

This perspective on enterprises as living, emergent systems is also reflected in more formal theoretical work on enterprise governance and engineering. In his book 'Foundations of Enterprise Governance and Enterprise Engineering', Jan Hoogervorst (2017) conducted an extensive study of the philosophical foundations of enterprise governance and enterprise engineering. He argues that these foundations have several important implications that we need to consider.

(1) Theories and concepts define reality

Interpreting and understanding social and business phenomena cannot be achieved without using concepts and theories that give meaning to these phenomena. The language we have at our disposal determines the space in which interpretation can take place. In this sense, the ontological model of a company is by definition, relative. This corresponds to findings from practice, which clearly show that an ontological model can only be as accurate as the knowledge – and the language that allows this knowledge to be expressed – available to those involved in the modelling process.

(2) Mechanistic view of companies: the belief in social determinism

Social determinism is based on the idea that humans can shape social phenomena based on causal relationships between directives, activities, and the resulting outcomes. In the business world, this specifically refers to a causal-deterministic relationship between planning, control, and business results. The extent to which strategic planning and other activities lead to predictable results is important. We are not claiming that there is no connection between planned activities and business results, but rather that there is no deterministic causal link between the two.

(3) Mechanistic view of companies: ignoring social interaction

Social determinism and the resulting mechanisation of companies leads to employees being viewed as instruments in the workings of a company that is seen as a machine. This idea ignores the reality that employees are first and foremost social actors in the relational dynamics of a company. Employees interpret reality within the company and give value to it by perceiving it through their individual mental lens. We will discuss this in Chapter IV where we talk about the individual and shared mental models that exist in a company.

(4) Moral considerations are unavoidable

The mechanistic view of companies highlights only one aspect of it, namely its profitability and the value it creates for its stakeholders. Abandoning this mechanistic view rightly opens the door to considering other ethical aspects of entrepreneurship.

(5) Truth and knowledge: the importance of coherence and harmony

When do employees experience characteristics of their company as genuine or true? When they see and feel coherence and harmony on the different moments they are in contact with their company. A characteristic of the company is perceived as 'real' if, for example, the behaviour of managers is consistent with company's published values. If the coherence and harmony are not perceived as 'real', this has a negative impact on employee well-being and ultimately on the company's performance.

(6) Truth and knowledge: implications in the context of change

In the search for solutions to meet strategic expectations, there is a pragmatic question of 'what works'. Given the social dimension of the company, this search is typically a process of social interaction, and the answer to the question 'what works' is formed by consensus among the employees involved. We will discuss this consensus when we talk about shared mental models.

(7) Interdependencies between employees, context and language

In the process of defining and redefining the characteristics of the company – including during design or redesign – it is important to be aware of these interdependencies.

Employees help to create the context of the company, but at the same time they are influenced by that context.

The same can be said about the language of the company. Employees can describe aspects of the company because they have a shared language at their disposal. At the same time, employees will help develop the language that is specific to the company. It is in this circular relationship – which is not recognised in the mechanistic view of entrepreneurship – that the success of the company is often determined.

(8) Lack of a common language for function and construction

There is no common foundation and no shared language for the functional perspective and the structural perspective of a company. Since this foundation is lacking, it is also impossible to make a formal, mathematical translation from the function to the structure of a system. In the context of enterprise engineering, this means that no straightforward relationship can be established between a single functional property of the system and a single structural property. It is also important to note that a functional property is not a property of the system itself, but rather of the relationship between a user and the system. A structural property, on the other hand, is a property of the system.

(9) Postmodernist doubt: recognising heterogeneity and diversity

Applying postmodernist ideas leads to pronounced doubt in many areas. In particular, it questions whether universal rationality exists, whether there is such a thing as universal human nature, and whether universal truth exists at all. The existence of well-functioning systems such as education, healthcare, and others is counterexamples to this fundamental doubt.

A key point in the context of this book is the knowledge that emerging forms of organisation are important and that there is a limit to the malleability of social reality. Within companies, it is also important to realise that heterogeneity and diverse lived realities are an unavoidable aspect of entrepreneurship.

(10) The mental glasses of language

Language exerts multiple influence on all processes that take place in a social context, including entrepreneurship. On the one hand, language within a single social context is the mechanism we use to describe that social context. At the same time, we must recognise that language creates the social context. Due to the dominant position of social determinism, our language in the field of entrepreneurship is also influenced...and our mental lenses are often limited. If we only know the word ‘hammer’, everything we encounter is a ‘nail’.

The above remarks, all based on the work of Jan Hoogervorst, are of crucial importance in light of the definition of a system, especially when we talk about a social system like an enterprise. Since this book is specifically meant to deal with enterprise transformation, we are not aiming for a generic system definition that would apply to all systems. Therefore, we will only provide a basic definition and add some remarks and concepts that are specifically relevant in the context of social systems like enterprises.

Using the definition of Jan Hoogervorst (2012, p. 12):

"*Essentially, a (real) system is viewed as a unified whole of elements that operates in an integrated manner pertinent to a certain goal. Unity and integration are core concepts within the system approach. Conversely, the system approach is considered essential for achieving unity and integration adequately.*"

In order to specify this definition further, we will add some concepts and remarks based on the work of Jan Hoogervorst (2009, 2012).

The first remark is about the necessity of a holistic focus in our system analysis. It needs to be focused on the whole, because in the understanding of the meaning of the whole we can find the necessary knowledge for understanding the meaning of the parts. This is clearly an anti-reductionist viewpoint. One of the characteristics of a systemic analysis is that it is holistic.

The second remark is related to the way the system interacts with the environment. In our case, dealing with enterprises, it is quite obvious that a closed or isolated enterprise would not make sense. It is in the interaction with its environment (suppliers, clients, governments, etc.) that an enterprise can deliver added value to its shareholders. Even in the most isolated monastery there exists interaction with the outside world. Hence, we regard the enterprise as an open system that interacts with the environment in order to be capable of delivering added value.

The third remark is related to limitations in approaches used for studying open systems. Both the mechanistic approach – seeing an enterprise as a machine – and the organismic approach – seeing an enterprise as a biological living being – have their limitations. Most of the limitations of the mechanistic approach have been explained above. Regarding the organismic approach, three limitations are important: (1) it implies that change is solely reactive to the environment; (2) the stimuli to act are reduced to system needs; and (3) the system is considered stable and unchanging.

The social systems theory views individuals and their behaviours as part of larger interconnected systems, such as families, communities, enterprises and societies. It emphasises that these systems are not just aggregates of individuals but are complex, dynamic wholes where the parts influence each other and the whole.

It remains a difficult task to fall back on a generic or generally accepted definition of a system, especially when studying complex systems like enterprises. The social systems theory should be the one closest to our object of study. Still, it remains important to realise that system models are often about the system structure (system elements and their relationships), the subsystems, and so on. Given the inherent nature of system thinking, the social system theory is committed to a positivist orientation and a highly objectivist view of the social world. Again, this is similar to the structural functionalist perspective (Hoogervorst, 2009).

We have had many discussions during the elaboration of this book, what we would use as subtitle. Two options remained possible: (1) A holistic approach to changing living systems and (2) A systemic approach to changing social systems. The most important reasons to choose for social over living systems are the following:

- The difficulties with the definition of the concept 'living system'. Living systems theory is a general theory that applies to all living systems, from cells to ecosystems and organisations.
- Social systems theory focuses specifically on social phenomena such as human behaviour, social interactions, and societal structures. It analyses how these elements form interconnected systems and how they influence each other.
- Our approach is strongly based on relationships between humans.
- Our scope of interest is enterprises in their environment.

Why we chose for 'systemic' over 'holistic' will be explained later in this chapter.

Two key perspectives of systems

When analysing a system, two perspectives are particularly useful:

1. **The functional perspective:** This focuses on what the system does – its production and the interactions with the environment. Think of it as a black box: attention is focused on inputs and outputs rather than on the internal processes.

2. **The constructional perspective:** Here, we explore the inner workings of the system – specifically, how components interact and which structures support which functions. This perspective is crucial for understanding how changes in one part might ripple through the entire system.

For our confectionery company example, the functional goal might be to enable customers to personalise T-shirts with ease. The constructional goal, however, might involve automating the design upload process to reduce manual intervention. Both perspectives are essential for effective redesign of the system.

If one wants to change a system, it is crucial to recognise, define, and thoroughly examine both perspectives. Not everyone looks at a system in the same way. Technically skilled people, such as engineers, technicians, and software developers, pay more attention to the way a system is constructed and how it works. Managers, on the other hand are mainly interested in the inputs and outputs of the system. They look more at overall system performance and throughput. This difference in perspective is the main reason why communication between managers and technically skilled employees can sometimes be challenging.

During design processes, the enterprise engineer will assess both functional and constructional requirements related to the new or revised objectives we want to achieve with the artefact. In addition to the requirements, the areas of concern regarding the system must also be addressed during design.

The Systems Engineering process: From vision to realisation.

In their book 'Grondslagen van de engineering' (Foundations of Engineering), Mannaert and Peremans, both professors at the University of Antwerp, Belgium, discuss the methodology for design (Mannaerts & Peremans, 2020). First and foremost, they make an important distinction between three categories of sciences:

- formal sciences, such as mathematics
- explanatory sciences, such as social sciences
- design sciences, such as medical sciences

Another author that makes the above distinction is van Aken (2013). In his view, an important task of the design sciences is gathering knowledge and realisation of artefacts. The realisation of these artefacts is not a purpose on itself but a step in a process to create new constructions and, not unimportantly, solving existing problems with constructions. Engineers, says Van Aken, are not so interested in knowledge to understand something, but rather to be able to create something. As the book progresses, it will become clear that this is our ambition as well.

How does one go from understanding a system to transforming it? Welcome to the systems engineering process, a proven framework that unfolds in four phases:

- **Concept definition:** Identify the mission and the needs of stakeholders. What are the goals, functional as well as constructional ones?
- **System definition:** Establish requirements, create logical and physical designs and analyse whether the system will meet the objectives.
- **System realisation:** Building and implementing the system.
- **Deployment and use of the system:** Testing, refining, and launching the system in the real world.

The simplicity of the four phases above might lead one to conclude that designing systems is a linear process. This is absolutely incorrect. Designing requires an iterative approach. In each iteration it is important to assess the performance of the new system against the concept or system definition where the objectives were defined. In the design process of systems, we establish a relationship between functional and constructional characteristics. A particular function of a system is made possible by one or more constructions. In the same way, one construction can be the solution for more than one functional characteristic.

Let us take a bicycle as an example. An important function of a bicycle is that it allows us to ride at a certain speed given a certain amount of effort. Between 1880 and 1890, the first bicycles were designed with pedals in the middle and a chain that drove the rear wheel. These bicycles had a constant speed-to-effort ratio. You could make a bicycle with a higher or lower constant by using different sprockets, but you could not change this ratio on a single bicycle.

At a certain point, the need arose to be able to ride the same bicycle faster or slower while the pace of pedalling remained the same. The designer of this innovation was familiar with the fact that the size of the sprockets on the bottom bracket and on the rear wheel axle determined the ratio. But how can he solve the problem of being able to use more than one sprocket on one or both axles?

Here you see two phases or steps in the design, the first is an innovative step and the second is a broadening step in which we reuse, deepen and broaden the innovation. To stick with the example of the bicycle. The innovative step is the transition from one sprocket on the rear axle to two sprockets. The construction devised for this was a metal glider that guides the chain and can change from the first to the second sprocket. In the broadening step, the idea was further developed with more sprockets having a greater variety of numbers of teeth, with electrically guided switching. This pattern of moments of breakthrough followed by generalising the new idea is also present in the activity of designing. It is one of the reasons why designing is not a linear process.

Coming back to the engineering process itself, we will focus mainly on the first two phases, where the transformation begins. In concept definition, we map out the enterprise's purpose and the needs of its stakeholders. For example, does our confectionery company's T-shirt initiative meet customer demand? In system definition, we turn these needs into actionable designs by starting with logical models that outline functionality, followed by physical designs that assign specific technologies and roles. The logical model of the target system helps to reduce complexity and keep the engineering process intellectually manageable. It includes logical architecture design, which defines the functionality and behaviour of the future system. Following this, the physical architecture design allocates specific physical elements to the logical structure. The final stage of the system definition phase is the system analysis, where engineers verify that all system requirements are fulfilled.

This process doesn't stop at a first design. As we already explained, iteration is key. Just like a sculptor refines their work with each pass, engineers go through cycles of analysis and adjustment until the target system's requirements are fully met.

The following three activities from generic systems engineering can enhance the preparation of transformation projects:

- the application of conceptual modelling,
- the use of architectural frameworks,
- the iterative process inherent in design and engineering.

Further in this book we will explain how these characteristics are put into practise within transformation projects.

Why it matters: design and governance

Great systems don't happen by accident. A well-designed system is easier to understand, manage, and adapt. Whether you're building a system from scratch or modifying an existing one, an effective design influences the outcome(s) and ultimately determines the success or failure of the change.

But design alone isn't enough. Governance – the way a system is controlled and aligned with its purpose – is just as critical. In technical systems, governance might be as simple as a switch on a lamp. In enterprises, it's far more complex. How do you ensure employees act in ways that support the system's goals? Training, policies, and accountability mechanisms (e.g., incentives, clear communication, effective leadership, etc.) become your tools for guiding employee behaviour.

In the confectionery example, governance might involve user-friendly software to guide customers through the design process, as well as clear protocols for handling complaints. Without such measures, even the best-designed system can falter.

Terminology agreements in the enterprise engineering domain

Before diving into the characteristics of social systems, let's align on the vocabulary. Clear definitions help avoid confusion, especially when terms can carry different meanings across fields. Think of this as setting the stage for a shared understanding – a crucial step for meaningful exploration.

- **Enterprise**: For our purposes, an 'enterprise' is any unified entity functioning as a system where people collaborate toward a shared objective. This might be a government institution, non-profit organisation, business, or even a hobby group. When we say 'enterprise', we are referring to the whole entity. To emphasise the social aspect of the enterprise we use the image of a human being to represent the enterprise.

Figure 2. Human shell: interface between system and environment

- **Organisation**: This refers specifically to the enterprise's organisational aspect, i.e. its organisational design. This includes structure, processes, policies, and procedures, as we know them from the structural-functionalist approach. Very important aspects to add are employee behaviour, management behaviour, organisational culture, and other social aspects of the enterprise. When we mention 'organisation', think of it as the skeleton, the nervous system of the enterprise.

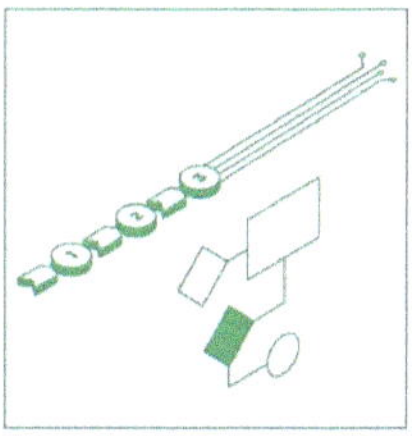

Figure 3. Inside the system: the organisation

- **Information**: Here, 'information' covers the informational design domain, i.e., all the data managed within the enterprise. Note that information technology systems fall under 'infrastructure' rather than 'information'.

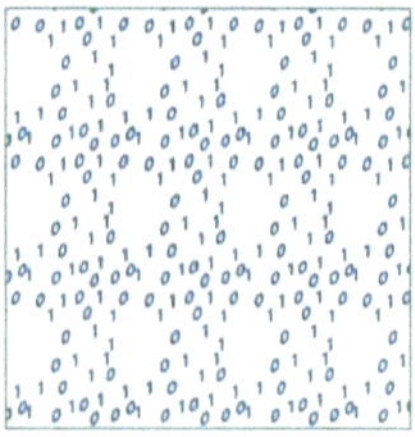

Figure 4. Inside the system: the information

- **Infrastructure**: 'Infrastructure' encompasses all technical resources essential for achieving the enterprise's goals. This might mean information technology systems, office facilities, or in specific cases like a dredging company, specialised equipment like vessels.

Figure 5. Inside the system: the infrastructure

Figure 6 illustrates how these domains interconnect. Enterprises interact with the world by procuring supplies, delivering services, and navigating relationships with entities like government bodies or banks. These interactions contribute to the function of the enterprise.

Internally, the enterprise's structure across information, organisation, and infrastructure supports its purpose. In other words, these constructs facilitate the functioning of the enterprise. When change is on the horizon – say, launching a new service – adjustments across these domains become necessary to ensure alignment.

Consequently, when initiating changes in the enterprise, it is essential to assess necessary modifications across each domain in advance. By ensuring alignment across these domains, we can maximise the likelihood of successful change implementation.

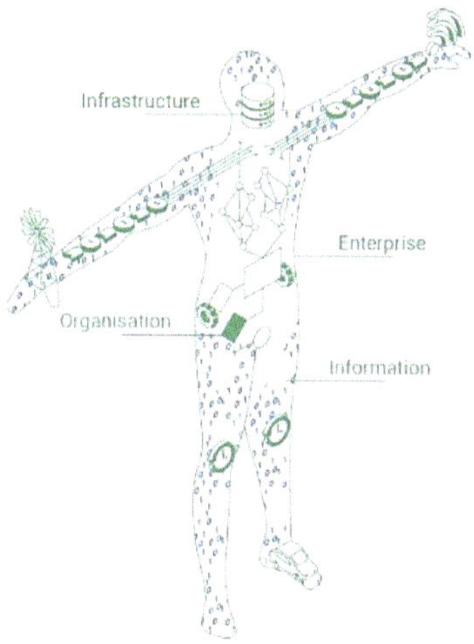

Figure 6. The enterprise as a whole: a social system

The organisation, information, and infrastructure are the constructional design domains of the enterprise.

How we Look at Enterprises

Over the last 20 years, we have increasingly started to view organisations from different perspectives. Some authors use metaphors and colours to make typical aspects of organisations more clear. Other authors look into organisations with a specific focus, like for instance the notion of power. Still other authors will describe how organisations are changing because of recent changes in society. All of these different views on organisations make clear that organisations are complex and that the human factor is at the same time cause and effect.

Authors such as Gareth Morgan and Frederic Laloux describe different types of organisations using images we are familiar with from everyday life. These images offer a perspective to better understand organisations despite their complexity.

In his book Images of Organisation, Morgan (2006) describes eight types of organisations by using metaphors. For each metaphor, he describes the dominant form in which such an organisation guides its employees and also how this effects employees:

- The **machine metaphor** sees organisations as highly structured hierarchical structures with a strong separation of labour. Employees in these organisations have clearly delineated roles.
- The **organism metaphor** sees organisations as living entities that can and must adapt to the environment in order to survive. Employees in these organisations are encouraged to be creative and flexible and have less delineated roles.

- The **brain metaphor** sees organisations as complex systems that rely heavily on the collective wisdom and intelligence of their employees. The latter are therefore strongly encouraged to share their ideas and perspectives with other employees.
- The **culture metaphor** sees organisations as groups of individuals who share a set of common values and beliefs. Employees in these organisations are expected to conform to the beliefs of the group they are in.
- The **political metaphor** sees an organisation as an arena in which different groups compete for power and influence over the organisation. Employees in these organisations have to unite in alliances and coalitions.
- The **psychic prison metaphor** sees an organisation as a place where myths and stories limit people's thoughts, ideas, and actions. Employees in these organisations allow themselves to be influenced by the stories they believe in.
- The **metaphor of domination** sees the organisation as an instrument of domination, as a means of imposing one's will on others and exploiting resources for personal gain. Employees in this organisation endure the domination of others unless they themselves belong to the dominant group.
- The **flux and transformation metaphor** sees an organisation as a constantly changing system that is inextricably linked to its environment. Change is a natural part of the organisation. Employees in this organisation are encouraged to embrace new ideas and new perspectives.

Understanding the different metaphors that underpin organisational structures can help in understanding behaviour and recognising strengths and weaknesses within different organisations.

Laloux (2014) uses colours rather than metaphors to distinguish the different types of organisations. He works with five different types while drawing inspiration from natural evolution.

- The **red organisation** organises itself according to the principle of the strongest, as in the harem structure of a group of gorillas with the silverback as leader.
- The **amber organisation** organises itself around the principle of rules, laws, and principles that are not up for debate, like monks in a monastery who have chosen the rules of the order.
- The **orange organisation** organises itself based on scientific management and division of labour. This type corresponds to the organisation as a machine from Morgan (2006).
- The **green organisation** organises on the principle of a family and bases itself on the search for harmony and empowerment. Achieving consensus is key here.
- The **green-blue organisation or teal organisation** attaches great importance to meaningfulness and making a social contribution. It organises itself along the

lines of a living system that is much more adaptable than the other organisational types. This type of organisation corresponds to the Flux and Transformation type from Morgan (2006).

Because change is often also related to power, it is important to also consider a completely different approach to looking at organisations and organisational change. Guido Maes, professor of 'organisational design' at the Catholic University of Leuven, Belgium, discusses this approach in his book 'Verborgen krachten in de organisatie' (Hidden forces in the organisation) (Maes, 2014).

His research starts from the observation that many changes fail. But the hypothesis he formulates is particular, namely that politics provide a better explanation for the failure or success of changes. There are few studies that make a clear connection between organisational change and politics. One of the interesting aspects of the book of Maes is that it does not shy away from the challenge of addressing organisational politics.

Guido Maes (2014) finds the solution to the complexity issue in systems theory, in which change itself is seen as a complex system. He describes various discourses and how they relate to organisational change and organisational politics.

In our book, we will not discuss the dimension of power and politics in organisational change. Not that we doubt their existence; on the contrary. If the people in the organisation who have a lot of power are not prepared to involve employees and middle management in the change, then the approach we propose is bound to fail from the start. However, because also people with power benefit from successful change, we are convinced that the approach proposed in this book can be successful.

In his book, Dancing with Change and Fluidity, Hans Schönfeld (2025) describes the concept of fluidity by giving examples at multiple levels. At the macro level, he sees examples such as the disappearance of cultural identity and industrial boundaries. These forms arise partly due to the influence of the internet and social media. At the meso level, he explains how organisations and institutions struggle with their identity. Finally, at the micro level, he points out how individual roles, identities and behaviour change.

He identifies three characteristics that mark examples of fluidity. The first is a clear blurring of boundaries or merging of objects, phenomena and concepts. The second is technology, which acts as a catalyst and enables change. The third is that fluidity leads to debate, escalating conflicts and – usually fruitless – attempts by the government to introduce regulations.

It is an interesting way to identify the causes of the changes that many of our organisations are struggling with. It also makes it very clear that this is an evolution that will not stop immediately and will certainly not be reversed. The fact that the examples of fluidity cause debate and conflict also indicate that many people and organisations are struggling with the increasingly rapid and far-reaching changes. They resist these new situations, which leads to heated debates. But it is wrong to think that this will stop the evolution.

In his book, Hans Schönfeld (2025) describes eight powers that can help organisations strengthen their capacity to adapt. We list them here to give the reader an idea of the direction they are taking:

- The power to recognise context and see multiple future alternatives.
- The power of digital fitness and cobots (collaborative robots).
- The power of creative innovation.
- The power of ambidexterity (exploring unpredictability and logic together).
- The power of quick decision-making.
- The power of an ecosystem.
- The power of continuous improvement.
- The power of rapid realisation.

The book describes an evolution that we also recognise in the field. As organisations, we need to be able to make decisions more quickly, even if we did not have the opportunity to fully assess the consequences of our decision. It becomes a trade-off between deciding with limited knowledge or not deciding, whereby not deciding is not really an option.

While some organisations are becoming fluid, we are also confronted with the opposite type of organisations, still shaped and developed from a mechanistic perspective. Therefore, in the following section we will discuss the origins and characteristics of mechanistic thinking in organisations in more detail.

We will also zoom in on the organisational forms that lean towards the teal or flux and transformation type. This is because this organisational metaphor fits much better with the systemic approach we have already discussed.

The Newtonian heritage: the machine-like enterprise

Even today, we feel the influence of Isaac Newton's worldview in our enterprises. He saw the world as a great mechanical timepiece, consisting of a set of separate parts, and ticking like a perfect machine. Guarded by the laws of physics, all the clockwork's properties and results were predictable.

Still too many managers rule over their segregated functional departments and plan for predictable results. They still look for further optimisation of the machine to achieve even higher efficiency.

In this view, the main responsibility of management is to design and program the machine while the role of employees is to deliver their efforts according to the machine's operation.

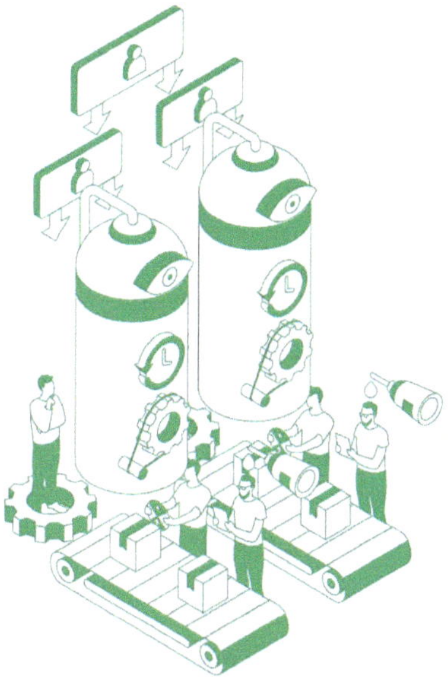

Figure 7. The machine-like enterprise

The above view emerged in the 20th century during the second industrial revolution. During that period of tremendous growth, there was a significant demand for higher production in the still relatively young factories. Frederick Winslow Taylor, an engineer in a metal factory in the United States, achieved very large increases in production with relatively small interventions in the way things were done. Probably without realising it himself, he was at the origin of a huge wave of organisational changes that can still be felt today. With this, Taylorism was born.

Taylor argued that in order to reduce process time:

- production methods should be adopted based on science
    - this way it became easier to dictate and prioritise activities in the production cycle
    - the scientific method is used by the manager to determine the best way of organising
- tasks should be separated according to the skills of workers
    - an analysis must be conducted to determine which employees are best suited to perform a specific job
    - training must be planned to ensure maximum efficiency is achieved
- work performance needs to be monitored

    - to evaluate the efficiency of employees
    - to guide employees whenever necessary
    - to ensure productivity
- a separation of functions between managers and workers is needed
    - managers should oversee planning and training
    - workers need to implement what they have been trained to perform

The above principles were perfectly defensible in the time frame and type of organisation in which Taylor worked. Afterwards these principles were used as examples and applied in work environments where they were much less appropriate, if at all.

When looking at an enterprise that is led based on a mechanistic view on management one will find the following characteristics:

- The organisational structure allows direction only from a central point, resulting in a one-directional control.
- The information in the organisation is available exclusively to management and decision-takers.
- Leadership is expertise-driven and control-focused, with little attention to informal dynamics or relational networks.
- Assumes organisational practices can be simply added together (A + B + C...), overlooking interdependencies.
- Leans on strict rules and procedures, leading to rigidity and a control-oriented culture.

Organisational change approach from a mechanistic view on enterprises

When we talk about organisational change, it seems impossible not to talk about John Kotter (2012), professor at Harvard Business School, Boston, United States, and a worldwide authority in change management. His well-known book, Leading Change, had its first edition in 1995 and a new edition in 2012. In between those two dates the ideas about social constructionism and social systems were already developed in full. Still the new edition does not elaborate on these new insights. The principles on which Kotter bases his approach stem mainly from a mechanistic view of organising.

According to Kotter (2012), leading change consists of eight steps. These eight steps will show that Kotter focused mainly on centrally driven organisations in which power and control is an important management mechanism.

1. **Create urgency**
   The first step he named 'create urgency'. With this he referred to the point that change will run much more easily when most of the management and employees want the change. Kotter meant that this step required an open and honest

dialogue between the stakeholders about why the change should happen. This allows the sense of urgency to grow in the organisation.
Some have named this step as 'create a burning platform'. Choosing this metaphor can lead to deliberate communication that presents the situation as much more serious than it actually is. This leans towards a form of manipulation of those involved in the change. Hence, the use of this metaphor is rather perceived as counterproductive.

2. **Form a powerful coalition**
   Convince employees and management that the change is necessary. Achieving this requires strong leadership combined with the support of key people in the organisation, like directors, engineers, founders. To lead the change, it is necessary to form a coalition, a strong team with influential people. This coalition helps create a high sense of urgency and use the momentum for the change.

3. **Create a vision for change**
   A clear vision will help employees and management understand why this change needs to happen. It is therefore important to integrate emerging ideas into a coherent vision for the whole organisation at an early stage. When people can relate the demand for change to a vision of the future, they are more likely to engage with the process.

4. **Communicate the vision**
   In an organisation, there are new messages at all times. For one's vision to rise above them, the message of change and the underlying vision must be communicated often and powerfully. While this can be achieved primarily by talking about it at every available opportunity, one can also use the vision as a rationale for active decision-making and problem-solving.

5. **Remove obstacles**
   Check that the people helping to articulate the vision or shaping the change are not hampered by any barriers. If yes, help them remove those barriers by adjusting processes and changing structures so that the first examples of the change are not hindered. In this way, the first-movers will be more motivated to continue the effort and make the change more likely to succeed.

6. **Create short-term wins**
   There is nothing more motivating than success. Let the organisation get a taste for progress, preferably as early as possible in the change process. This is why it is important to define a number of 'quick wins' and make them happen. Once these have been achieved, it is important to include them in the change

communication as well. Every positive example helps to motivate the whole organisation.

7. **Build on the change**
   Real change runs deep. Do not celebrate the success too early, but build further change on the foundations of the initial victories. This requires continuously developing the improvements needed to make the transformation permanent.

8. **Anchor the changes in corporate culture**
   Ultimately, any change must integrate into the day-to-day functioning and be embedded in the core of the organisation. Only then is change assured. At that point, there is no longer any need to talk about the change, but rather about the new normal. Even then, it remains important to pay due attention to the new way of working.

As we mentioned earlier, Kotter's approach to organisational change is a global success. Most likely, one of the main reasons is the simplicity of the eight-step plan.

The post-modernistic heritage: see the relations in social systems

Between 1985 and 2010, the influence of post-modernist thinking began to make itself increasingly felt in the social sciences and in the practices of organisational development and change.

A characteristic of postmodernism is the radical ontological and epistemological scepticism toward, first, the concept of truth as asserted by self-legitimising systems, and second, the notion of 'romantic' authenticity.

The deep distrust in the great ordering principles like religion, politics, science and art, has the effect of questioning the existing beliefs in the human sciences. As a result, new beliefs are formulated in numerous practices including most social and human sciences.

One of the most important changes in the field of social and human sciences is the development of social constructionism. This philosophical movement focuses on human meaning and significance. It emphasises the importance of coming to a shared perception together without eroding a person's uniqueness. In doing so, it uses some central presuppositions such as:

- Objective reality is elusive to individuals, and to the extent that it exists, it is socially constructed.
- Knowledge is historical, socio-culturally specific, and determined by context.
- Knowledge arises from interpersonal communication processes.

Kenneth J. Gergen, Professor in Psychology and the President of the Taos Institute (Dallas, USA), is internationally known for his contributions to social constructionist theory. He influenced thinking in domains like technological and cultural change, innovative views on aging, on education, and on relational theory and practices. From Gergen's perspective, all human intelligibility (including claims to knowledge) is generated within relationships. It is from relationships that humans derive their conceptions of what is real, rational, and good (Gergen, 1994). From this perspective, scientific theories, like all other claims about reality, should not be assessed in terms of truth, but in terms of pragmatic outcomes. Such assessments are inevitably wedded to values, and thus all science is morally and politically weighted in implication. As he saw it, this same form of assessment also applies to social constructionist theory. The question is not its accuracy, but its potential for humankind.

The impact of the social constructionist claims on the field of organisational development is very important. It invites us to question the classical silo-like structures of organisations and to look for other more flexible, flatter, people-friendly structures. It invites us to question the classical top-down approach in leadership and to look for a more egalitarian approach. It suggests rethinking business processes from a more holistic point of view.

It is therefore, in this zeitgeist, that the space arises to start looking at organisations with different metaphors, like 'flux & transformation like systems' or 'living systems,' or with new colours like the 'teal organisation.'

Philippe Bailleur, founder of Living Systems Coaching and author of several books in the domain of organisational development and coaching, describes the characteristics of a living system as follows (Bailleur, 2021):

- Organisational design enables direction from the most suitable sources, allowing for bi-directional flow.
- Information is shared widely, supporting self-regulation.
- Leadership acknowledges both the visible (upstream) and invisible (underlying) dynamics, fostering relational connections.
- Recognises that practices multiply (A x B x C...) in impact, understanding that misalignment can neutralise benefits.
- Encourages continuous adaptability within guiding principles, with mobility as a core value.

How to Deal with the Complexity of Social Systems

Enterprises don't operate in isolation. They're dynamic, adaptive systems, constantly interacting with unpredictable environments. The complexity of a system reflects the difficulty in predicting its behaviour or anticipating the consequences of modifying it. Complexity arises when there is no straightforward relationship between the actions of individual components and the outcomes of the entire system. This is particularly evident in systems that incorporate adaptation or problem-solving to meet their objectives across varied scenarios.

But how do we manage this complexity? Two models offer useful maps for navigating this terrain. The first model, derived from Weinberg's work, highlights the types of interventions suited to different levels of complexity (Weinberg, 1975). The second, the Cynefin framework developed by Snowden & Boone, refines these interventions further (Snowdon & Boone, 2007).

Weinberg's complexity spectrum

Weinberg (1975) categorises systems into three levels of complexity:

1. **Organised Simplicity** – Predictable and linear.
   Think of a single machine with one switch to turn it on and off, executing one action that delivers a clear result. Organised simplicity refers to a level of complexity that is easily analysable, where cause-and-effect relationships are apparent. Within this context, system behaviour remains predictable.

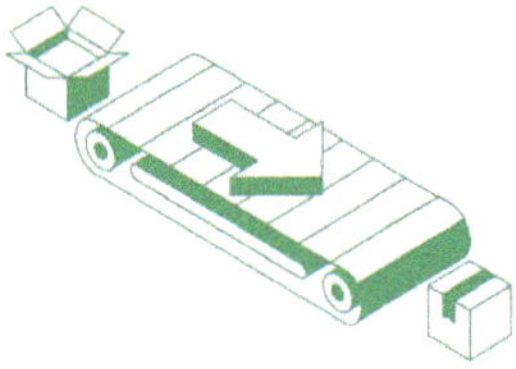

Figure 8. Organised simplicity

2. **Unorganised Complexity** – Random but statistically predictable.
   Think of a technical device: we know that it will occasionally fail, but we do not know when. If we record enough instances of this failure over a given period, we can calculate the probability and predict the likelihood of future occurences. Unorganised complexity describes systems with random cause-and-effect relationships that are amenable to statistical analysis. Here, statistics allow us to predict system behaviour effectively.

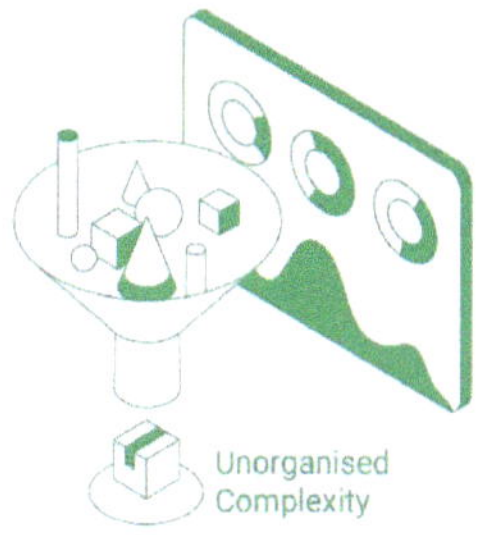

Figure 9. Unorganised complexity

3. **Organised Complexity** – Too intricate for simple analysis, yet too structured for randomness.
   Think of a traffic intersection where cars, cyclists and pedestrians cross each other. There are clear rules in the traffic regulations that determine how each group of users should behave. These rules are designed to minimise the risk of accidents. However, the users of this intersection may not always follow these rules, for a wide variety of reasons. In addition, conflicting situations can arise due to design limitations. Sometimes these conflicts end well, sometimes they do not.
   Thanks to the rules, user behaviour is not entirely random; implying that statistical models can only be applied to a limited extent. Due to the unpredictability of user behaviour, it is also impossible to make predictions based on the rules alone.
   This is where we find our enterprises, making it a good reason to further investigate how we can manage this level of complexity.

Figure 10. Organised complexity

Between organised simplicity and unorganised complexity lies the realm of organised complexity: a domain too intricate for straightforward analysis, yet too structured for statistical prediction. Enterprises typically embody organised complexity, requiring a blend of scientific and intuitive approaches. Systems located in this complexity level are to be designed in such a way that it is automatically clear to those in the system what is expected of them. Good design leads to easy-to-use devices that have an intuitive user interface. Good design also leads to easy-to-apply business processes that require no explanations or procedures. Enterprises are systems characterised by organised complexity. They need to be designed correctly in order to function properly.

How can we improve the road intersection we used as an example of a system in the realm of organised complexity? What is the objective of this improvement? Let us say that we want to improve the area of concern 'safety' for the users of the intersection without blocking mobility. The latter remains the higher objective of our traffic system. We propose two options, a design solution and a governance solution.

The design solution creates a new intersection with two levels, one with only cars using it and the other one dedicated for cyclists and pedestrians. It comes with a serious development cost but a very low maintenance cost. In the governance solution, the intersection is not changed. Every day two policemen are needed to govern the correct use of the intersection, two hours during the morning and two hours during the evening traffic. This solution comes with a zero development cost but with a very high maintenance cost.

The above example shows what kind of possibilities we have in cases of organised complexity. Depending on the nature of the problem at hand – sometimes a design solution can aid final improvement(s) whereas sometimes governance has to step in. Every situation has to be analysed to gauge what the options are. We suggest that governance should be implemented only when complexity cannot be removed through design. Examples of governance include: carrying out content validation, controls, operational audits, checking sickness of absent employees by a control physician, conducting inspections, and so on.

What all governance practices have in common is (1) that they cost manpower, time, and money, and (2) that once started, it becomes hard to stop them. It is sometimes claimed that 'good design' is expensive, but in the long run, 'good governance' is usually even more expensive.

To effectively govern enterprise behaviour within organised complexity, comprehensive governance is essential. For overall/ultimate success, enterprise governance and enterprise engineering must function in tandem.

The Cynefin framework: navigating domains of complexity

David Snowden's Cynefin framework (2007, 2020) offers another model on how to deal with different types of challenges within enterprises. His framework can easily be applied to all kinds of difficulties that occur where people work together to obtain a common goal. It refines the complexity spectrum (Weinberg, 1975) and gives a clear framework on how to act. The framework provides four domains of complexity:

1. **Simple or known**: Clear cause-and-effect relationships. Use best practices.
2. **Complicated or knowable**: Cause and effect are separated. Rely on expert analysis.
3. **Complex**: Relationships only become clear in hindsight. Experiment, adapt, and learn.
4. **Chaos**: No discernible patterns. Act quickly to stabilise.

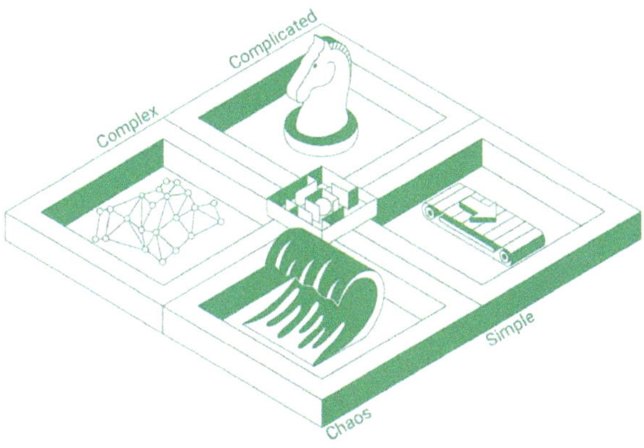

Figure 11. The Cynefin framework

How does the Cynefin framework work?

Let us dig a little deeper into this approach. We can be brief about the simple or known problems a manager may encounter. The knowledge to solve it is there; good operational procedures exist. So, getting started is the motto here.

Things get a little more difficult when we get into the realm of complicated problems. The knowledge is not present in the department, but perhaps in the company, or outside the company. The expert can clarify the cause and the expected outcome, draw up a plan to solve this technical problem, and explain to those involved what needs to be done. Most managers will be happy with this solution.

What we typically see when managers are confronted with a complex problem is that they do not act differently than when confronted with a complicated problem. Maybe this is related to the fact that their judgement of the complexity is incorrect? Maybe it is related to the fact that the manager doesn't like situations in which they have less control or no back-up of an expert?

We call the problems in the complex domain 'adaptive challenges'. They cannot be solved in the same way as a technical problem. They demand iterative experimentation, collective buy-in, and a willingness to learn as you go.

Unlike technical problems, adaptive challenges involve shifting beliefs, values, and relationships. They require:

- Acknowledging the problem (often denied).
- Changes across multiple domains – individual, group, and systemic.
- Leadership from within, as external solutions won't suffice.
- Experimentation and a focus on learning, not just outcomes.

Consider how a shared assumption – like the belief that 'budgets will always come through' – anchors an organisation in outdated practices. Addressing this requires more than policy updates. It demands a shift in collective thinking, achieved through persistent dialogue and iterative progress.

In the complex domain, cause-and-effect relationships can only be discerned retrospectively. This domain requires iterative experimentation: probe, sense the results, and adapt based on emerging patterns.

In the chaotic domain, cause-and-effect relationships are indiscernible. Rapid action aimed at stabilisation is critical to prevent paralysis, with crisis management playing a vital role. Here, immediate action is followed by observation and response based on novel practices.

The Cynefin framework in management coaching

Widely used in organisational coaching, the Cynefin model aids managers in decision-making by clarifying how to approach different situations. The distinction between complicated and complex problems is especially challenging for many managers, as complex issues often require an emergent approach, necessitating decisions without a clear solution upfront. Therefore, it is important to focus on the distinction between 'technical solutions' and 'adaptive challenges' and make sure that we use the right approach for each problem.

- Technical Solutions for Complicated Problems
  Technical solutions, informed by expert knowledge, effectively address

complicated problems.
Characteristics of complicated problems include:
  - Clear identification
  - Resolution through straightforward technical solutions
  - Potential for expert-led, outsourced solutions
  - Limited change required within defined parameters
  - Minimal resistance to technical solutions
  - Easy implementation
  - Presence of a defined end state when resolved
- Adaptive Challenges for Complex Problems
  Managers may struggle to accept that the cause-and-effect relationship in complex problems is not obvious. Attempts to apply technical solutions to complex issues often fall short. Complex problems necessitate an emergent approach, as in Appreciative Inquiry, where solutions evolve rather than being predetermined.
  Characteristics of adaptive challenges include:
  - Difficulty in identification and frequent denial
  - Requirement for changes in values, beliefs, roles, and relationships
  - Necessity for the problem owner to lead initial progress
  - Changes that span multiple areas, potentially beyond organisational boundaries
  - Often met with resistance, even before the challenge is fully accepted
  - Necessity for experimentation, discovery, implementation, and integration
  - A focus on developmental direction rather than an end state, aiming for improvement rather than definitive resolution

The key takeaway? To navigate complexity, enterprises must embrace systems thinking. They must treat shared mental models as levers for change, knowing that sustainable transformation stems from within.

A Systemic Approach to Changing Social Systems

Why systemic?

In the paragraphs above we have been paying attention to almost all the terms in the subtitle of this book. We discussed different types of systems and how underlying theories influence the way we look at them. We addressed the adverb 'social' to explain how different specialists look at this aspect of systems. We gave the enterprise, the subject of our book, a place in these different approaches. We addressed the different levels of complexity and explained how we can try to master it in a change approach. The one term we have not yet addressed is 'systemic'. More specifically, why do we emphasise the fact that the approach to, should be systemic?

A systemic approach is a method for analysing or addressing complex situations by considering the entire system, rather than focusing on individual parts or isolated elements (Senge, 1990). This approach emphasises the interconnectedness of different components within a system and how their interactions influence overall behaviour and outcomes.
It is often used for complex problems where a holistic perspective is needed to understand the situation and develop effective solutions. Five key aspects characterise a systemic approach:

- Holistic perspective
  A systemic approach looks at the entire system, including its various components and their interrelationships.
- Interconnectedness
  The elements within a system are interdependent and changes in one part can affect other parts.
- Emerging properties
  Systems can have properties that arise from the interactions between their parts, which cannot be predicted by looking at the parts individually.
- Focus on relationships
  Emphasis is on understanding the patterns of interaction between different elements within the system.
- Focus on the long term
  Systemic approaches often consider the long-term consequences and implications of actions and changes within a system.

Why our approach is classified as a systemic approach will become clear in the rest of our argument in this book. Here, we will outline a few characteristics of our approach that point to its systemic nature.

In the first place, the fact that we are looking into all the design domains of an enterprise. We are not only working on changes regarding products and services delivered by the enterprise – the business perspective. Instead, we also derive the implications of the changes in the business to the three constructional domains: organisation, information and infrastructure. What responsibilities need to be organised internally to achieve commitments to external partners?

In the second place, the fact that we are not only making models that describe how the future enterprise should be constructed, but that we also define guiding principles how the enterprise should be implemented and managed. Defining these guiding principles is an important aspect of the approach and serves as the compass for all decisions related to building the enterprise. During the definition of these principles, we use the enterprise's new objectives and the areas of concern as input to guide the transition from the current state to the desired future state.

In the third place, the fact that the above products (models and guiding principles) are created in a generative process. In this process, all necessary knowledge and expertise are brought to the table so that all perspectives are taken into account in developing the company's future vision. In the workshops we ask the participants first to (re)discover the strengths of the enterprise and then to project these strengths in a vision of the future of the enterprise. Using these visionary statements on the new enterprise, we will then start redesigning.

In the fourth place, the fact that we create a new foundation on which the employees and the management of the enterprise can start building its new future. By implicating employees and management in this generative approach, new ways of thinking which fuel change are discovered. We explicitly do not work on the enterprise's culture as a whole. We discover during the process which are the shared mental models that have changed during all of the structured dialogues between employees and management. The new way of thinking provides the foundation on which the new company can be built.

The combination of models regarding the future construction, guiding principles that help to take the right decisions during implementation, vision that is built using the knowledge of the whole system, and the new ways of thinking that fuel of the change, allow enterprises to go through real transformation.

Introduction to the coming chapters

In this introductory chapter, we have discussed the relevant scientific foundations in the domain of social systems that are enterprises. These are important as background for the chapters that follow.

In the next chapter, we will briefly discuss the current problems we see in initiatives related to enterprise transformation. This discussion will also clarify the relevance of the research that preceded this book.

In the third chapter, we will discuss in detail the two methods we use in our approach: Appreciative Inquiry and Enterprise Engineering. The appreciative inquiry method helps us to shape the process in which we allow new visions to emerge in a structured manner. We use techniques such as conceptual modelling and architecture in the design phase of AI. We combine the products from the enterprise engineering methodology in the appreciative inquiry process. By integrating practical examples into this explanation, we make it accessible to readers.

In chapter four, we discuss why our approach is successful in transformational change. The approach is characterised by several forms of dialogue between the employees involved, and this related to different aspects of the change. By embedding these conversations in a generative dialogue, we build new foundations on which the subsequent change can grow. New ways of thinking will lead to new ways of acting. In today's digital world, every enterprise transformation has an impact on existing information technology solutions. To support change in the right way, it is important to make the correct choices in this technical domain as well. Either the change will lead to significant adjustments to existing information technology systems, or new systems will have to be purchased.

In chapter five, we first discuss how we integrate these decisions in the preparation of the transformation projects. We will also emphasise the importance of achieving the necessary level of shared understanding in the different phases of the preparation, the implementation, and the roll-out of these information technology systems in the organisation. To achieve a coherent result over different design domains, we will argue that transformation needs to be driven by a dedicated governance agent which we will call the transitional organisation.

Finally, in chapter six we will summarise the whole approach based on a real-life case in which we have applied this approach.

In the epilogue, we will emphasise some important, very recent, evolutions. It is not always clear to pinpoint the exact starting point of these evolutions. They have been propelled into our lives and work through global events like the COVID pandemic, wars, and important changes in the global political and economic environment.

Chapter II: The Heart of Enterprise Transformation

A guide to enterprise transformation cannot be clear unless we first have a shared understanding of the concept of enterprise transformation. That is why, in the following paragraphs, we will explain how to recognize the difference between change and true transformation.

In the second part of this chapter, we will also look at the results of transformation initiatives in general. It is difficult to call these results successful, which is the main reason why we started the research and wrote this book.

Characteristics of Enterprise Transformation

When can we classify a change as a transformation? Is an IT project by definition a transformation? In the next sections we will try to formulate an answer to these questions.

What happens when an organisation outgrows its past?

Picture a publisher, once renowned for its encyclopaedic legal tomes, stepping into the digital age with online databases. Or a retailer with hundreds of bustling storefronts launching an online marketplace to reach customers beyond the city limits. These aren't mere steps forward; they are leaps that reshape the essence of how these enterprises operate.

Welcome to the world of enterprise transformation, where change goes far beyond surface-level adjustments – it cuts to the core.

Each of these examples share a common thread: transformation ripples through every corner of the organisation. It's not just about introducing a new product or tweaking a process. Instead, it demands a recalibration across four critical domains:

1. **Business Domain**
   Transforming products and services requires addressing everything from innovative market strategies to online payment systems and redesigned sales incentives. A simple tweak isn't enough – it's a wholesale reimagining of how value is created and delivered.

2. **Information Domain**
   What does the system need to know that it didn't before? Managing customer data, streamlining invoices, or handling disputes – all of this calls for rethinking the way knowledge is structured and utilised within the enterprise.

3. **Organisation Domain**
   New skills demand new roles, which in turn work in new processes. It's a delicate dance of attracting talent while ensuring that the current systems don't collapse under the weight of change.

J. De Winter, *Concise Guide to Enterprise Transformation*,
The Enterprise Engineering Series, https://doi.org/10.1007/978-3-032-29931-4_2

4. **Technical Infrastructure**
   Outdated tools and facilities often become relics overnight. Whether it's repurposing underused warehouses into digital fulfilment hubs or equipping employees with modern devices, transformation in this area sets the stage for all other changes.

Transformation impacts every aspect of an enterprise, meaning success hinges on collaboration across teams and domains. But that's only the beginning. Every enterprise transformation, regardless of its complexity, follows a journey – a blueprint for transformation. This journey includes six crucial phases:

1. **Vision Building**
   Where are we going, and why? This is the North Star that guides every step.

2. **Design**
   If the vision is the 'what', the design phase is the 'how' – mapping out what needs to change.

3. **Business and Process Analysis**
   Reality check: Is the design translated into clear business definitions of goods and services? And what responsibilities do we have to set up in order to produce these goods and services?

4. **Procurement and staffing**
   This involves procuring the right tools to support the above responsibilities and the related business transactions. Buy-in the necessary services or organise them internally and make sure that we hire or train our collaborators so that they are equipped for the journey.

5. **Implementation**
   This is the point where the rubber meets the road – realising the necessary information technology projects helping to deliver the expected solutions and integrations. Preparing the collaborators to start working in the renewed organisation.

6. **Rollout and Change Management**
   Change is only complete when people, your collaborators and your clients, fully embrace the new way of doing business. This phase ensures that the transformation is deeply embedded.

While these phases may seem straightforward, they are often overlooked. We still encounter too many cases where these crucial steps were not implemented. Why? Sometimes, what begins as a minor adjustment snowballs into something far more complex. So, at the beginning, there was no reason to put so many resources in what was supposed to be a little project. At other times, management underestimates the scale of change, mislabelling it as a simple technical fix. The result? Missed opportunities, misaligned systems, and crises that could have been avoided.

Evidence from Practice: Why Transformation Projects Stumble?

Change initiatives in companies do not have a good track record. Cases of major transformations that fail to deliver the expected results regularly make the news. Let's see if we can talk about success and what the causes are.

Some first indications on the results of transformation projects

The truth is, transformation projects fail at an alarming rate. Research paints a sobering picture:

- A McKinsey study found that 17% of large transformation projects were so disastrous they threatened the survival of the company (Bloch et al., 2012).
- A Geneca study revealed that at the outset, 75% of project teams doubted their projects would succeed (Geneca, 2011).
- The Standish Group discovered only 36% of over 50,000 projects worldwide hit their targets for time, budget, and scope (The Standish Group, 2016).

Let us look deeper into this evidence. Before we start explaining our approach to enterprise transformation, it is important that we have a clear view on the real success rates in larger transformation projects.

Why large transformation projects can threaten the very existence of your company?

The 2012 study executed by McKinsey and the University of Oxford, is based on the analysis of the outcomes of over 5,400 large transformations spread over a large set of economic sectors. They defined projects as large if they had an estimated cost of at least $15 million.
A first look at these projects showed that, on average, 45% of these projects exceeded their anticipated budget; 7% required more time than anticipated; and 56% delivered less value than initially projected. Additionally, it was found that the projects pre-estimated as long-term were more likely to exceed both time and budget estimates. Furthermore, they were able to show that 17% of these projects were so poorly executed that they even threatened the survival of the entire company.

From the results of this study, the researchers distilled the following advice to improve the chances of success of large-scale transformation projects. They proposed that the key to success lies in mastering four broad dimensions, which together form a methodology for large-scale transformation projects that they call 'value assurance'. This approach consists of the following elements:

- focus on managing strategy and stakeholders rather than focusing exclusively on budget and planning
- controlling technology and project content by securing critical internal and external talent
- building effective teams by aligning their incentives with the overall goals of the project
- excelling in core project management practices, such as short delivery cycles and strict quality controls

According to survey responses, inability to manage the first two dimensions causes about half of all cost overruns, while poor performance on the two dimensions that follow is responsible for another 40% of spending overruns (Bloch et al., 2012).

Geneca study from 2017 reports up to 75% of transformation projects will fail.

This study based on a survey of 600 business and information technology managers focused mainly on why teams continue to struggle to meet business expectations in custom development projects. The researchers, all from the software development company Geneca, argue that many executives feel exhausted by confusion over the objectives of projects and recognise the need for more involvement from business stakeholders.

Participants were quizzed on topics such as the definition of requirements, accountability, and measuring project success.

"*There is no question that the overall survey results show that our greatest opportunity for performance improvement lies in a more business-centric approach to requirements*", a researcher claimed, "*unfortunately, bad practices in defining requirements have become so common that they are almost tolerated*" (Geneca, 2011).

The classic chaos report of the Standish Group

For over 30 years the Standish Group has conducted research on success and failure of projects worldwide, thereby maintaining a database of thousands of projects each year. In their yearly 'Chaos report' they publish findings on the performance of all types of projects along with explanations on the sources of their success and failure.

Triple constraint theory at the basis of their reports

From the start of their research, they have used the parameters of the triple constraint theory to determine whether projects are successful. The theory states that every project will include three constraints - budget, time, and scope - all of which are interconnected.

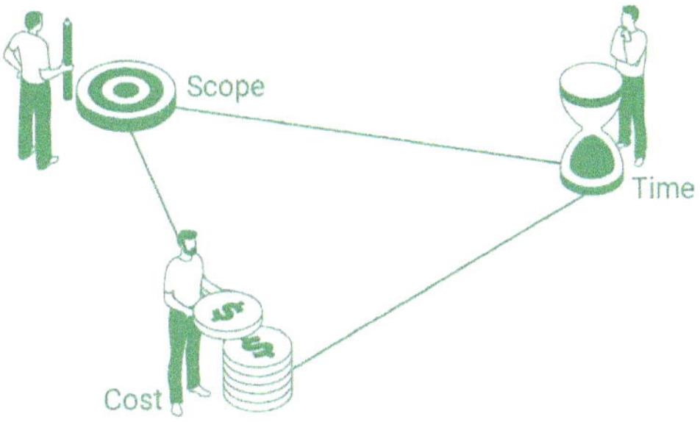

Figure 12. Triple constraint theory: the project triangle

A project that delivers the expected results on time and within budget is deemed successful. Conversely, a project that does not deliver and that is neither in time nor within budget is considered a failure. Meanwhile, a project that delivers the expected results but fulfils only one of the remaining criteria – either staying on time or within budget – is referred to as a challenged project.

Using the above criteria, the Standish Group classified all projects included in their research over the past 30 years. This allowed them to identify trends across various factors, such as project size, the methodologies used, the industry involved, etc.. We will first discuss the results of the 2016 Chaos Report, which was still organised in the classic style used between 1995 and 2015. Then we will also investigate the most recent Chaos Report which is the one of 2022, where we will also explain the differences with the traditional style.

In the 2016 Chaos Report, The Standish Group reported the results for all projects over the FY2011 until and including FY2015 (The Standish Group, 2016). These reports include the results of more than 25,000 projects with an average of 5,000 projects per year. The percentage of successful projects varies between 36% and 41%; these projects score positively on all three constraints. The percentage of failed projects varies between 17% and 19%. All other projects, varying between 40% and 47%, were challenged, which means that they did miss one of the constraints but still delivered at least some results.

Any reflection on these results, regardless of the setting, should humble us. It cannot be argued that program and project management theory and practice are so novel that we can excuse a lack of knowledge on how to manage them. Neither can we say that we were not aware that there is a high risk that programs or projects might fail. The Standish Group alone is telling us this for thirty years.

What is it that hinders us to do it in a different way? And what is the right way? Given all the data they have gathered, The Standish Group is definitely capable to tell us something that can help.

What are the key reasons for transformation project failure?

Based on their massive data on project success and failure, the Standish Group is one of the authorities worldwide that can help us understand what the most important reasons are for success or failure. In their 2016 Chaos Report, they identified five key success factors that together accounted for 80% of successful projects, referring to these as 'the winning hand'. In order of importance, the winning hand comprises of:

- Size of the project: small projects are more successful than larger projects
- Method used: agile projects are more successful than waterfall projects
- Executive sponsorship: projects having an experienced sponsor are more successful than those lacking good sponsorship
- Environment in which the project is executed: emotionally mature environments allow better projects than emotionally immature environments
- Technical skills: projects with highly skilled staff are more successful than projects with less skilled staff

The other remaining factors (six in total: user involvement, clear business objectives, emotional maturity of stakeholders, optimisation of scope, standard software infrastructure, and formal project management expertise) determine only 20% of the result.

These results might be surprising since there is a common belief that the skills and expertise of the program or project manager are also very important. But maybe our mind is tricking us here, as we are conditioned to believe that if a project runs well, then it must be driven by a skilled project manager. However, the data tells us another story, since the impact of a skilled project manager counts five times less than the impact of the size of the project or the method used.

Are the triple constraints the right parameters to measure success?

There is some criticism on the way of measuring the success of a project. In their book 'Do you have your information and technology under control?' (Mulder et al., 2018), add another parameter in evaluating the success of a project. The reason they do so is because a challenged project may bring more value to the business than a successful one.

Let us use their example to illustrate this. A first project was budgeted at € 100K, with an expected value of € 400K if successful. At the end of the project the real value for the organisation was calculated at € 300K, while the project cost ended up being € 150K, resulting in a € 50K overrun. According to the triple constraints, the project is considered challenged, but the value of the project remains very positive, at € 250K. The second was budgeted at € 250K and after completion, the costs amounted to only € 200K. The project delivered the expected result in time and within budget, so according to the triple constraints the project is a success. However, the solution that the project brought appeared to generate no value, and after a year it was taken out of service, incurring an additional cost of € 125K. Therefore, despite the fact that the project was a success, the company face a loss of € 375K.

Hans Mulder argues that it is better to use a value-driven parameter to evaluate the success of a project instead of a cost-driven one. The focus should be on how much value (business value – project cost) did the project deliver instead of what the project cost.

One can argue of course if it is the responsibility of project management that the solution didn't bring any value. This discussion can only be sorted out if one knows who was responsible for the preparation of the project and the decision to build the solution the way that it was done. In other words, was it a business decision or a project decision? Why is this so important? Because it points out that something obviously went wrong during the preparation of this imaginary project.

In the next paragraph we will find out that the researchers of the Standish Group used the above critiques to further improve their interesting reporting.

The new – 2022 – chaos report of the Standish Group

Between the 2016 Chaos Report and the recent one of 2022 lies a period full of change and innovation. Agile project management became the most chosen project approach; cloud applications and cloud computing definitely became the standard choice; mobile first for individual usage shifted to professional usage too; robotics and automation of repetitive administrative work start to be replaced by artificial intelligence applications. So intuitively, should the 2022 Chaos Report show a large growth of successful projects due to the technical and organisational changes over the last ten years?

No, looking at this longitudinal research report, there is no improvement at all between the results published in 2022 and the ones published in 2016. When using the same evaluation criteria for projects, there is no change in the success rate between 2015 and 2020.

It is intriguing, to say the least, that the aforementioned changes in project approach, technology choice and user-friendliness do not make a significant difference to the success of projects.

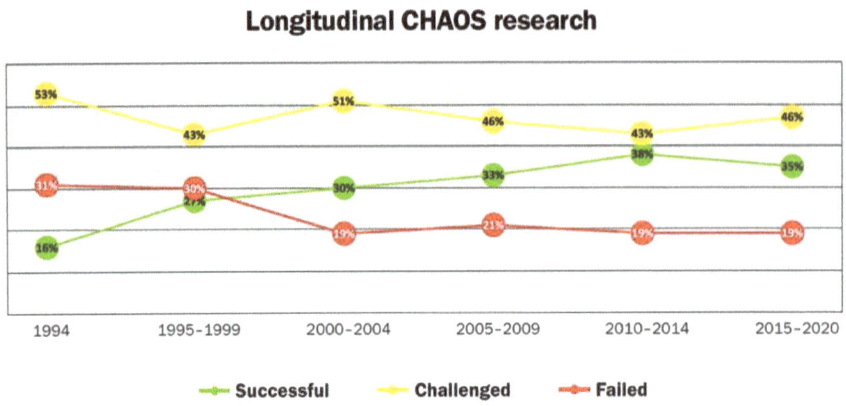

Figure 13. Longitudinal CHAOS research.

Reproduced with the permission from James Johnson, 2026, CHAOS Report: Beyond Infinity, (2022)

Each of these developments is said to be an improvement, but this is apparently not reflected in the results of projects. In the following paragraphs, we will see how The Standisch Group has dealt with this. However, it is also important to realise that transformation also requires a change in the way employees and the organisation think. We will discuss this in more detail in Chapter IV.

From project management metrics to comprehensive evaluation of project success

In the same period of time – between the results of 2016 and 2022 – The Standish Group has been rethinking the approach to evaluate projects. Already in 2016, Johnson (2016) acknowledged that the triple constraint theory was limited, and introduced the idea of focusing on *value and stakeholder satisfaction* as a secondary evaluation criterion. Focus in 2016 was still on finding the right 'winning hand', a combination of key success factors helping to beat the odds of failure.

In the 2022 Chaos report, The Standish Group has broadened the evaluation approach with multiple benchmarks. Next to the traditional measurement (triangle of constraints), they introduced customer satisfaction and delivered value as extra criteria. Their argument was that time, budget, and scope are good project management metrics, but not true success metrics.

Perhaps an even more important change in the 2022 report is the introduction of emotional maturity and decision latency as root causes of project outcomes. The maturity of the projects is based on three separate maturity assessments. First the maturity of the sponsor, second the maturity of the project team and finally, the maturity of the environment in which the project is taking place. The introduction of these evaluations allowed the Standish Group to deliver completely different insights into the underlying reasons for project success and failure.

The results are striking when one uses decision latency as a criterion for the success and failure of projects. Poor decision latency leads to 10 times more failure than good decision latency - 43% versus 4%. Therefore, the ability of a project to make decisions quickly is crucial to success.

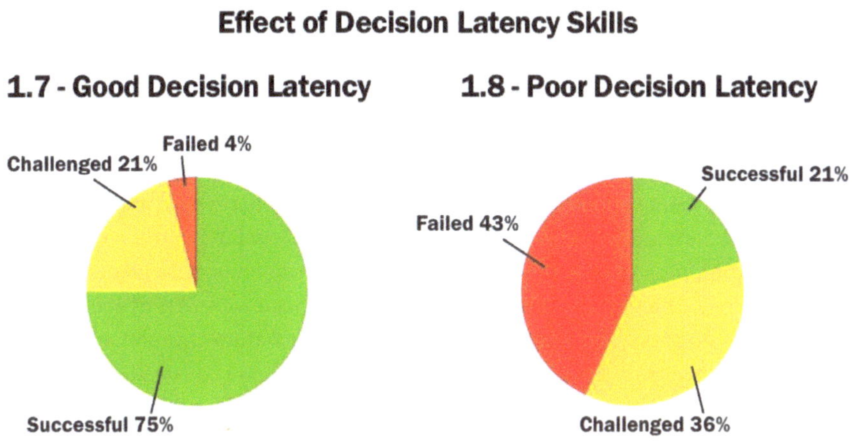

Figure 14. Decision Latency Effect.

Reproduced with the permission from James Johnson, 2026, Chaos Report: Beyond Infinity (2022)

Two important remarks can be made regarding the concept of decision latency as it is used in the Chaos Report. First it is important to understand that the quality of the decision is not part of the decision latency skill of a project. The Standish Group does not consider the decision latency of good decisions alone. Instead, they also consider the time it takes to decide and all quality levels included.

Second, decision reconsidering, meaning coming back on a decision that was taken earlier, triples the decision latency. Obviously, there is a correlation between an organisation's decision latency and its tendency to reconsider decisions.

As pointed out by the decision latency, there are important differences between success and failure ratios if one starts to dig deeper into the characteristics of projects, specifically the people they work with. The Standish Group evaluates project outcomes against three human-centred maturity factors: the sponsor, the team, and the environment (also called the 'place'). Each of these is rated on a maturity scale (Highly Mature, Mature, Moderately Mature, Not Mature), and the results are linked to the triple constraint theory.

Highly mature sponsors steer 67% of their projects to success, only 7% to failure, and 26% of their projects are challenged. Whereas, not mature sponsors score totally differently: 18% of their projects are successful, a large 33% fail, and 49% of their projects are challenged. Obviously, the maturity of the sponsor is very important for the success of the projects he or she is steering

A similar result is found if we look at the success ratio compared to the maturity of the project team. Highly mature teams bring 66% of their projects to success, only 8% to failure, and 26% of their projects are challenged. Not mature teams achieve only 11% of their projects in a successful way, over 1 in 3 fail (35%), and 54% are challenged. Similar to sponsors, team maturity strongly correlates with outcomes. An immature team has only an 11% chance of success, while a highly mature team succeeds two-thirds of the time.

A mature environment supports better outcomes, but its impact is less pronounced than sponsor or team maturity. Highly mature environments allow 50% of the projects to be successful, 10% fail and 40% of the projects in this environment are challenged. The difference with not mature environments is less pronounced with 23% of success, 31% of failure and 46% of projects challenged. Even in a highly mature environment, success rates peak at 50% versus ~66–67% for highly mature teams and sponsors.

The above statistics are clear, but the most important question still needs to be answered: Why are these numbers so striking?

To answer these questions, The Standish Group sought to identify the skills and behaviours that support 'good sponsor', 'good team', and 'good environment'. These skills and behaviours correlate strongly with project success. Based on these analyses, they succeeded in substantiating 'good sponsor' with 10 principles. Each principle is further explained with five behavioural attributes.

The same has been done for 'good team' and 'good environment'. For a complete and detailed overview of these principles and behavioural attributes, we refer to The Standish Group's report Chaos 2022: Beyond Infinity. In our book, we will focus on the outcomes that are relevant to the development of our argument.

What a project sponsor does naturally influences what the project team does. And a good sponsor also influences the environment in which the project takes place. This is an important reason why there is an overlap between the underlying principles of sponsor, team and environment.

That is why we will limit ourselves here to the ten principles that contribute to the maturity of a project sponsor. We also believe that these principles largely correspond to the principles for a project manager and certainly for a programme manager. So what are the key principles that enable a project sponsor to be classified as a mature project sponsor?

1. Decision latency,
   the ability to create an effective environment in which firm and quick decisions can be made.
2. Vision principle,
   the ability to inspire the implementation team, stakeholders and end users.
3. Principle of smart working,
   ability to create habits that make him and the project team more efficient in the process.
4. Principle of daydreaming,
   ability to form new ideas and concepts for objects and services that have not yet been realised.
5. Influence principle,
   ability to create and maintain favourable interactions and relationships and to be influential in doing so.
6. Passion principle,
   ability to create and maintain an intense and driven sense of conviction for the project.
7. People principle,
   ability to bring the right people together for the right job at the right time.
8. Tension principle,
   ability to constructively create a healthy tension with the project team.
9. Torque principle
   the soft power that the sponsor uses to deliver a high-quality product or service.
10. Progress principle,
    ability to understand the project management process and stimulate the actions and events that lead to completion.

The above principles are thus decisive for the success of projects. They determine whether we can label the sponsor as mature, and that maturity ensures that the project runs smoothly. This is partly, of course, due to the significant influence that the sponsor has on the functioning of the project team and the relationship between the project and its environment. If we examine these ten principles in the light of the approach we propose in this book, we can emphasise the following points.

Firstly, projects are started to achieve things that are by definition unclear and involve uncertainty. There is no obvious solution, so it is important that a sponsor can inspire the project team to look for less obvious solutions. This is reflected in the principles of vision, passion, daydreaming and also influencing.

Secondly, projects run the risk of getting bogged down in research, deliberation and inaction. It is therefore important for the sponsor to keep an eye on this. This is reflected in the principles of decision latency, progress and smart working.

Thirdly, projects require the art of bringing together the expertise necessary to understand the problem and come up with a solution. It is therefore important to bring together knowledge and expertise, but also to let them work together. This is reflected in the principles of people, torque, vision, and daydreaming.

Fourthly, like in other forms of organisation, in a project people are brought together to achieve a specific goal. Bringing people together also requires the organisation of leadership and management. This is reflected in the principles of tension, progress, influence, passion, and smart working.

What we do not see reflected in The Standish Group's studies in the list of causes for failure are causes such as technical complexity and technical, legal or other limitations. Some readers may be surprised by this, as these reasons are often used in everyday project life as 'dry' reasons for the failure of a project.

I agree with The Standish Group on this point: these 'technical' reasons are almost never the real reasons for failure. If they were, this would have become clear during the feasibility study. Usually, they are simply a more acceptable reason to explain the failure.

What does become very clear from The Standish Group's research is that project performance is primarily a matter of people, rather than a matter of tooling.

From 'better projects' to 'infinite flow'

Between the report of 2016 and the report of 2022 the vision of The Standish Group regarding future developments changed drastically. In the 2016 report, the vision was still project-centred, saying 'let us do projects better'.

The measures they promoted were still related with the organisation of the project, like a smaller scope, agile methods, strong sponsors, and better governance as ways to increase project success. 'The Winning Hand' metaphor suggested success is about playing your cards right within the project framework.

Two years before the 2022 report, Jim Johnson and Hans Mulder introduced the concept of 'Infinite Flow' (Johnson & Muller, 2020). They describe 'Infinite Flow' as a state where software or information systems are no longer treated as discrete projects with fixed beginnings and ends, but as continuous streams of evolution. Influenced by new theory and practice in software development the idea emerged that software is no longer 'growing old' and has to be replaced by 'new, younger software'. In this old paradigm, projects are needed to replace the old software by new software.
In the 2022 report, we see a radical shift towards the 'end of projects' and the beginning of 'Infinite Flow'. The idea is that software is infinite, while projects are finite and artificial. The future lies in continuous daily pipelines, not projects.

The Standish Group strongly emphasises a future where there are no project managers, no plans, and minimal overhead. Evolution of software comes with continuous micro-delivery and constant modernization, and organisations must invest in sponsor/team/place maturity and emotional maturity. In their vision 'Infinite Flow' will dominate the software development era of the next 20 years. But with 'Infinite Flow' come also conditions, principles, or mandatory practices:

Non-project-based delivery but continuous, incremental modernisation

Instead of defining fixed projects, scope, timeline, budget per project, there exists a pipeline of continuous work. Legacy or core applications are modernised in small, incremental pieces rather than ripping-and-replacing or large-bang rewrites.

Service-oriented pipeline approach with frequent feedback and user involvement

There is a pipeline where new features, improvements, fixes flow through continuously, rather than waiting for a project to finish. The work is delivered frequently, often in small increments. Users or business stakeholders are involved regularly, to give feedback, adjust priorities, etc. Avoiding long delays between an idea or change request and seeing it in production.

Reduced overhead through reduction of project management

Many of the traditional artefacts of project management (big scope docs, fixed plans, long timelines, etc.) are minimised. Focus shifts to managing the pipeline rather than managing discrete projects.

Organisational readiness and maturity in skills and culture

The Standish Group readiness appraisal consists of a large set of skills to assess whether an organisation is prepared to operate in Infinite Flow. These include items like team autonomy, ability to accept continuous change, strong feedback culture, failure tolerance, appropriate architecture, etc.

Application architecture and technical capabilities

To support continuous small changes, the technical foundation needs to allow it. It has to be modular, decoupled (meaning no combinatory effects), highly testable and deployable, amongst other requirements. Otherwise, even with the right culture, the technical debt or architecture would bottleneck things.

Budgeting and financial model suited to continuous change

If budgets are always defined on a per –project basis, practise will force you back into a project-centric mode. Infinite Flow, in contrast assumes that budgeting and funding are aligned with the overall workflow or pipeline, rather than allocated discretely to individual projects.

Lean governance / light process

There needs to be enough governance to ensure alignment, prioritisation, strategic value, etc., but not so much that it slows down the flow. Governance must be aimed at managing value and risk, not at managing projects.

So, before a company can declare that it has reached 'Infinite Flow', it needs to:

- Have replaced their old, non-evolvable information technology with evolvable software.
- Be capable to build evolvable solutions to support new activities
- Run its software delivery through continuous, daily task pipelines (no big projects).
- Have small, autonomous, cross-functional teams (producers and actors).
- Continuously modernise and refactor its systems.
- Use feedback loops (steppingstones, retrospectives) to adapt daily.
- Have governance, sponsorship, and budgeting aligned to flow, not projects.

One may reasonably ask how many companies, at the end of their research, have reached this state of infinite flow. Here The Standish Group is obviously more cautious. First of all, in their 2022 report, they don't provide a specific percentage of companies that have already reached the state of 'Infinite Flow'. They emphasise that very few are there yet. Most are still in project-based delivery, with some adopting agile/DevOps practices that are steps toward 'Infinite Flow'.

It is clear that the idea of 'Infinite Flow' is a logical continuation of the longer evolution that information technology projects are undergoing. It started with large waterfall-like projects to implement information technology systems that demanded very well-elaborated blueprints before development could even start. Decades later agile project approaches allowed to shorten the time between defining and delivering the solution, also because only since that moment the technology allowed to work in this way. That we are now evolving towards even shorter timings between idea and delivery is a certainty. However, just like in the change towards agile working, it will only be possible if the solutions themselves allow to evolve in such a continuous way. And that, for sure, is not yet the case for all information technology solutions.

Therefore, it is fair to say that at this moment only a small minority of organisations operate this way and that, probably, quite some are experimenting with parts of it. The Standish Group explicitly says in its 2022 report that the 'flow period' started somewhere around 2020 and predicts that organisations will move from project-based software development to 'Infinite Flow' over the next 20 years or more.

Before you Continue Reading

Before we continue to present our approach in the following chapters, it is important to summarise the situation we currently find ourselves in – today, first half of 2026.

At any given moment in time, people reflect on how quickly everything is changing, much faster than it used to. We must make the same observation today. The only constant is change, and this also affects our companies. The current (geo)political instability and related insecurity, force many business owners to reconsider their offering, organisation and positioning. From a technological point of view, Artificial Intelligence (AI) offers a whole realm of new possibilities which can both be seen as a threat and as a possibility. But whether we choose it or not, we *must* change.

What we learned from the past is that companies that fail to evolve in time to a new expression of themselves are in danger of disappearing at a rapid pace. Some well-known examples are:

- Blockbuster (2010) – Filed for bankruptcy after failing to adapt to digital streaming.
- Kodak (2012) – Filed for bankruptcy after failing to commercialise their own digital camera.
- Nokia (2014) – Innovative and very successful in the first mobile era, but missed the switch to smartphones; then sold their mobile division to Microsoft.
- Toys 'R' Us (2017) – Filed for bankruptcy due to e-commerce disruption.
- Yahoo (2017) – Sold core assets to Verizon after missing key tech opportunities.

We believe that the timeframe within which a company must adapt to changing circumstances and expectations is becoming increasingly shorter.

A second observation that we cannot ignore is that today's companies are, at the very least, hybrid companies, if not already fully digital. Hybrid or digital, without a solid information technology foundation, a company is unable to survive. Combined with the first observation, this means that companies are pushed to change at two levels at the same time.

A good example of automation where one would not expect it is a fully automated dairy farm that works with milking robots, also known as automatic milking systems. Here, cows decide for themselves when they want to be milked. The milking robot recognises the cow with a sensor and checks whether she is 'ready to be milked'.

The robot then automatically cleans the teats and attaches the teat cups using cameras and sensors. Each teat is milked separately, and the milk flow is continuously measured. Next, the robot removes the cups and disinfects the teats. All data on milk production and the health of the cow are automatically recorded in the data management system.

In the example of this modern dairy farm, the information technology solution can still be reasonably isolated to the boundaries of the farm.

It is quite different if a healthcare service provider decides to replace its core applications. This decision has a significant impact on information technology integrations with external partners. The existing links with government platforms will have to be rebuilt or adapted to ensure legal reporting and compliance. Data exchange with healthcare institutions, service providers and suppliers (invoicing, certificates, files) will also have to be revalidated. Furthermore, the interfaces with insurance partners and internal systems for customer management and payments are directly affected.

And last but not least, the new systems have to be rolled out in the organisation. The failure of information systems in a hospital can have serious consequences. Given the large number of interdependencies between systems and the consequences in the event of problems, implementation in a hospital may be spread over several years. In this period, different departments work on different systems, with different processes. This requires a thorough redesign of the integration architecture, migration of data flows and intensive testing with all chain partners. Without a robust integration plan, both the continuity of service and legal compliance are at risk.

Hopefully, it is clear to the reader that a decision to start the above project cannot be made without thorough preparation. This preparation will require analyses to identify all the underlying changes that are needed, which systems will have to be replaced, but also which processes will change. In complex companies, these preparations can take several years.

A concrete example is the replacement of the accounting system of a major banking institution. The preparation for this project took more than five years. Now that it is ready and the budget has been approved, the bank is hesitant to actually start the project. The largest part of the team that investigated and prepared the new solution e.g., by setting up different proofs of concept, have moved on with their careers. The employees in the financial departments of this bank, that were not involved in the preparation, are not convinced of the choice of the new solution. The management fears that the project will be more difficult because of the possible resistance that the change will cause.

Surely it cannot be the intention that, after more than five years of preparation, the management of this bank's finance department should conclude... 'We forgot to involve our people in this story'. Just as it cannot be the intention that an entire appreciative inquiry summit is organised and people are free to come up with ideas that cannot be implemented because no thought has been given to the technical impact of all these good ideas. That would mean that they go back to the start of the five-year preparation period.

This brings us to the third observation, which is of a completely different order. On the one hand, we have organisational studies: this is an interdisciplinary field of science that investigates how organisations function, change and develop. It combines insights from social sciences, psychology, economics and management to improve both the human and economic dimensions of organisations. This field includes organisational development, human resource management, industrial and organisational psychology, personnel & organisation and human capital management.

On the other hand, we have enterprise design studies, also called enterprise engineering: Enterprise Engineering is an interdisciplinary field that focuses on designing, improving and integrating organisations and their supporting information systems. It encompasses methods and practices such as enterprise architecture, IT architecture, process improvement and business analysis, with the aim of making companies goal-oriented, efficient and agile. This domain combines insights from organisational science, information systems and management to optimise both the functioning of business processes and the connection with technological solutions.

Both scientific domains have grown significantly over the past fifty years. Both domains study the same phenomenon, namely enterprise transformations, but from a different starting point. And the representatives of both domains believe that the other domain adds little value. At least, that is the only meaningful explanation we can come up with for the fact that both parties are doing virtually nothing to work together to develop even better methods for the challenge we all face.

In the following chapters, we will attempt to lay the stepping stones that both domains can use to explore the neighbour's terrain. You will be surprised by the number of common backgrounds. Each one is an interesting element to be used in a shared approach. On the other hand, you will also discover gaps that leave room for developing new ideas. So, there is certainly still uncharted territory, ideal for new research.

I invite you to put all your preconceptions aside. You may encounter ideas that challenge your current perspective – embracing discomfort is part of the process. If you are willing to make that effort, the knowledge in this book will automatically open up to you. Do not expect this to happen automatically, because the deeper your knowledge is anchored in one of the two domains, the greater the effort will be to open yourself up to the other.

I have been fortunate, partly due to my urge to seek out the least travelled paths, to get to know the other world – a pursuit that has truly paid off for me.

Chapter III: A Positive Approach to Vision Building, Design, and Architecture.

In Chapter I, we provided an overview of the relevant perspectives on social systems. In the second chapter we explained the reasons why transformations of those social systems are not particularly successful. These introductions serve as a general framework for what follows.

In Chapter III, we embark the explanation how our approach works. First, we highlight both parts of our approach separately. Next we will zoom in on the reasons why these methods fit together so well.

Combining Two Distinct Methodologies

What happens when we combine the strengths of two different ways of working? This chapter takes you on a journey where enterprise engineering (EE) meets appreciative inquiry (AI), blending structure with creativity to address complex organisational challenges. By synthesising these methodologies, we unlock a powerful framework to envision and design enterprise transformation.

Let us start with enterprise engineering. Wikipedia (2025) defines it as:

- "*The body of knowledge, principles, and practices employed to design an entire enterprise or specific parts of it.*"
- "*A life-cycle-oriented discipline focused on identifying, designing, and implementing enterprises, alongside their continuous evolution, supported by enterprise modelling.*"

Figure 15. Enterprise Engineering: Modelling and Architecturing

J. De Winter, *Concise Guide to Enterprise Transformation*,
The Enterprise Engineering Series, https://doi.org/10.1007/978-3-032-29931-4_3

Enterprise engineering's roots are grounded in information systems development and enterprise architecture, and it surfaced first at the University of Maastricht in the Netherlands in the early 1990s. Over time, its scope has expanded to include business processes and other enterprise design topics.

Key persons in this domain include Jan Dietz, Jan Hoogervorst, Hans Mulder, and many others.

Now, consider appreciative inquiry (AI), a discipline defined as (Wikipedia, 2025):

- "*A model aimed at engaging stakeholders in self-determined change, focusing on strengths and capacity building.*"
- "*A strengths-based approach to transformation that fosters cooperation and vision by uncovering shared potential.*"

Pioneered within Case Western Reserve University (Cleveland – United States), AI emerged as a counterpoint to problem-focused organisational development – a method that often traps organisations in cycles of deficit thinking. AI shifts the lens to what works, inviting participants to dream big and design futures that inspire.

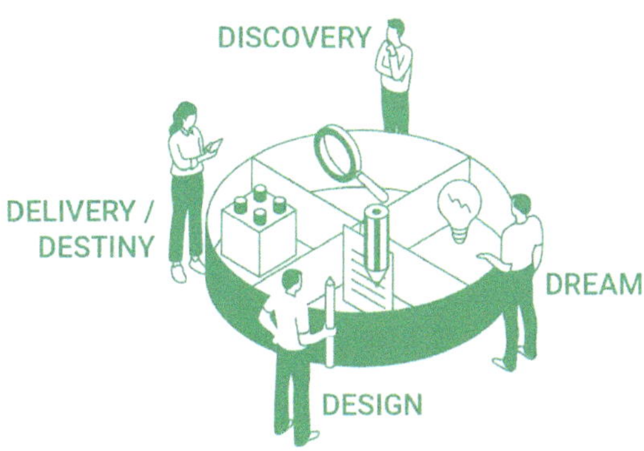

Figure 16. Appreciative inquiry: 4-D cycle

Key contributors to AI include Ronald Fry, David Cooperrider, Gervase Bushe, and many others. Together, their work highlights how storytelling and shared visioning can lead to profound change.

When paired, EE and AI create a dynamic synergy. EE brings precision to the design phase, providing tools to craft actionable models. AI, on the other hand, ensures that the vision is bold, human-centred, and grounded in collective strengths. This combination can turn ambitious dreams into practical blueprints.

Appreciative Inquiry: Enabling Transformation

The appreciative inquiry method is an approach to facilitating change based on a positive view of the existing situation. Whereas other methods start by investigating what is going wrong, AI starts with what is working well.

One of the fundamental aspects of AI is its objective of developing capacity. Barret & Fry (2005) make the following distinction between AI and deficit-oriented methods in organisational development. In the deficit-oriented approach the starting point of the intervention is a problem that needs to be solved. The intervention will investigate the problem and propose a solution to solve it. The aim of the intervention is to change something that is not OK into something that is OK. Once the problem has been solved, there is no further need for improvement.

If, on the other hand, the intervention starts from the idea that the organisation has existing strengths and that the intervention aims to build further on these strengths, the frame of mind is different. The aim is not to solve a problem and to restore the system to normal or reliable functioning. In fact the intervention starts at normal or reliable functioning and investigates pro-actively if extension is possible. The aim is to have the system grow to an excellent or flawless state. In that process of growth the problem will be solved as well, even if we did not focus on it at the start.

In order to steer the intervention towards capacity development, there are a few important attention points that we must carefully monitor.

First and foremost is the affirmative topic – a positive, compelling theme that serves as the foundation for the inquiry. Establishing this topic requires thoughtful reflection with a the steering group responsible for the intervention.

Based on the affirmative topic, the steering group needs to investigate who is required in the inquiry exercises in order to have a fruitful discussion on the chosen topic. This is the second attention point. The result of the inquiry can only be as rich as the knowledge that is represented in the group of participants. This also applies in the opposite direction: if there are not enough participants with a certain expertise, it is better to adjust the topic. Discussing a topic with an incomplete group of participants will only lead to an incomplete result.

The third attention point concerns the structure of the intervention itself. The starting point is the 4-D cycle, that consists of:

1. **Discovery** – Identify and celebrate strengths.
2. **Dream** – Envision the best possible future.

3. **Design** – Co-create the path to achieve that future.
4. **Destiny** – Implement and sustain the vision.

A typical approach to organise these four steps is the AI-summit, a large gathering of all the participants. During this summit participants share stories during discovery, express visions on the future during the dream phase, and translate what they want to achieve into how they envision this during the design.

In the following sections, we will explain the appreciative inquiry method in more detail. We will start with an explanation of the main characteristics and principles of AI. We will then zoom in on the appreciative approach in the context of enterprise transformation. We will discuss in detail what happens in the various steps of this approach. For each step, we will illustrate it with a concrete example based on one of the projects in which we have applied AI. In the last part we will explain why AI works in enterprise transformation. This explanation is particularly interesting because it forms the basis of the scientific rationale behind our approach.

What is Appreciative Inquiry?

Barrett and Fry describe AI as follows:

"AI is a strength-based, capacity-building approach to transforming human systems towards a shared image of their most positive potential by first discovering the very best in their shared experiences. It is not about implementing a change to get somewhere; it is about changing... convening, conversing, and relating with each other in order to tap into the natural capacity for cooperation and change that is in every system" (Barrett & Fry, 2005, p.25.).

This description may seem abstract or unscientific, particularly to those unfamiliar with AI. The vocabulary used is different from traditional change management terminology, but it reflects the core principles of AI. To make this concept clearer, the following aspects of AI are crucial:

- **Strength-based**: Unlike most approaches, AI does not begin with problem-solving. Instead, it focuses on identifying the strengths of the organisation and building upon them.
- **Capacity-building**: AI not only facilitates change but also equips organisations with the capacity to continue evolving independently, fostering a self-sustaining enterprise.
- **A shared image of their most positive potential**: AI is a participatory, solution-focused approach that uses human creativity to envision a positive future. In the 'Dream' phase, the group collaboratively develops a shared vision of the future at its best.

- **Discovering the very best in their shared experience**: In the 'Discovery' phase, participants recall and share moments of strength from their past experiences, helping the organisation rediscover its most positive moments.
- **Changing through convening, conversing, and relating**: AI aims to build change capacity by bringing members together (convening), engaging in dialogue (conversing), and fostering connections (relating).

Key principles of Appreciative Inquiry

To explain AI effectively, one must cover several key aspects: its socio-rationalist perspective, the six core principles, the reasons AI works, and its fundamental characteristics.

The socio-rationalist perspective

AI, an alternative form of action research, was introduced by Cooperrider and Srivastva (1987) to counter the problem-solving focus of traditional action research. They highlighted three main critiques of conventional action research: (1) its overemphasis on problem-solving, (2) its assumption of a stable and objective social reality, and (3) the underestimation of the influence of theory on research outcomes.

AI, grounded in the socio-rationalist paradigm, aligns with social constructionism, recognising that social and psychological realities are fluid and open to continuous reconstruction. Moreover, Cooperrider and Srivastva (1987) advocate for using theory in a generative way to create fresh alternatives for social action.

The six principles of Appreciative Inquiry

Based on the socio-rationalist perspective, Cooperrider (2003) developed five foundational principles for AI, with Barrett and Fry (2005) later adding a sixth principle:

- The **Constructionist Principle**: The language and symbols we use significantly impact the outcomes we achieve.
- The **Poetic Principle**: Organisations are dynamic systems open to multiple perspectives. The choice of research topics shapes organisational growth in the chosen direction.
- The **Principle of Simultaneity**: Change begins the moment we ask a question. Inquiry itself is an intervention.
- The **Anticipatory Principle**: Positive images of the future can help transform human systems. The collective vision of the future influences present actions.
- The **Positive Principle**: Positively framed questions foster cooperative capacity and sustain generative dialogue, which is essential for building and maintaining social systems.
- The **Narrative Principle**: Storytelling during AI exercises is powerful in creating committed relationships and shared mental models, enhancing the cohesion and effectiveness of change efforts.

Applying each of these principles individually adds value to interventions aimed at transformation. In a well-designed AI-based intervention, all these principles work together to create a workspace that invites participants to engage in the intervention.

Participants in such a well-organised AI intervention can recount years later exactly what they discussed with whom. This workspace greatly facilitates the further steps in the intervention. The downside is that participants are very disappointed if it later turns out that the AI intervention has led nowhere.

The appreciative approach to change

The Antwerp against poverty project

To make the approach to change using AI more concrete, we will refer to the project on poverty reduction in Antwerp, Belgium. In this project, we worked with an AI summit involving 135 people. But first, let us explain the context of the project.

In the city of Antwerp, five organisations where poor people have a voice, have been working side by side for many years. Each of these organisations have grown out of different religious or social movements and are still financially or logistically supported by these movements. Next to this support, these organisations, which operate according to clearly defined principles, are individually entitled to government subsidies. The fact that there are five such organisations in the city of Antwerp, led to fragmentation in the eyes of the city administrators and therefore they were asked to merge. Taking such a step would guarantee the city's subsidies, but other financial support would probably be lost. In addition, they would also lose part of their identity, which meant that they were not really keen on the idea of a merger.

So they were looking for a way to combine their efforts without losing their individual strengths. The idea they had in mind was to establish a network organisation with the five organisations as founding members. This way, the founding members could continue to exist independently, and the city's request for a single point of contact would also be met. The embryonic idea of the future organisation for poverty reduction in Antwerp was based on scientific research on network organisations and network governance by Patrick Kenis, then Academic Dean of the Antwerp Management School, affiliated with the University of Antwerp, Belgium who was involved in this project.

In his research, Patrick Kenis (2008) works with complex organisational forms - labelled network organisations - in which two organisational forms can be distinguished: (1) the individual organisations that are part of the network and (2) the network level itself. In the example of poverty reduction in a city, we also recognise these two organisational systems: (1) the individual organisations (five organisations where the poor have a voice), (2) the network organisation established by these five organisations.

Referring to the definitions of systems in Chapter One, we know that every system exists within an environment. From the perspective of each individual poverty organisation, this environment consists of all possible actors that play a role in poverty reduction in an urban fabric (companies, schools, health institutions, police, street workers, etc.). So the network organisation is also an actor in the environment, be it one with whom the individual poverty organisations have a privileged relationship.

There is a world of difference between the idea of setting up a network organisation and actually implementing one. This is especially true for organisations that are obliged, both by their statutes and by their funders, to do everything in a participatory manner with both their employees and their target group, people living in poverty. This is why they bear the title of associations 'where the poor have their say'.

Together with Professor Kenis, we set out to find an approach to guide this transformation. Ultimately, we opted for the approach described in this book, with the caveat that no information technology was involved.

In the following sections, we will describe the approach and then explain how we implemented it in the "Antwerp against poverty" project.

The affirmative question or topic

As previously explained, Appreciative Inquiry is grounded in social constructionism, and the selection of the inquiry topic holds significant importance. Cooperrider elaborates on this, stating: "*It is a fateful decision ... problem-focused study builds organisational knowledge, wisdom, and capacity about those problems... To understand Appreciative Inquiry at a fundamental level, one must grasp two key points. First, organisations evolve in the direction of what they study. Second, Appreciative Inquiry consciously chooses to focus on the best aspects of an organisation, its positive core*" (Cooperrider, Whitney & Stavros, 2008, p. 33).

Selecting the topic for Appreciative Inquiry is crucial. "*It is termed the affirmative topic because it represents positive affirmations of the organisation's strengths and the potential it aims to explore, learn from, and embody*" (Cooperrider, Whitney & Stavros, 2008, p. 41).

When individuals are tasked with choosing a research topic, they often identify problems to be solved. The first step in the Appreciative Inquiry approach is to translate the problem into a positive or affirmative inquiry topic. Appreciative Inquiry does not aim to ignore problems; rather, it asks us to first consider what the desired outcome looks like once the problem is solved. This is what is meant by focusing on the situation's most positive potential.

Crafting the affirmative topic is typically the responsibility of a small group preparing for a larger workshop, often referred to as an AI summit. During this process, the 4-D cycle is already in use, making Appreciative Inquiry an iterative co-creation approach. The initial outcome is the affirmative topic, which serves as the foundation for the next phase of co-creation.

How did we manage this in the Antwerp against poverty project?

Each organisation was asked to appoint one person to the steering group, which would supervise the entire process. In addition to the representatives of the five organisations involved, there was also a representative from the city and from the local university, since these bodies were also providing financial support for the project.

At the start of the project, we had two objectives: one, to start with the actual content as soon as possible, and two, to give participants an immediate taste of the appreciative inquiry method. Therefore, we organised an AI discovery and dream exercise at the first meeting. The topic for this first session was based on the objective of the first meeting itself, namely to assess whether there was sufficient support for the desire to achieve better cooperation and how we would go about this.

By taking this highly interactive approach to identifying common strengths and gauging expectations, we immediately achieved several important benefits:

1. The members of the steering group got to know each other in an open and positive way through their success stories.
2. The common strengths of the five organisations became much more visible.
3. The members of the steering group also learned about the strengths and weaknesses of the AI method.
4. The members of the steering group were able to imagine much better what an AI summit is and what they still needed to prepare in order to make it happen.

In the subsequent working meetings of the steering group, the focus was mainly on the following points:

- Working out the details of the question and the topic of the summit
- Considering who should be invited to this summit (the whole system in the room) in order to have all the knowledge and skills needed to address the topic of the summit
- Discussing the practical organisation of the summit in all its details

The ultimate goal of the transformation was to establish a network organisation. This is a complex organisational form that requires extensive consultation on the roles, responsibilities, and powers of the founding associations on the one hand, and of the network organisation itself on the other. It is evident that the design of this organisational form cannot be realised at a two-day AI summit.

Therefore, it was decided to focus primarily on the discovery and dream phase during the AI summit. The design phase would then start after the AI summit and make use of all the ideas that were brought up during the AI summit. This also allowed us to limit the AI-summit to one full day instead of two days.

Given the nature of these organisations, where poor people have a voice, there was an extra dimension that we had to take into account – a possible communication gap. The disadvantage of the AI summit is that it is an activity that requires a high level of language skills from participants and that such a large gathering can be quite intimidating. These are precisely two issues that people living in poverty often struggle with, especially when it comes to generational poverty.

We solved this by organising a limited AI summit with only people living in poverty and their support workers. The same process was set up with exactly the same questions. This ensured that the people living in poverty who participated in the large AI summit were sufficiently prepared and felt at ease.

In the end, 135 people participated in this AI summit. Among them were people living in poverty, employees of the five organisations, city employees, people from the education sector, people from the business community, employees of other civil society organisations, etc. Not quite the entire system, but still a good start.

Discovery

"The primary task in the discovery phase is to identify and appreciate the best of 'what is'" (Cooperrider, Whitney & Stavros, 2008, p. 41). During this phase, participants are encouraged to share stories of positive experiences, instances where both individuals and the organisation excelled. These narratives highlight the most valued moments in the organisation's history – periods that participants would like to experience again.

Figure 17. Appreciative Inquiry: Discovery

As positive stories are shared, relationships within the organisation are (re)constructed. Strengthened relationships are crucial for achieving the organisation's vision, mission, and goals.

A common question arises: why doesn't Appreciative Inquiry focus on situations where things are not at their best? The decision to focus solely on positive experiences is intentional. It serves several purposes:

- It encourages participants to introduce themselves in a positive light, fostering stronger bonds.
- Recalling positive experiences elicits emotions and energy, empowering participants to dream and imagine future possibilities.

- The collected stories offer insight into the conditions that contributed to the organisation's past successes. These conditions can inform critical success factors for future initiatives.

In the Antwerp against poverty project, we worked this out as follows. Based on the profiles of all invitees, participants were divided into 15 tables of nine participants. Each table had a tenth person who guided the participants at the table and ensured that the process ran smoothly. Having a coordinator at each table is not a requirement in itself. Given the presence of people living in poverty, the desire to have a report of what happened at each table shortly after the AI summit, and, last but not least, the fact that it was a large summit (15 tables), their presence was fully justified.

Why nine participants per table? Because this facilitates the process during the discovery and dream phases. We prefer to start the discovery phase with three people, each with one role: one person tells their success story, one active listener helping the storyteller and one person who takes notes. After the first story, the second is told, followed by the third; in each iteration, the roles are reversed.

When all the stories have been told, the three groups of three come back together at the table. There, the nine stories are shared with the whole table. The reporter tells the story (briefly), but emphasises why this story was successful. The names of the storyteller, the story and the reason for its success are noted by the table coordinator on the flipchart.

The aspect of intimacy is very important in this approach. Even though there are 135 people in the room, telling your story to just two people empowers even the shyest participants to speak up and to feel that their voice is as important as that of the most extroverted person in the room.

Dream

"The dream phase amplifies the positive core and challenges the status quo by envisioning more valued and vibrant futures than are currently imagined by organisational members and stakeholders. The purpose of the dream phase is to broaden people's sense of what is possible" (Cooperrider, Whitney & Stavros, 2008, p. 44).

Figure 18. Appreciative Inquiry: Dream

A key aspect of the dream phase is that it builds on the organisational strengths identified in the discovery phase, setting it apart from other visioning methods. The result is a compelling and vivid image of the future, one clear enough for participants to mentally walk through.

Let us look how we did this in the Antwerp against poverty project. The layout of the tables during the dream phase remained the same as during the discovery phase. There were two reasons for this. Firstly, redistributing participants to different tables between the discovery and dream phases would be an additional difficulty for people living in poverty who were taking part. They, and all other participants, would then have to cope with an additional change in a very short period of time (a break between two exercises). The second reason has more to do with the process itself and specifically with what we call 'bonding'. By going through the discovery phase together, an often unexpected relational process develops in such a trio. By listening to each other's stories, these three people grow closer. Giving this fledgling relationship further opportunities during the dream phase is an advantage both for the phase itself and for all future collaborations. It is striking that people who have been in such a trio seek each other out again, even months later.

Just as in the discovery phase, participants sit down in groups of three to first tell their dream story in a smaller group and only later share their dream with the whole group. The process, guidance and reporting are very similar to those in the discovery phase.

There are two important components to the question for the dream phase. On the one hand, there is the invitation to dare to talk about the moment that arises after the project work has been completed. We know that a lot of work still has to be done before we reach this dream situation, but it is important not to be overly influenced by it. The reality is actually the other way around: you can only correctly estimate the work that still needs to be done if you know where you want to end up afterwards.

Design

"The design phase involves creating the organisation's social architecture, embedding it through provocative propositions, also known as possibility statements or design principles, that reflect the organisational dream in ongoing activities... Successful design identifies the organisational elements that need rethinking and crafts propositions that integrate the ideals of discovery and dream into these elements" (Cooperrider, Whitney & Stavros, 2008, p. 45).

Figure 19. Appreciative Inquiry: Design

It is not explicitly stated that the design phase must be part of the AI summit, but in most case descriptions in which an AI summit is organised, we see that the design phase is also part of the summit. In the case of less complex changes, this is certainly possible. The advantage of this approach is that the participants are still fully immersed in the positive flow of the AI summit and that the ideas in terms of design will be more closely aligned with the elements that emerged in the dream.

When the transformation involves complex changes in terms of both IT, business and organisation, the design phase during the AI summit is too limited. What is possible, of course, is to take preparatory steps during the AI summit for a more in-depth design process to be organised at a later stage. This could involve establishing the content-related division of the design results to be delivered, or jointly establishing a number of design principles, also known as provocative statements.

In the following chapters in this book we will explore the design phase in greater depth, focusing on how enterprise engineering principles can enhance the Appreciative Inquiry process.

In the Antwerp against poverty project, we had decided very early in the preparation that the design phase would only start after the AI summit. We were going to work in smaller task forces on the three aspects of the organisational form to be developed. The content of the AI summit was intended to provide the task forces with input from the broad network of actors who had been invited to the AI summit.

We set up three task forces. The first worked on substantive innovation, in particular the development of new 'products and services' for the network organisation. The second focused on internal cooperation within the network, in particular defining the responsibilities of the individual organisations vis-à-vis those of the network organisation. And the third worked on new possible forms of cooperation with external actors in the environment.

Destiny

Initially termed the 'delivery' phase, this stage was later renamed 'destiny' to reflect a more improvisational approach, which was found to yield greater results. "*The destiny phase realises the new vision of the future and is sustained by fostering a collective sense of purpose. It is a period of continuous learning, adaptation, and improvisation (much like a jazz ensemble) – all aimed at shared goals. The momentum and potential for innovation are exceptionally high. With a shared positive vision, everyone is encouraged to align their actions to co-create the future*" (Cooperrider, Whitney & Stavros, 2008, p. 45).

Figure 20. Appreciative Inquiry: Destiny

In this phase, ideas are implemented within the organisation. It is essential to maintain momentum, and one approach is to embed an 'appreciative' mindset into organisational systems and processes. In their research on 20 successful Appreciative Inquiry cases, Bushe and Kassam (2005) concluded that the most significant transformations occur when participants change their way of thinking, rather than simply changing their actions.

Let us look a last time into the Antwerp against poverty project. Something particular happened during the destiny phase of this project. In the last two months of the project, just as we were preparing the landing for the three task forces, municipal elections were held in Belgium. For organisations that depend on municipal subsidies, such elections can have an impact on their funding, especially when there is a change in the power distribution in the city council. A few months after the appointment of the new mayor, it became clear that subsidies would be cut, including those for associations representing the poor.

It was not surprising that this would have an impact on the ongoing project. Setting up a network organisation, even if it is low-profile, has a certain cost. Faced with subsidy cuts and redundancies in the five organisations, the project was halted just before we reached the finish line.

Six years later, we contacted the client for a reference interview.

I had had no contact in the intermediate period. What we heard then exceeded my expectations. Two years earlier (four years after the sudden halt to the intervention), a spontaneous discussion had arisen at another meeting in the network on poverty reduction in Antwerp about the whole process that the organisations had gone through. This conversation revealed that perspectives had evolved in the meantime, but also that the whole idea of building a network organisation had not disappeared, quite the contrary. In a very short time, the five organisations resumed talks and effectively established the network organisation.

In the next paragraph, where we explain why AI works, we will come back to this particular outcome of the Antwerp against poverty project. Also in the case of the National Geographic Institution in Chapter VI, we will report a similar outcome.

Why does Appreciative Inquiry work?

In this section, we will focus on the underlying reasons why AI is so effective in the context of organisational development. The study on which we will mainly focus has played a pivotal role in the further development of the scientific domain of organisational development. It is also an important link in the development process of the method described in this book.

Gervase Bushe (2005, p. 161) noted that "*while Appreciative Inquiry was becoming an increasingly popular method for organisational change, there was a lack of research explaining why it works*". Apart from studies by Whitney & Trosten-Bloom and Bushe himself, little scientific research exists on the effectiveness of Appreciative Inquiry.

Whitney & Trosten-Bloom's research (2003) identified six essential conditions, termed the 'six freedoms', that contribute to Appreciative Inquiry's success:

- Free to be known in relationships:
  Appreciative Inquiry encourages genuine, individual-to-individual interactions, fostering authentic relationships.
- Free to be heard:
  Active listening throughout the inquiry process ensures participants feel acknowledged, stimulating innovation and idea-sharing.
- Free to dream in community:
  Appreciative Inquiry provides a platform for collective dreaming, offering a safe space where diverse groups can share their visions.
- Free to choose to contribute:
  Participants have the freedom to contribute, and this choice strengthens their commitment.
- Free to act with support:
  Appreciative Inquiry cultivates a supportive environment, encouraging experimentation and learning.
- Free to be positive:
  It encourages individuals to adopt a positive outlook on their work, achievements, and future goals.

Bushe conducted an intensive study on 20 cases where Appreciative Inquiry (AI) was applied to social systems change (Bushe & Kassam, 2005). Because of the importance of this research in arguing why AI combined with enterprise engineering is such a powerful tool for enterprise transformation, we will discuss this research in more detail.

To carry out this research, he evaluated each case using predefined parameters to identify them as AI cases. This aspect of the research is notable, as the practice of AI had grown significantly over the recent years, with various approaches being implemented. The challenge lies in determining whether these different approaches are still comparable and whether they can all still be classified as 'Appreciative Inquiry'.

1. Bushe's first criterion for categorising the cases was the adherence to AI's core principles. He examined whether these principles were present or were absent.

2. The second element of the case evaluation relates to the intervention model, with the most significant being the 4-D cycle. Bushe assessed whether the 4-D cycle was applied.

3. The third element concerns the narrative approach of AI. The most common approach is collecting stories during the discovery phase.

4. The fourth element addresses the focus of the AI intervention, distinguishing between a focus on 'figure' versus 'ground'. This concept relates to AI's goal of not only delivering change but also building the capacity for ongoing change. Traditional organisational interventions often result in specific changes, referred to as 'figure', while AI aims to create new 'ground' – a new foundation for a broader range of future possibilities.

   Since this fourth element is especially important in the light of transformational change, it is vital to understand the way Bushe explains this distinction: "*It is difficult to define what qualities, ideas, or processes are figural or ground in the abstract. Ground concerns the substructure that influences what people think and do. In enterprises, this can range from physical spaces to mental maps, from emotional fields to semantic fields*". (Bushe 2013, p. 89)

5. The fifth element of evaluation involves the working methods in the change process. Traditional organisational development approaches often emphasise action planning, progress monitoring, and implementation strategies. In contrast, the appreciative approach seeks to avoid these conventional methods.

   Bushe describes this as follows: "*Instead, the first three D's of Appreciative Inquiry should create a set of images and ideas that are so compelling to system members that they voluntarily find ways to transform their social and work processes. By allowing this transformational process to operate from the ground up, creating systems for supporting local initiatives without requiring consensual or hierarchical validation, some AI theorists argue that much more change takes place, much faster, than through any attempt to control and implement something new*" (Bushe & Kassam 2005, p. 177).

   This idea of bottom-up, free of control emerging initiatives is particularly intriguing. Given our earlier definition that enterprises are complex social systems, deliberately designed to achieve goals, it may be challenging to accept emerging ideas as the sole means of rapidly enacting change. This aspect of AI will be further explored when discussing Appreciative Inquiry and design.

Bushe's analysis focused on two key outcomes when examining the cases, both concerning whether the approach resulted in transformational change:

1. "*Did the AI intervention result in new knowledge, or, as seen in traditional organisational development, simply in new ways of doing things? Did it create new perspectives, models, or theories for addressing existing issues?*" (Bushe & Kassam, 2005, p. 165).

2. "*Did a generative metaphor emerge from the initiative*?" (Bushe & Kassam, 2005, p. 165). Generative metaphors are provocative phrases that inspire new possibilities for previously unconsidered action (Schön 1993).

Using these variables, Bushe evaluated the 20 cases together with multiple independent evaluators. The results were surprising. Although all cases were deemed successful, only seven were categorised as 'transformational' according to Bushe's criteria. All these transformational cases generated new knowledge, introduced a new metaphor, and created new ground. Of these, five employed a bottom-up emerging approach during the destiny phase, one was clearly implementation-focused, and the orientation of the final case was ambiguous.

In the 13 cases that did not result in transformational change, the findings were even more striking:

- none of them created new knowledge.
- only 8% introduced a generative metaphor.
- only 8% created new ground.
- only 16% utilised a bottom-up emerging approach.

Conclusion of the analysis

Bushe offered the following insights from his research: "*Two key insights emerge from this analysis of AI cases in practice. One is that transformational change is more often associated with the more radical change prescriptions of AI advocates. A focus on changing how people think, rather than merely altering what they do, significantly differs from conventional enterprise development practices. ... Perhaps even more radical is the recommendation to relinquish control in planned change efforts and foster a more improvisational approach to the action phase in action research... The cases reviewed here suggest that if we create a collective sense of what needs to be achieved, develop new models or theories aligned with people's inherent motivation in relation to organisational life, then significant change, leading to enhanced organisational performance, can occur when individuals are empowered to take the initiative*." (Bushe & Kassam, 2005, p. 178).

The importance of this statement will become very clear in the next chapter where we will investigate the advantages of combining appreciative inquiry with the enterprise engineering tools that we will discuss in the coming paragraphs. Given the complexity of social systems such as enterprises, it is crucial to reduce this complexity to create a collective sense of direction that is intellectually manageable. We will argue that the design phase of Appreciative Inquiry can be enriched by tools that help simplify this complexity.

Enterprise Engineering and Enterprise Governance: Unlocking the Power of Transformation

When embarking on a transformation project, enterprise engineering and enterprise governance provide us with the essential tools to reimagine and rebuild our organisations. Two pivotal practices from the domain of enterprise engineering – conceptual modelling and architecturing – form the backbone of this transformative process. Next to engineering, we also need governance to manage the transition. Therefore we will provide the concept of a transitional organisation.

Let us first dive into how these engineering practices can shape the journey, reduce complexity, and align stakeholders to a shared vision of success.

Conceptual modelling is the formal description of certain aspects of the physical and social world around us for the purpose of understanding and communication. A conceptual model is often an abstraction of things in the real world, both physical and social. The variety and scope of conceptual models are due to the range of purposes for which they are used. We use the illustration in figure 21 to picture the activity of conceptual modelling. It is a group of people sitting at a round table and reflecting and discussing how to carve the conceptual model out of the massive block in between them.

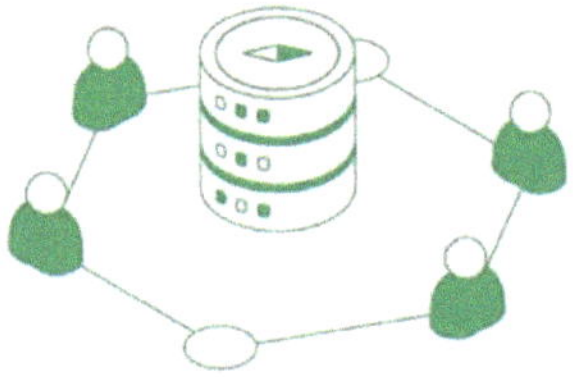

Figure 21. Enterprise Engineering: Conceptual Modelling

Most people are familiar with architecture from the world of construction, such as the rules that determine whether you can build three or four storeys high. The rule exists and is laid down in the urban planning department of the city or municipality where you want to build.

Just as there is architecture for building in cities, there is also architecture for enterprises. We call this enterprise architecture, which consists of a large set of rules. When you want to change as a company, the existing rule may no longer be appropriate because it leads to the wrong behaviour. We refer to the process of drawing up new rules as architecturing. A formal explanation of the concept 'architecturing' can be the following: the activity of defining the fundamental structures of a system together with the principles and rules that guide its design and evolution (Maier & Rechtin 2009; ISO/IEC/IEEE 2011; Rozanski & Woods 2012).

The set of rules or guiding principles determines the course of change; they form the compass, hence the following illustration (Figure 22).

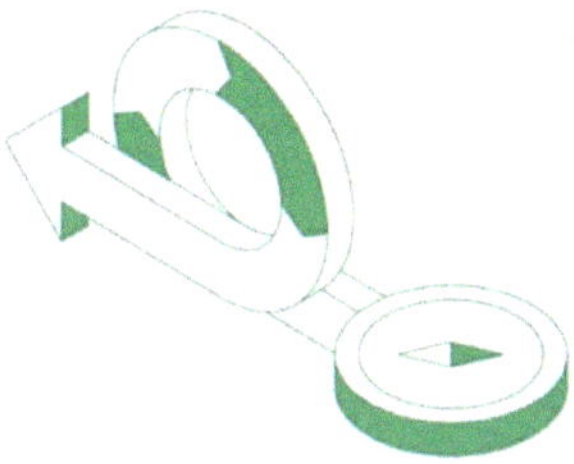

Figure 22. Enterprise Engineering: Architecturing

Before delving deeper into ontology and architecture, it is important to address two more aspects of the transformation. The reference context we are working in and the transitional organisation we need.

A clear and shared understanding of the reference context is a prerequisite for creating ontological models and designing the right architecture. However, experience in change projects reveals that the reference context of an organisation undergoing transformation is not static. Often, the reference context, or elements of it, is itself subject to change, especially when the transformation is driven by major external changes.

Here are some examples of questions that might help the reflection process on the reference context:

(1) what is the type of change that is occurring in this enterprise?
(2) are there other changes occurring in the enterprise or in the environment the enterprise is in?
(3) what is the experience of the enterprise with respect to changes in the past? what is the culture of the enterprise like?
(4) is there a momentum for change that can be expected?
(5) how will the change affect the relationship between the organisation and its environment?

Furthermore, during the reflection process, the reference context will probably be challenged. Open and innovative discussions about overcoming challenges or brainstorming new organisational strategies can lead to questioning established norms and values. It is essential to remain receptive to such challenges during the initial phase of the change process, which demands several iterations of inquiry. However, at a certain point, the questioning must cease, and the process of defining the new enterprise in a deterministic manner must begin. Identifying the exact point at which this transition occurs is one of the intriguing elements explored in this text.

Last but not least we need a transitional organisation. This is some form of committee, task force, group of people with the authority to make decisions on the activities to prepare the change, on the changes in the organisation themselves, on the budget, resources and time that can be spent on the preparation of projects and on the execution of approved projects.

Conceptual modelling using DEMO

The design of enterprises should be comprised of goal-oriented and deliberate actions. Incidental, emergent processes with unpredictable outcomes are insufficient to build or change enterprises effectively. One of the conditions for successful enterprises is their ability to rely on a structural-functional foundation, in which certain relationships between elements of the enterprise can be described unambiguously (Hoogervorst 2009, 2012).

However, we will argue in Chapter IV that creating this structural-functional foundation is an appreciative and emergent process that requires participation from the entire system, yet is neither incidental nor unpredictable. It involves an inquiry, leveraging the necessary know-how and know-why to determine what future constructions will support the desired functionality of the transformed enterprise, as well as how stakeholders will need to act within the new enterprise to ensure the change is sustainable. Within the enterprise engineering framework, valuable elements emerge that can assist in mastering the change process.

The Role of Ontology in Enterprise Transformation

The word 'ontology' has been used in this book several times already. Here is a good place to explain it properly. Ontology (from the Greek ὀν = *being* and λόγος = *word*, *teaching*) is another word for the study of being. It is the branch of philosophy that considers what 'is' and what can be defined as 'being'. Ontological theories consist of concepts and categories that define the properties of 'things that exist' and describe the relationships between them.

In the field of enterprise engineering, the term ontology, or enterprise ontology, is used to describe the essence of an enterprise. Regardless of all the choices made during implementation, what is the 'being' of this enterprise? In other words, what are the essential responsibilities that make this enterprise what it is?

One of the key reasons for our choice of enterprise ontology for operationalising implementation-independent models is that its underlying theory is based on a constructionist belief. As Dietz (2006, p. 8) explains, "*Intersubjective reality (i.e., what is real between two subjects) is constructed and continuously adapted through negotiation and achieving social consensus among subjects*".

We regard ontology as the foundation for meaningful communication about a particular reality, which is continuously shaped and reshaped through communication.

Since an enterprise is an artefact created through social interaction during its design, it can only be changed through a similar process of interaction. Therefore, the theory and methodology used to support enterprise change must accommodate this constructionist viewpoint.

A second important aspect of enterprise ontology, as defined by Dietz, is its focus on shared conceptualisation. The purpose of ontology is to create shared understanding, which is achieved through clear and explicit communication. Natural language, due to its inherent ambiguity, is insufficient for this task; thus, ontologies must be formal and precise.

Thirdly, the concise nature of ontological models is crucial for managing the complexity of enterprises. Enterprises are inherently complex, heterogeneous systems, and changing them can introduce additional complexity. To improve the success of transformation projects, it is essential to drastically reduce this complexity, allowing for meaningful discussions about the current situation and the desired future state of the enterprise. The transaction and distinction axioms play a vital role in achieving this.

Conceptual model for both function and construction?

The enterprise engineering framework suggests the need for an implementation-independent conceptual model, encompassing both the function (teleological model) and the construction (ontological model) of the enterprise. For the functional perspective, further research is required to develop an appropriate modelling method. Jan Hoogervorst's earlier work (2012) provides a preliminary graphical representation of the relationships that define the enterprise's interaction with its environment.

Discussions about the future business definition of an enterprise can go in all directions and produce very conceptual and abstract results. To better structure these discussions, we use a pragmatic approach in which the following aspects are defined:

- the market the enterprise wants to be in;
- the products and services the enterprise wants to offer;
- the formula the enterprise wants to use to approach the market;
- the dominant orientation of the enterprise (for instance product-oriented versus market-oriented).

The combination of the answers to these questions constitutes a high-level strategic matrix of products and markets. Although this matrix is very useful in real cases, it is not an implementation-independent conceptual model. It is not implementation independent and it is not a conceptual model. However, our experience shows that they are very useful.

For the constructional perspective, DEMO has been selected as the preferred methodology. DEMO stands for Design and Engineering Methodology for Organisations and was developed by Jan Dietz (2006). The methodology is currently promoted and maintained by the Enterprise Engineering Institute. In our book, we will focus on the key elements of DEMO that are used in our transformation approach, such as the transaction pattern and the distinction axiom.

DEMO: the Universal Transaction Pattern

Reducing complexity and making enterprise transformations intellectually manageable are essential to increasing the success of transformation projects. The universal transaction pattern significantly contributes to these objectives.

The transaction axiom states that the operation of an enterprise consists of activities performed by actor roles, which are elementary units of authority and responsibility, executed by individuals. These individuals perform two types of acts: production acts and coordination acts, which result in production facts and coordination facts, respectively (Dietz 2006).

The transaction axiom, which explains how these acts take place, posits that the complete transaction pattern is universal. Every transaction follows a course through this pattern, consisting of at least four coordination acts and one production act organised in three phases - the order phase, the execution phase, and the result phase.

As shown in figure 23, the transaction initiator – here presented as a lady – requests the execution of the production, and the executor – here presented as a man – promises to carry it out. This concludes the order phase.

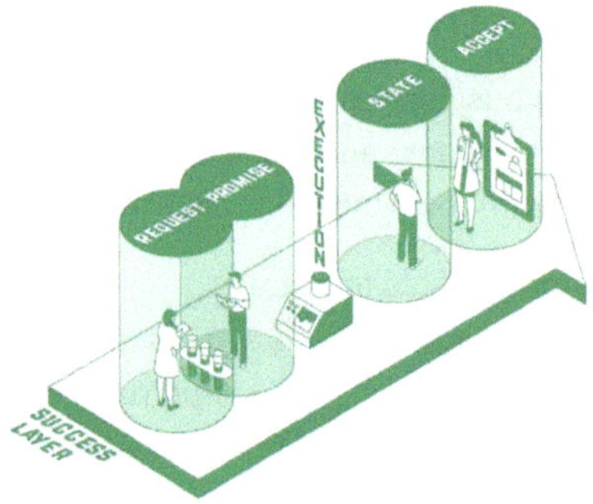

Figure 23. Universal Transaction Pattern: Success Layer

In the execution phase, the executor performs the production act. The transaction then enters the result phase where the executor declares that he has accomplished the task.

When the initiator accepts the successful execution, the transaction is completed and the production is a fact (Dietz 2006).

Let us take a simple and straightforward example to clarify how the transaction pattern works. The hot bakery in the village where I live bakes nice fresh bread every day. When I step inside the fragrant shop, I request a sliced round, grey peasant bread. The baker nods affirmatively, takes a round grey loaf from the rack, walks to the slicer and cuts the bread. Then he puts the sliced bread into a bread bag. He looks at me and says, "Please, a grey peasant bread sliced. Would you like anything else?". I reply, "No thanks, this is it," and accept the bread.

By accepting the bread, the transaction is closed and the delivery of the bread is a fact. The above example describes the success layer of the transaction, so named because all the steps have a positive outcome.

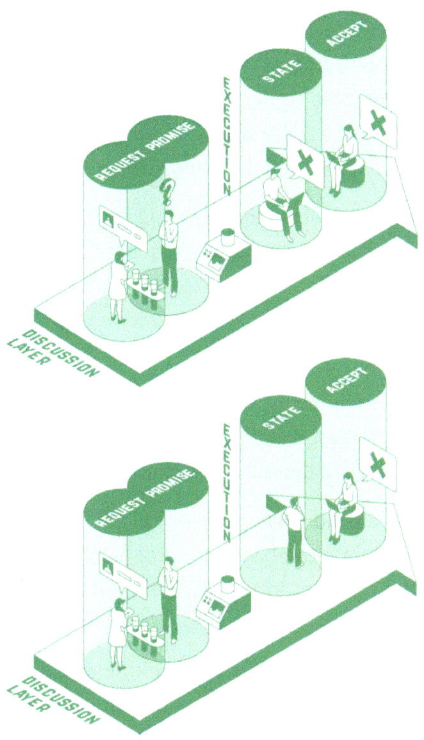

Figure 24. Universal Transaction Pattern: Discussion Layer

Next to the success layer of the transaction there is also a layer of discussion. The discussion layer describes the possible states of the transaction when both parties do not agree in one or another phase of the transaction. Both actors will try to reach an agreement through effective communication. If they don't, the transaction will not be completed successfully and will imply a decline/quit/reject or a stop.

In figure 24 you will see the discussion in the order phase (top of the illustration) and the other type of discussion in the result phase. In the illustration the discussion remains unresolved and leads to a halt, marked by an X.

Let us go back to the baker to demonstrate what the discussion layer means. The next day, I return to the local bakery. Like the day before, I request a sliced round, grey peasant bread. This time the baker shakes his head and says, "Excuse me, but I just sold my last grey peasant bread there, I'm sorry. Instead, can I offer you a long brown bread?" I think for a moment and reply, "Rather not, just give me a sliced rye bread." "That will do," says the baker and he takes a rye bread from the rack, cuts it and then says "Please, anything else?" "No, thank you," I say, "this will do" and I accept the bread.

Since the baker had no more peasant bread available, he was unable to provide me what I requested. However, after some questions we found a new, slightly different agreement. The same process can happen between the declare and the acceptance stages, after production. The baker states that he has produced what I requested, but I saw that he made a mistake and therefore I am not willing to accept it. Again, we start a negotiation which may or may not lead to a successful transaction.

Next to declining instead of promising, and rejecting instead of accepting, there exists the phenomenon of revocation. It is possible that a request that was initially made is revoked. For instance, a customer of our bakery ordered twenty pastries for their daughter's birthday party. On the day itself, the daughter is ill and the party is cancelled. They revoked their order.

A revocation can be the case in each of the coordination acts. In European law, every person that buys a certain product has the right to return it (provided that it is unused and undamaged) within seven days of the purchase and is eligible to request a refund.

Next to the success and discussion layer there is also a third layer, the layer of discourse. Here, the parties will renegotiate the basic conditions of their collaboration. Most likely this happens after serious changes in the environment or after repeated discussion in transactions between them.

Let us return to our local bakery example to demonstrate this. Every day, for two weeks, I stop by the bakery to buy a round, grey peasant bread, but each time the baker tells me that he has no more bread, not even white bread. After two weeks I get so tired of passing his store for nothing that I ask him why he never has any bread left when I arrive. He says that he decided to bake less peasant bread because he wants to be sure that at the end of the day all his bread is sold. Not at all satisfied with his explanation, I tell the baker that I understand and that in the future I will be going to the baker in the next village.

How to use the transaction pattern?

The transaction pattern has an important advantage in the fact that it brings structure to the business communication. Knowing that the pattern is universal, describing all possible states of the business communication between two parties, it is not necessary to describe all possibilities for each transaction that can take place between the enterprise and its environment, at least not at first. Thanks to the transaction pattern, the complexity of the enterprise can be reduced and can be made intellectually manageable. The compact oversight of the transactions describing the enterprise in this first phase of our change process facilitates consensus over a large group of stakeholders.

Figure 25 shows the transaction symbol as it is presented in the DEMO conceptual modelling language. Each transaction takes place between two actors, the initiator and the executor. The executor is indicated with the little red block. The symbol of the transaction shows both the communication (circle) and the execution (diamond) and the four spaces between the communication and the executions represent the four coordination actions (request – promise – declare – accept).

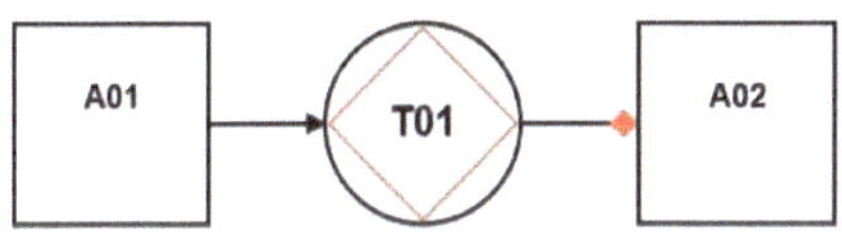

Figure 25. DEMO symbol of one transaction between two actors

DEMO related illustrations can be viewed via the QR-code and the related url:
https://enterprise-transformation.com/book-cgtet/version-1/image-25/

What is not visible in the symbol of the transaction is all the possible steps and facts that exist in the discussion layer. But since we know that the transaction pattern is universal, we don't need to draw them in the construction diagram. This helps considerably to focus the business analysis only on the important information (the essential transactions) and to avoid premature discussion of all details and exceptions.

Expanded with the discussion in the order and result phases, the same transaction pattern in figure 26 immediately shows the result of a first simplification of the transaction pattern.
The initiator starts the transaction with a 'request'. Once this has been made, the status of the communication is 'requested', indicated by 'rq' in the circle between the two actors.

The same can be seen after the executor has made the promise and also later during the result phase.

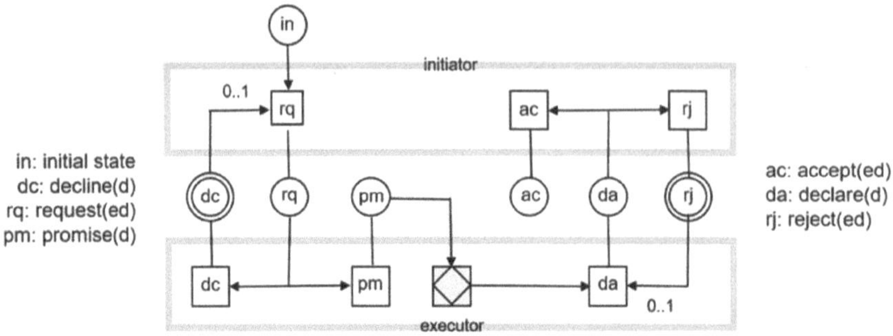

Figure 26. Transaction Pattern with Success and Discussion Layer.

Reproduced with Permission from Jan Dietz, 2026, Enterprise Ontology (2024)
DEMO related illustrations can be viewed via the QR-code and the related url:
https://enterprise-transformation.com/book-cgtet/version-1/image-26/

Next, in the realisation of the change, the transaction pattern gives great advantages because it guides the further detailed analysis and decision process. For each transaction, the analyst can use: (1) the basic transaction pattern to investigate the exceptions and (2) the revocation patterns to investigate how the enterprise deals with these revocations.

In the middle of figure 27, you see the success layer with the production in the middle. For each coordination step in the success layer, you also find the related revocation and the possible outcomes of the discussion.

Since the conceptual model uses the vocabulary of the business and is easily understandable for non-technical stakeholders, it is a great tool to structure the completion of the business analysis. For each transaction the analyst uses the complete transaction pattern as a guideline for their questioning and step by step, in a very structured way, additional details of the analysis are added.

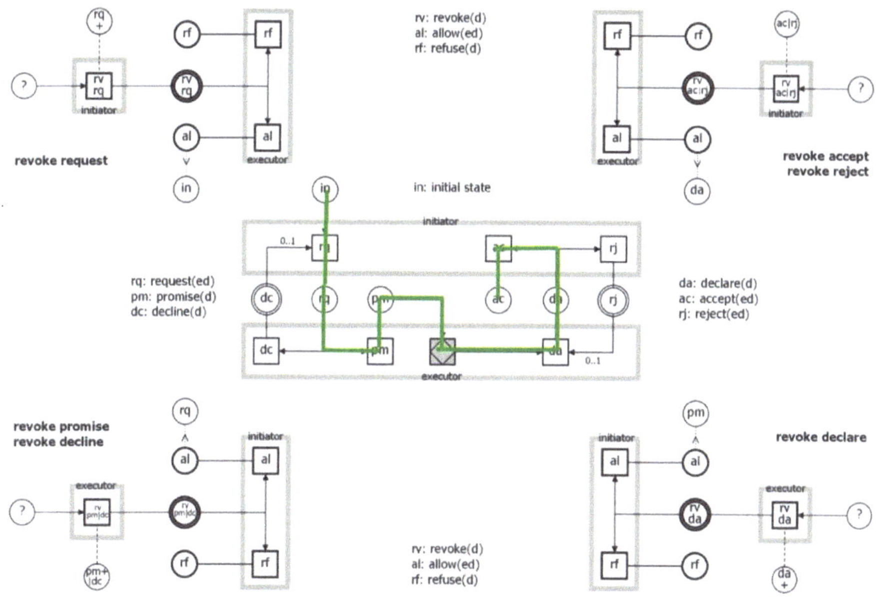

Figure 27. General Transaction Pattern

Reproduced with Permission from Jan Dietz, 2026, Enterprise Ontology (2024) DEMO related illustrations can be viewed via the QR-code and the related url: https://enterprise-transformation.com/book-cgtet/version-1/image-27/

In practice, we are often confronted with systems in the testing phase that have been built on an incomplete analysis. What strikes me is that very often the discussion layer of the transactions has not been explored in sufficient depth. This is not entirely surprising, given that we know that most analysts and developers do not conduct a structured inquiry into the possible discussions in a transaction. As a result, only those exceptions that are indicated by the business owner come to light. But forgetting an exception is, of course, human. A memory aid in the form of a transaction pattern can be a great help.

For the preparation of operation and the definition of operational rules, the transaction pattern brings extra structure as well. Knowing the structure of the transaction pattern, it is clear that there are two kinds of rules - coordination rules and production rules, that are related to coordination acts and production acts, respectively.

The distinction axiom

Emphasis is given to the distinction axiom for two reasons. First because the distinction axiom will also help to further reduce the complexity. Secondly, it also explains the constructionist stance of the underlying theory and the way it deals with communication. This is an important element in the advantage of DEMO in change projects.

In the distinction axiom Dietz makes a distinction between three human abilities that are important in the way actors operate (Dietz 2006). The first one is called 'forma' and is about the form aspect of communication, the uttering and perceiving of information. In human communication, an example of the form aspect is the language we use. If people use different languages, there is miscommunication based on a problem in the form. Related to enterprises, the form aspect deals with the structure of information and is about the datalogical actions (copying, storing, transmitting existing information).

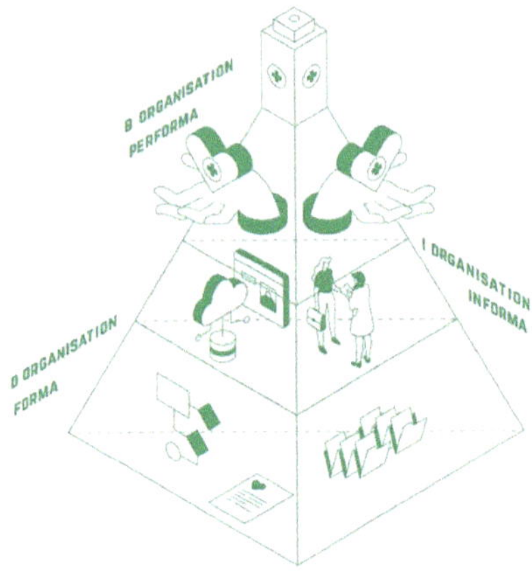

Figure 28. DEMO: the distinction axiom

The second ability is called 'informa' and is about the content aspect of communication, namely the formulation and interpretation of thought. An example of informa is the shared understanding of a term. If an organisational specialist talks to an information technology specialist about change management there is a certain risk that they both use the same word but that they are talking about completely different activities. If people use the same words without sharing the same meaning and are unaware of this, we talk about miscommunication at the content level. Related to enterprises, the content aspect deals with the content of the information and is about infological actions (computing, deducing, reasoning).

The third ability is called 'performa' and is about the purpose aspect of the communication, namely the commitments we express to and accept from others. Representatives of enterprises (for example a salesperson of company A and a purchase specialist of company B) that are preparing a business deal are communicating with each other with a specific purpose. The final goal of both representatives is to close the deal, but the purpose of the salesperson will probably be to maximise his margin, and the purpose of the purchase specialist is related to minimising their total cost.

A misunderstanding based on a difference in purpose is obviously of a different nature. In the example, both parties are probably aware of the purpose of their interaction, but this will not always be the case. Related to enterprises, the purpose aspect deals with the purpose of our actions and is about ontological actions (deciding, judging, producing, etc).

DEMO and the Theory of Communicative Action

In the phase of the transformation process where conceptual models are developed, the primary goal is to reduce complexity to a level where all stakeholders can actively participate in the discussion. Therefore, the models must capture the essential aspects of the enterprise. Key questions include: what commitments is the enterprise making to its external environment (functional perspective), and what internal activities and responsibilities must be organised to ensure it can fulfil these commitments (constructional perspective)?

Reducing complexity and rendering the subject matter intellectually manageable are crucial prerequisites for involving all stakeholders and achieving a shared understanding. As with any social system, such as an enterprise, communication is the primary mechanism by which things happen. Through communication, actors accept or reject proposed products and services, make decisions, and move processes forward.

For this reason, it is vital to understand what communication entails. One of the reasons DEMO is so compelling for enterprise transformation projects is its foundation in communication theory with a constructionist approach. DEMO is grounded in Habermas' 'Theory of Communicative Action' (Habermas, 1981).

While a detailed explanation of Habermas's theory is beyond the scope of this book, several aspects are particularly relevant to enterprise transformation. Habermas distinguishes between three 'worlds' that influence and are influenced by communication: the objective world, containing elements that exist independently of any subject; the subjective world, unique to each individual; and the social world, which is shared by a specific group of individuals who have collectively created it.

In the context of enterprise transformation, this distinction is critical. A new vision for a specific aspect of the enterprise is only real for those who were involved in its creation; it exists in their shared social world. For other members of the organisation, this vision simply does not exist. Even when it is documented and disseminated, individuals not involved in the creation process will interpret it through their own subjective lens, which may differ significantly from the original intended meaning. As discussed earlier in this text, Appreciative Inquiry is based on a similar constructionist stance.

A second important element of Habermas' theory of communicative action is the concept of 'Verständigung', a German term that is difficult to translate into English. It is often rendered as 'communication', but a more precise interpretation would be 'aligning subjective mindsets'.

According to Habermas (1995 [2017], p.57):

Verständigung "*functions as a mechanism for coordinating action only when participants in the interaction agree upon the validity of their assertions. This requires mutual recognition of each other's claims to validity, which are intersubjectively acknowledged.*" In this sense, 'Verständigung' is an essential component of efficient and goal-oriented communication. Participants in a communicative act must:

a) indicate which 'world' they are referring to,
b) make validity claims about it, and
c) intersubjectively accept or dispute these claims.

This process, which Habermas refers to as the 'Verständigungsprozess', must be repeated. We might argue that 'Verständigung' (or aligning subjective mindsets) is a prerequisite for initiating communicative action, or at the very least, it is a vital component of communication that supports the coordination of social action.

The Aspect Models of DEMO

In DEMO, the enterprise is represented through various models, each highlighting different aspects of the organisation. These are referred to as aspect models. DEMO distinguishes four key aspect models: the construction model, the process model, the state model, and the action model. DEMO utilises a conceptual modelling language to describe the enterprise in a concise and unambiguous manner. The notation or language used for modelling will not be detailed in this document, and reference is made to Dietz's earlier work (Dietz, 2006). More recently Jan Dietz and Hans Mulder (2020) published a new version of the fundamentals of DEMO.

The construction and process models are the most pertinent in the context of the approach we propose. These two models are closest to the everyday reality of employees and managers. They are also the most helpful in capturing the complexity in an understandable model. The construction model (CM) is divided into two sub-models: the interaction model and the interstriction model.

The interaction model visualises the interaction between actors at an essential level. The enterprise and its external environment are illustrated by depicting the actors and their transactions (with all possibilities of the universal transaction pattern represented by a single symbol). Consequently, the construction model is often referred to as the 'actor-transaction diagram'. Before going further into the interaction model, we will give a short explanation of the interstriction model.

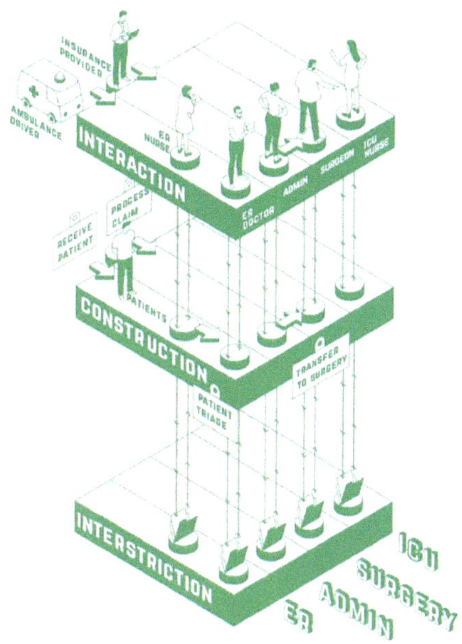

Figure 29. DEMO: construction model with interaction- and interstriction layer

The interstriction model, illustrates the information sources actors require to perform their transactions. In other words, it restricts the actors' freedom of action based on the information available.

The model is called the interstriction model because it imposes restrictions on activities. The method by which information is made available is dependent on implementation and is not modelled, as aspect models are designed to remain implementation-independent.

A short example will make this clearer. The nurse in the emergency room (ER nurse) gets access to parts of the data in the medical record of the patient that are available for their role. While executing the triage typical for an ER-admission, she can add data to that same medical database. The people working in the patient administration department will not have access to the same data as the ER nurse. Their access is restricted to act on tasks related to their role and therefore they are allowed access only to the necessary data. The responsibilities in the interaction model impose access or no access to data, which is managed in the interstriction model.

Having discussed the interstriction model, we now turn our attention to other characteristics of the interaction model.

To represent the enterprise and its relationships with the external environment, the enterprise is drawn as a black box, with the focus placed on transactions involving external actors. This is known as the Global Actor Transaction Diagram (GATD). It centres on the products and services delivered to the external environment, and can serve as a starting point for the functional conceptual model.

By 'opening the black box' representing the enterprise in the GATD, the detailed actor transaction diagram visualises the transactions and responsibilities required to fulfil the enterprise's commitments to the external environment. At this stage, the enterprise is represented as a white box, and all internal actors and transactions are defined. This model is called the Detailed Actor Transaction Diagram (DATD) and forms the constructional conceptual model of the enterprise.

The following example demonstrates the simplicity of the DEMO construction model by describing the essential conceptual model of my local bakery. The external environment includes three actors: the client, the supplier, the government. For the sake of simplicity of this example, the different suppliers and government agencies are represented as one actor. For the bakery to deliver bread to me as a client, it has to purchase the ingredients for the bread.

As you can see, the payment transactions are modelled as a separate transaction. The first reason is the fact that the initiator of the payment transaction is different, it is the bakery that asks to be paid, while it is the client that asks to receive the bread. The same applies to the delivery of ingredients. The second reason is that the timing and the frequency of the payment might not be in sync with the timing and the frequence of the delivery. The supplier will send an invoice – the request to start the payment transaction – only once a month, including all deliveries of that month. Depending on their agreement with the bakery, the same may be the case for regular clients.

The government, the supplier and the client are outside of the scope of the detailed actor transaction diagram. This means that the model does not detail how they organise their responsibilities internally. There are five key transactions with these external parties, resulting in the following outcomes: the bread is delivered, the bread is paid, the ingredients are delivered, the ingredients are paid, and the tax payment is executed.

Let us now examine into the responsibilities that need to be organised within the bakery in order to achieve the commitments the organisation made to its external relations.

Figure 30. DEMO: Global Actor-Transaction Diagram Local Bakery

DEMO related illustrations can be viewed via the QR-code and the related url: https://enterprise-transformation.com/book-cgtet/version-1/image-30/

As an essential actor can only be responsible for executing one transaction, my local bakery requires seven essential actors that will probably be organised in four departments. The dough maker and the bread baker will be working in the bakery workshop, the bread deliverer will be serving the clients in the local store and in the financial department we discover the three clerks. The ingredients purchaser works in the procurement department. The existence of these departments will of course depend on the size of the enterprise. If it is a large bakery chain with a centralised factory and 50 stores, then all the responsibilities will be executed by different employees. But if it is my local bakery with only one store, where the baker and his wife are the only employees, then one person will be executing the responsibilities of more than one actor.

The interaction model provides a concise representation of the responsibilities (actors) and coordination of production acts (transactions) necessary to achieve the enterprise's objectives. It significantly aids in reducing the complexity of the enterprise and is often the starting point for further modelling activities. By focusing on the essential level, it also helps to establish consensus on the enterprise's fundamental aspects, which is particularly important in enterprise transformation projects.

The process model provides a description of the sequence of relationships between transactions. Two types of relationships are identified: conditional and causal. In a conditional relationship, the successful completion of the second transaction is a prerequisite for completing the first. In a causal relationship, the first transaction triggers the initiation of the second. The process model also allows for marking certain transactions as optional. This model offers a concise view of the enterprise's essential business processes, making it a valuable component in defining new operational strategies during enterprise transformation projects.

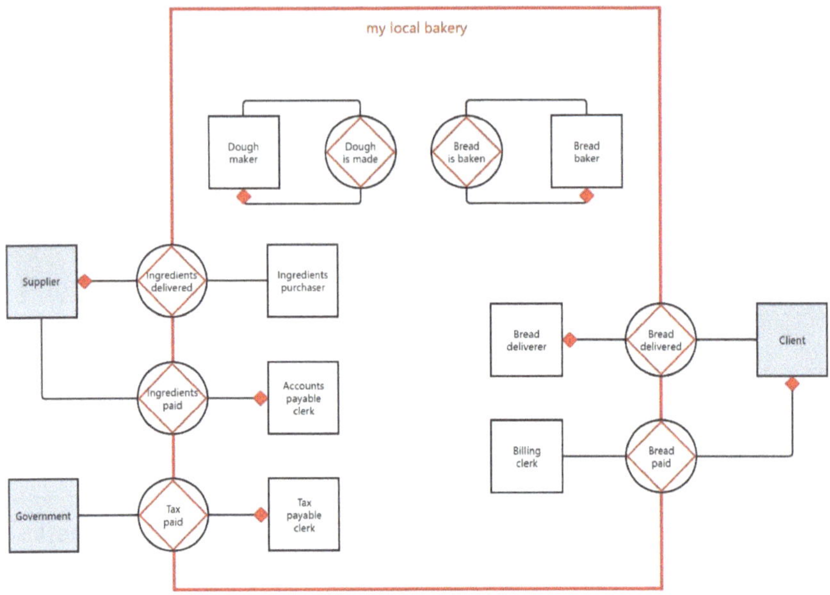

Figure 31. DEMO: Detailed Actor Transaction Diagram

DEMO related illustrations can be viewed via the QR-code and the related url: https://enterprise-transformation.com/book-cgtet/version-1/image-31/

The state model provides an overview of the lawful states of business objects within the enterprise. It is closely related to the interstriction model, as the latter visualises the information sources required by actors, while the state model describes the essential information structure. Since information management is often crucial in enterprise transformations, the state model becomes an integral part of the enterprise's evolving description.

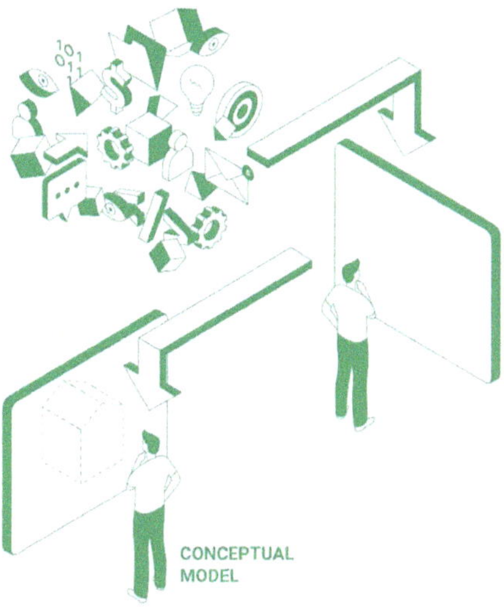

Figure 32. Process of conceptual modelling

The action model outlines the coordination rules (Dietz, 2006) at an essential level. This model is the most detailed, as it specifies the coordination rules for each step in a transaction. In enterprise transformation projects, completion of the action model occurs in a later phase. It is critical to first reach consensus at a higher level of abstraction before elaborating on the action model. Too much detail at the early stages of the change process may hinder reaching consensus. However, as the process progresses, the detailed coordination rules become necessary to ensure proper guidance of the enterprise's operations.

Defining architecture in enterprise transformation

Imagine a sailing ship navigating stormy seas. Although the captain knows the destination, he must adjust the sails, read the stars, and steer through treacherous waters. Without a clear compass – a shared understanding of the direction and guiding principles – the crew risks chaos. Similarly, in enterprise transformation, architecture serves as that compass. Not just a blueprint, but a dynamic process that engages people, clarifies purpose, and ensures everyone is moving in the same direction.

Why Architecture Matters in Transformation

Change is hard. On a personal level, it requires intention, attention, discipline, and often uncomfortable adjustments. Scale that up to an enterprise, with its tangled systems, competing priorities, and diverse people; the challenge becomes monumental. Architecture and the act of architecturing itself, offer a way through this complexity.

At its core, architecture consists of guiding principles – those non-negotiable truths that anchor decisions and actions during transformation. These principles are not handed down from on high; they are forged in deep conversations about what truly matters. They emerge from questions like: *What does success look like? What behaviours must change? What must stay constant?*

But the power of architecturing lies not just in the principles themselves. It's in the process of their creation. When leadership teams engage in these discussions, they build alignment and trust. They confront assumptions, share aspirations, and co-create a shared vision. In this way, architecturing is as much about shaping the culture as it is about designing the future.

Given the topic of this chapter, we will only explain how we approached the creation of the organisational architecture.

A practical example to make architecturing more tangible.

In order to make the process of architecturing clearer we will use the example of the Social Secretary for Enterprises (SSE).

First, some information on the context. Belgium has a unique type of HR service provider which is called a Social Secretary for Enterprises (SSE). Their core activity is calculating the salaries of their clients' employees. In addition to calculating wages in the strict sense, an SSE can also be responsible for the operational implementation of its clients' communication and payments to the various government agencies. For example, they not only calculate the withholding tax and national insurance contributions for the employee, but they also pay the calculated amounts to the appropriate government agencies. It goes without saying that the functioning of an SSE is largely dependent on properly functioning information technology systems and in particular, on the payroll calculation engine which must be able to handle the various exceptions that occur in different sectors and companies. The end-to-end process of wage calculation is particularly complex in the Belgian context.

The mission of this SSE is to support enterprises in the process of remuneration of their employees. Starting from managing the personnel data from the clients' employees, the SSE takes over the calculation of the gross salaries based on the performance of the workers, the gross-to-net calculations, the net payments, the social and fiscal declarations, and finally the payments of all declared amounts, including taxes and other amounts due.

The services delivered are based on highly automated information processing in combination with company-specific advice and services delivered by some 400 payroll consultants (PRCs). At the moment of the intervention, the organisational structure in which the PRCs were working was still based on the existing structure of two SSEs that had merged some years earlier. The goal of the intervention was to deliver a future-proof organisational design that would allow the integration of all PRCs in a single service structure.

In order to deliver this organisational design, we first worked on the following items:

- a conceptual model of the responsibilities of the SSE
- an organisational architecture
- a prototype of one organisational unit
- several implementation approaches of the prototype in a company-wide organisation

The conceptual model of the responsibilities of an SSE

The core activities of an SSE are highly complex. An SSE must be able to calculate the wages of different companies across many sectors. This involves a large number of variables, each of which is complex in its own right. These may include, each with its own specific regulations, for example, different types of contracts, in different regions, in different joint committees and, finally, in different companies. Each of these levels has rules that may or may not have to be followed at a lower level.

This makes discussions about system requirements particularly difficult. First because there are more exceptions than rules, and second, because subject matter experts and analysts tend to get lost in the maze. Several attempts by Belgian SSEs to build a software solution for calculating salaries have ended without result.

It is therefore very important to find a solution to control this complexity. The conceptual model we developed for this SSE, aimed among other things, to provide a clear overview of responsibilities and decisions that needed to be organised when calculating the salaries of self-employed company managers since their calculations are slightly less complex than those of their employees.

We will not discuss this model in detail, but we have decided to include it in this book because it shows that large and complex environments can also be perfectly modelled using DEMO. In the project in question, the model mainly contributed to:

- developing a shared understanding of what needs to be built
- better management of the sprint plans of the various development teams

- better coordination of the work between the representatives of the business and the representatives of the development teams
- providing more structure in the detailed business analysis, mainly when investigating the exceptions
- better scoping of the partial results to be delivered

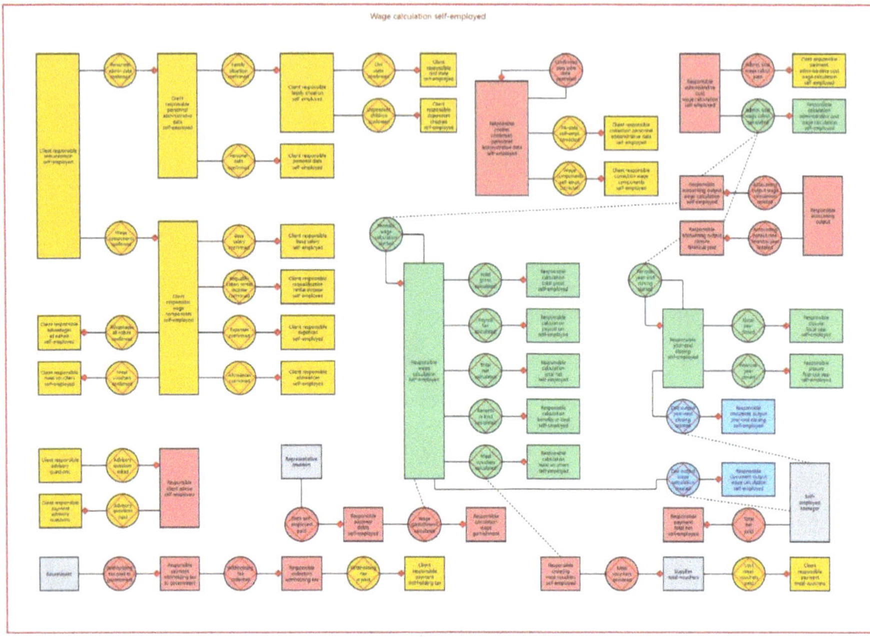

Figure 33. The construction model of wage calculation for self-employed company managers

DEMO related illustrations can be viewed via the QR-code and the related url: https://enterprise-transformation.com/book-cgtet/version-1/image-33/

The Impact of Architecturing

1. **Building Team Cohesion**: Architecturing compels management to grapple with fundamental questions: What are our goals? How do we achieve them? These discussions aren't just intellectual exercises – they are team-building moments.

Leaders emerge from these sessions with a clearer understanding of each other's perspectives and a unified approach to leading the organisation.

2. **Creating Shared Mental Models**: Every individual brings a unique mental model – a lens through which they see the world. Architecturing helps align these lenses, creating shared mental models that guide collective action. It's not enough to write down principles; the conversations that shape them are what drive meaningful change.

When these principles are codified and communicated, they ripple out to the broader organisation, embedding the new ways of thinking into daily operations.

Architecturing as a Social Construct

Guiding principles are not static rules carved in stone. They are living agreements, shaped by negotiation and consensus. While some principles draw on science or regulatory standards, their real power comes from the dialogue behind them. Why does this principle matter? How does it connect to our shared purpose? These conversations transform principles into a rallying cry – a call to action that resonates across the entire enterprise.

Architecturing starts with defining areas of concern.

Borrowing from Jan Hoogervorst (2009), architecture can be seen as a normative concept – a coherent set of principles and standards that guide design and decision-making. Architecturing is the act of crafting these principles. It starts by understanding the enterprise's goals and areas of concern – the gaps between the current state and the desired future state. These Areas of Concern (AOC) might include reducing costs, improving employee satisfaction, or speeding time-to-market.

The process of architecturing is iterative and reflective. As teams identify the AOC, they refine their understanding of what's needed to bridge the gap. This emergent approach ensures that the architecture is deeply rooted in the organisation's unique challenges and aspirations.

In order to properly support the impending change, it is important that the AOCs are tailored to the difficulties that this company will encounter with this specific change. There is little point in searching for AOCs on the internet and using them, for two reasons. Firstly, because every organisation and every change within that organisation is unique, so generic AOCs are not ideal. The second reason is even more important: by asking a group of employees to think and talk together about the change and the difficulties it will bring, the AOCs really become *their* concerns.

At our SSE, we put together a group comprising all possible roles within the organisation that were involved in the change. We had them work in the morning in a typical appreciative inquiry (AI) setting with a discovery phase and a dream phase, as explained in the sections on AI. We then asked them to think about the potential difficulties that could arise on the path between the current and the desired situation.

Based on their input, the workshop facilitator translated the difficulties to be overcome into positively described goals to be achieved. This result was discussed and validated by the employees involved in a short second workshop.

At our SSE, twelve AOCs were selected, which is really the maximum. Eight to ten AOCs are more manageable, but ultimately it is the decision of the employees involved.

Typical AOCs are: 'employee confidence is high', 'our SSE chooses its challenges carefully', but also 'the decision-making circle must be closed'. Each AOC is clarified by a short definition so that it can also be understood by people who did not participate in the process.

The Four Design Domains

To make sense of complexity, enterprises are divided into four primary design domains:

1. **Business Domain**: How the enterprise interacts with its external environment – delivering products, managing customer relationships, and responding to competition.
2. **Organisation Domain**: How activities are structured internally – including processes, policies, and culture.
3. **Information Domain**: How information is managed and used – ensuring it is relevant, structured, and of high quality.
4. **Infrastructure Domain**: The technological and physical systems that support the other domains – from information technology systems to production facilities.

Guiding principles address specific AOCs within these domains, ensuring that design decisions align with the enterprise's transformation goals.

Since we were working on organisational architecture at our SSE, we were particularly interested in the organisational design domain. We decided to divide it into the following subdomains:

- Capabilities
- Employee behaviour
- Management behaviour
- Structure
- Resources
- Processes
- Policies
- Culture

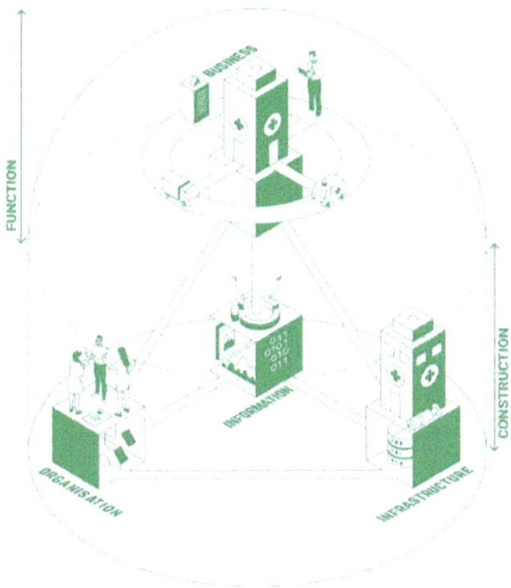

Figure 34. The enterprise and its four design domains

Defining a coherent and consistent set of principles is not an easy task. It requires collaborators to engage in discussions about the fundamental principles they will adopt to manage the future enterprise. How will they ensure that their goals are met? What guiding principles will help achieve consistency in decision-making? Since these discussions are focused on what the organisation aims to achieve (through the positive identification of areas of concern), the process of architecturing actively supports the transformation process.

Given the difficulty of the task of crafting good guiding principles, it is the workshop leader that starts with some examples. These examples are then used to explain the way of thinking needed in order to describe a principle that is addressing one or more AOCs in a specific subdomain.

We defined 32 guiding principles and for each principle we defined which AOCs they addressed in which design domain. The principle named 'simple organisational structure' is defined as: "*The organisational structure must be simple and transparent, making it immediately clear who is responsible for what within our SSE, both for employees and customers*". This principle addresses various AOCs within the 'structure' design domain. It will reduce complexity and contribute to crystal-clear roles and responsibilities, as well as to three other AOCs.

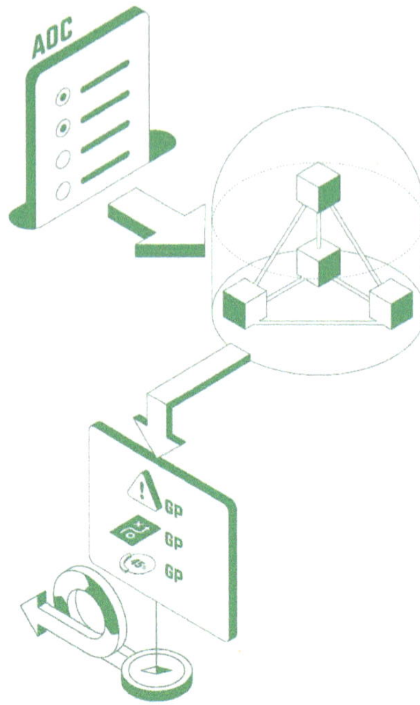

Figure 35. The process of architecturing

The outcome of this architecturing process is a coherent and consistent set of principles, systematically documented. Coherent distribution of architecture principles plays a key role in establishing the new way of thinking required to support the transformation process. It is vital that the results of the reflection are embedded in the enterprise's information systems and made accessible to all members of the organisation.

The structure of the principles for the distribution draws on Hoogervorst's framework. For each principle, it includes the following elements (Hoogervorst, 2009):

1. **The Principle Statement**: A clear articulation of the rule or guideline.
2. **The Rationale**: Why this principle matters and how it supports the transformation.
3. **The Implications**: What the principle requires in terms of actions, resources, or changes.
4. **Key Actions**: What do we need to do to embed the principle in the organisation.

This format makes the new shared mental models behind the principles explicit, enabling members of the enterprise who did not participate in the creation of the architecture to understand and apply the principles. Often, the principles identified are not yet embedded within the organisation, so defining key actions is crucial to initiate the necessary steps to implement the principle in the future.

The areas of concern (AOCs) related to the transformation specify what must be in place to facilitate the shift from the current state (A) to the desired future state (B). Examples of such concerns include 'lower production costs', 'higher employee satisfaction', or 'faster time to market'. It is essential that the AOCs are framed positively, stating clearly what the organisation seeks to achieve, and that they are directly related to the transformation process. Thus, they are not only specific to the enterprise but also to the transformation it is undergoing.

A Practical Framework

A guiding principle addresses one or more AOCs within a particular design domain. It helps ensure that the organisation remains aligned with its objectives throughout the design and realisation phases, while also maintaining consistency with design decisions made in other domains.

The architecturing process results in a matrix that maps principles to AOC and design domains. This ensures comprehensive coverage – every critical aspect of the transformation is addressed. For example, the organisation domain might be broken into subdomains like employee behaviour, structure, resources, and culture. Each subdomain must have at least one guiding principle linked to it. If a gap is identified, the team revisits the architecture to address it.

The Bottom Line: from Principles to Action

Architecturing doesn't end with defining principles. The real work begins when these principles have to be operationalised. They must be embedded in systems, processes, and behaviours. Leaders must champion them, and teams must see their relevance in daily decisions. Only then can the enterprise truly transform – not just structurally, but culturally and behaviourally.

Enterprise transformation is a journey – one that requires clarity, alignment, and shared purpose. Architecturing provides the map and the compass. But more importantly, it fosters the conversations that bring the crew together, ready to navigate uncharted waters. In the end, transformation is not just about reaching the destination; it's about how the journey reshapes the enterprise, making it more resilient, cohesive, and purpose driven.

Defining and installing the transitional organisation

In an unpublished article, entitled 'Enterprise Engineering: shortcomings of the dominant conceptual focus', Jan Hoogervorst (2025) wonders whether sufficient attention is being paid to employees within organisations in the field of enterprise engineering. Because the vast majority of applications in practice and scientific research in the field of enterprise engineering today focus on the relatively stable, operational side of the organisation, only limited knowledge has been developed about organisational adjustments or changes. There is also little input into the field of enterprise engineering from other scientific fields such as social sciences or organisational development. With this book, we aim to bring about some changes in this regard.

The article mentioned above is also particularly interesting for this book because Jan Hoogervorst describes a conceptual model that helps us understand the relationships between operation and transition in organisations on the one hand and enterprise governance and enterprise engineering on the other.

All companies are confronted with new or changing phenomena, both within the company itself and in the environment in which they operate. They have no choice but to deal with these new situations, and they can do so in various ways. They can integrate new emerging ways of organising and emerging work patterns into their operations without making big changes. In this case, the core of their way of working remains the same while dealing with the changing environment. They can also choose to improve their own processes and organisation in order to cope with the changes and they can opt to initiate a strategic change in order to prepare for even more and greater changes that they perceive to be coming.

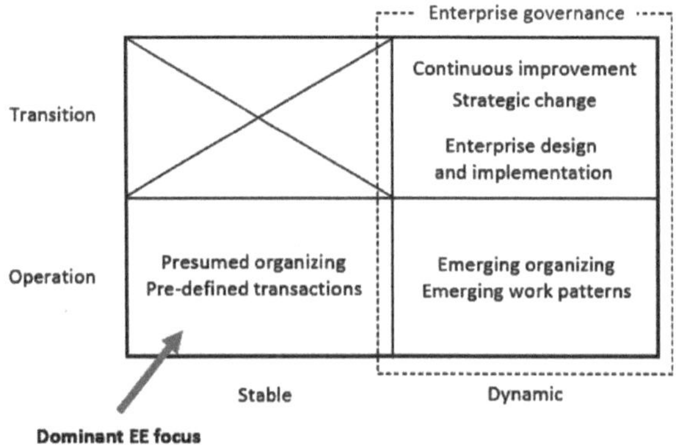

Figure 36. Focus of Enterprise Engineering.

Reproduced with Permission from Jan Hoogervorst, 2026. Unpublished

The difference between these different approaches lies in the extent to which a new design for the organisation itself is chosen. This is particularly the case with the penultimate and final approaches.

The difference between these different approaches lies in the extent to which a new design for the organisation itself is chosen. This is particularly the case with the penultimate and final approaches.

To bring some structure to this discussion, we will explain two perspectives. The first perspective with regard to companies is the operational perspective. It looks at the realisation of the business objective from the perspective of the current social organisation of the company. The second perspective is the transition perspective, which aims to achieve the same business objective by changing the operational processes and thus also changing the social organisation.

In figure 36, you find both perspectives in the rows of the quadrant. In the columns, we distinguish the state of the environment – internal as well as external – in which the enterprise is situated. Stable is defined as an environment in which activities follow a predefined way of working, while dynamic refers to an environment with emerging phenomena to which the enterprise needs to react organisationally. Since the perspective of transition cannot coincide with a stable environment, only three of the four fields of the quadrant are filled.

Reflecting on this figure, it is important to make the following remark related to the concept of enterprise governance. As one can see the enterprise governance concept covers both the dynamic quadrants and not the stable quadrant. Jan Hoogervorst adheres to a very broad definition of enterprise governance, saying that it refers to the enterprise competence (unified and integrated whole of skills, knowledge, culture, and means) for continuously inciting adequate control in operational and transitional processes in view of enterprise purpose and goals, as well as for the coherent and consistent operationalisation of enterprise reshaping initiatives through enterprise (re-)design and subsequent implementation.

Given this definition, it would be logical to extend the scope of enterprise governance to the stable environment also. However, he did not for two reasons. First, the governance of the stable enterprise operational environment can almost entirely be offered based on the operational rules. Second, the goal of the article was mainly to explain what the enterprise engineering community has been missing out because of the dominant focus on the stable operational environment.

Given the focus of our book, we are mainly interested in the enterprises that are situated in a dynamic environment. On the intersection of dynamic environment and operational perspective we find the enterprises that try to deal with the changes in their internal and external environment, while maintaining their operational approach.

In the remaining quadrant, a dynamic environment and a transitional perspective, we find the enterprises that start improvement projects or strategic change initiatives to deal with the upcoming changes in their environment. Consequently, they will also be changing their social organisation, and they will have to rethink their enterprise design.

Both perspectives or approaches, operational and transitional, can only be realised if there is an organisational form that supports this approach, namely the operational and transitional organisation. We are all familiar with the operational organisation; it is the organisation that installs the resources, procedures, and processes that enable operations. The people in the operational organisation are focused on the daily results, and if all is well designed, they act fully synchronised as suggested in figure 37.

Figure 37. The operational organisation

The transitional organisation is not as recognisable, yet it is also important in terms of business adaptation and change, resulting in a new social organisation. Failed change initiatives are often caused by a lack of attention to the transitional organisation.

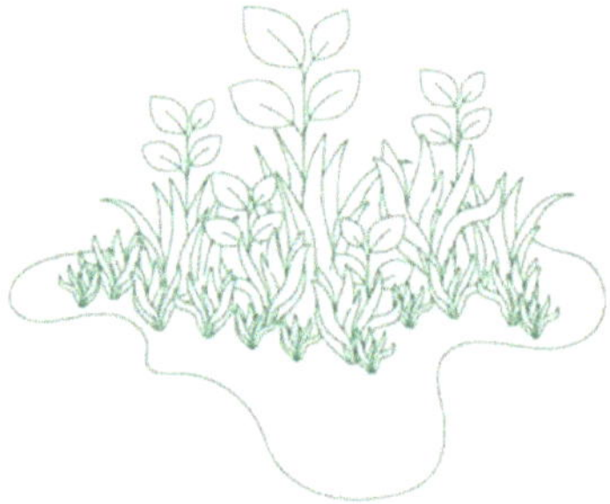

Figure 38. The transitional organisation

Decisions that need to be taken in order to achieve organisational change can have a negative impact on the running operations or on the effectiveness of the operational organisation. If these decisions need to be made by the operational organisation, because of the non-existence of a transitional organisation, chances are higher that the decision is negative.

The goals and the activities of the transitional organisation are totally different from the ones of the operational organisation. The transitional organisation exists to pick up emerging changes in- and outside of the enterprise, to reflect on the possibilities arising from those changes and to foster the interesting ones. The images that pop up while thinking of such an organisation are much closer to a gardener that is trying out new cultures on different soils, expecting that some fast-growing plants will lead to new revenues.

Conceptually it is not so difficult to see the difference between the operational organisation and the transitional one. But in the field, it is very difficult to clearly recognise both organisations. As we said already, in a lot of organisations there is no transitional organisation. Maybe there is a steering committee responsible for steering a change project. That is already something, but it depends of course on how this committee is acting and on what exactly is its responsibility. And since there is a steering committee, there is obviously already a project. So, in this particular case, a large part of the responsibility of the transitional organisation is already in the past. Was there a transitional organisation at the moment the enterprise started to prepare for the project?

The concept of a transitional organisation that is responsible to organise and steer the transition is of great importance for the success of the transition. But, let us be honest, it cannot be seen as completely separate from the operational organisation. In most organisations where transition is important, the reality will be that the operational and transitional organisation are intertwined. Some people will have a clear operational focus while some might have a pure transitional one. But in most enterprises the people responsible for transition will also be responsible for some operational activities. Reality today is that in most companies there is no dedicated transitional organisation, managers are expected to steer operations while being perceptive and receptive to change initiatives.

If one is convinced that it is really necessary for the success of a transformation to have a completely separated transitional organisation, a solution might be to carve out a part of the operational organisation and put it in the market as a separate enterprise with little to no links with the existing organisation.

A known example of this approach is the installation of Syensqo in 2023. Solvay split into two independent companies in December 2023: **Solvay**, which focuses on essential chemicals like soda, ash and peroxides, and **Syensqo**, which inherited Solvay's specialty businesses, including specialty polymers, composites, and solutions for clean mobility and materials. This strategic demerger was completed on December 9, 2023, following shareholder approval, with the new Solvay aiming for cost leadership and sustainability in essential chemicals, while Syensqo pursued innovation in specialty materials.

Figure 39. Operational and transitional organisation are often interwoven

In some cases, the transitional organisation is organised as a department directly under the responsibility of the chief executive officer, operating under the supervision of a chief transformation officer. If this 'transformation' department has the responsibility to prepare transformation initiatives, the power to steer transformation projects and to invite the right skills in these projects, then there is already a good basis to start. The next question of course is if these transformation projects are funded correctly, if they are supported by their sponsor in the right way and if they manage to deliver results that allow to start new initiatives.

A very important aspect of the transitional organisation is its capability to capture interesting ideas that emerge from within the own organisation. Experienced collaborators, next to enthusiastic clients, are the best sources for creative business ideas if they are stimulated to share their expertise.

In the case of the National Geographic Institute (chapter VI), a very practical example of the transitional organisation will be explained. It has been truly instrumental to achieve the transformation.

Chapter IV: The Link between Appreciative Inquiry and Enterprise Engineering

In chapter three, we described the methods that form the basis of the approach proposed in this book. Appreciative Inquiry, Enterprise Engineering and Enterprise Governance form the basis of the proposed way of working.

In this chapter, we want to explain why the combination of these methods is successful and how they reinforce each other.

First, we will explain social constructionism. This philosophical movement has had a very strong influence on all sciences in which humans play a prominent role. This certainly includes all practices related to organisations.

A second theme concerns the theory related to mental models. This theory stems from the scientific domain of organisational learning. We will zoom in on the concept of 'mental model' and how it provides insight into the behaviour of people in an organisation. We will also discuss the relationship between 'mental model' and organisational culture.

A third, and important relationship is that with the dialogical approach to organisational development.

To conclude this chapter, we will explain how each part of the proposed approach fits into the dialogical approach to organisational development.

All these connections will give the reader insight into the reasons why this approach is a successful one. They also offer additional opportunities to achieve similar results by using methods based on the same or similar principles.

Social Constructionism: The Foundation of Transformation

Imagine your organisation as a vibrant ecosystem teeming with relationships, routines, and unspoken agreements. Now imagine trying to change it. You quickly realise that transformation isn't just about moving the pieces around; it's about shifting the underlying patterns that hold everything together. That's where *social constructionism* comes in – a lens that reveals how the shared realities within organisations are built and, more importantly, how they can be rebuilt.

Social constructionism is a theoretical framework suggesting that various facets of social reality are shaped by ongoing interactions and negotiations between members of a social group. The theory of social constructionism posits that much of what we consider to be real is in fact the result of a dynamic construction process between human beings, influenced by social conventions which may differ depending on the social structures and contexts in which they exist.

J. De Winter, *Concise Guide to Enterprise Transformation*,
The Enterprise Engineering Series, https://doi.org/10.1007/978-3-032-29931-4_4

These constructions have a significant influence on both the behaviour and perceptions of individuals and are often internalised on the basis of cultural narratives, regardless of whether these are empirically verifiable. In this two-way process of reality construction, individuals not only interpret and assimilate information through their social relationships, but also contribute to shaping existing social narratives.

Since the late 20th century, systemic approaches have been steadily transforming fields as diverse as organisational development, coaching, and enterprise engineering. They share a core insight: to change a system, one must first understand – and then reimagine – the mental models that sustain it.

This book intentionally adopts this perspective. Social constructionism informs everything from **Appreciative Inquiry (AI)**, which draws out new visions through collective wisdom, to **Enterprise Engineering practices** like DEMO (Design and Engineering Methodology for Organisations) and architecture development. These tools share a philosophical foundation, recognising that change happens not just through systems and strategies, but through the narratives and shared understandings that people co-create.

With the social constructionist approach as a foundation, the following sections will clarify how the different elements in this proposed approach are related to each other. To achieve this, we must delve into the scientific work of Daniel Kim (1993, 2001). His research on individual and organisational learning is essential to understand why the systemic approach combining appreciative inquiry and enterprise engineering has succeeded consistently when applied. We will then link this to the latest developments in Dialogical Organisational Development, pioneered by G. Bushe (2009, 2015).

The power of shared mental models: turning culture into action

Organisational culture often feels like a convenient scapegoat to explain why changes are not successful. Why? Because culture is elusive. It's easy to name but hard to change. But what if we reframed culture not as an abstract force, but as a collection of shared mental models? Suddenly, it becomes more tangible – and beyond that, more manageable.

To learn more about shared mental models, we turn to an interesting article titled 'The Link between Individual and Organisational Learning', written by Daniel H. Kim in 1993. The author addresses a significant issue in organisational learning: the challenge of effective transfer of individual learning to the organisation or enterprise. To elucidate this transfer, the author employs the concept of 'mental models,' which can be categorised as either individual or shared, and further distinguished by whether they pertain to know-hows or know-whys. Mental models constitute the active component of memory; they influence the behaviour of both individuals and enterprises. In contrast, the passive aspect of memory can be viewed as a database where knowledge is stored and retrieved, without exerting direct influence on behaviour.

Figure 40. Individual mental model

Individual mental models are specific to a single person, whereas shared mental models pertain to a group of individuals, such as employees of an enterprise, members of a department, or even members of a family. Shared mental models emerge from a process of social construction within a group and can therefore reflect the culture of that group.

Figure 41. Shared mental model

The active component of memory significantly influences our behaviour and decisions. What drives us to act in a particular way, and why might others behave differently in the same situation? The answer lies in our memory, specifically the mental models that underpin these choices. Mental models may be operational, guiding us on how to perform tasks; or conceptual, explaining the reasons behind our actions. This is illustrated in figure 42.

In addition to individual mental models, which influence an individual's behaviour, there are also shared mental models. These shared mental models influence the behaviour of a group of people. There are also mental models that are shared by the employees of a single enterprise.

Let us take the example of a company that has the experience that a certain approach to convince a specific group of clients is very successful. This company created a training for all sales staff to explain this specific way of working. The goal of that training is to strengthen this particular way of working, thus spreading this operational shared mental model or, in other words, developing a shared routine.

Mental model	**Individual**	**Shared**
Operational	routines	shared routines
Conceptual	framework	weltanschauung

Figure 42. Four types of mental models

Within an enterprise, numerous shared mental models are encountered. When new members join an organisation, they undergo a series of onboarding activities designed to familiarise them with the existing operations and shared mental models. This process is crucial for employee integration into the organisation.

In our approach, we utilise shared mental models as a method to operationalise the culture of an enterprise. An organisational culture is composed of numerous shared mental models, possibly hundreds. While some shared mental models may be irrelevant to a particular transformation, others could impede the desired changes.

To illustrate this point, consider, for example, a group of mathematics teachers in a school, all teaching the same grade. Together, they form a professional team, making decisions about exams, selecting textbooks, and determining how to achieve the objectives their students need to meet. The group includes both seasoned teachers and younger colleagues, all with at least five years of experience in the school.

In their meetings, decisions are made smoothly because they understand how each person thinks about specific aspects of their work, having had similar discussions in the past. As there are no new factors to consider, they know what the group decision will be. The shared mental model prevails because no one feels the need to argue for a different decision.

Now imagine the same group a year later, with some changes. One teacher has retired, another has moved to a different grade, and two younger teachers have joined the team. When the group meets to decide on textbooks for the next academic year, one of the new members questions the preference for textbook A, suggesting that textbook B would be a better choice. A discussion ensues, and it becomes clear that:

- The new teacher is not alone in preferring textbook B.
- The debate is not really about A versus B, but about the use of digital teaching materials accompanying the textbooks.

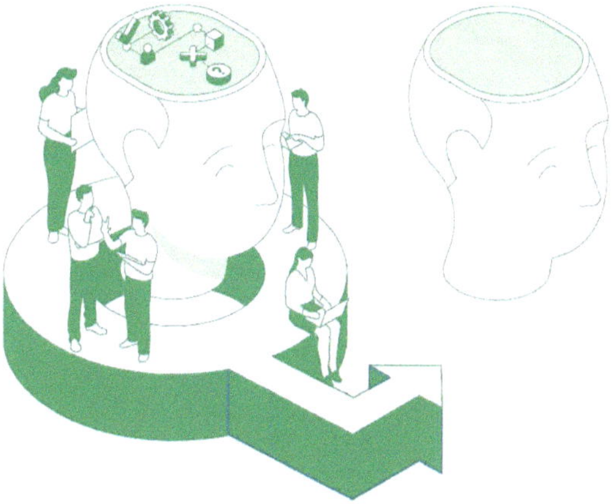

Figure 43. Process of changing a shared mental model

The question arises: Will the existing *shared* mental model prevail in the face of this challenge, or will it change in response to the new *individual* mental model? What we know is that a shared mental model will only change when it is challenged by a different individual mental model. In this scenario, it seems likely that some members of the group will be convinced to switch to textbook B. Over time, two groups might emerge within the team, each advocating for their preferred textbook.

The only process capable of altering shared mental models is dialogue – specifically, bidirectional discussions that focus on why outdated ideas must be replaced with new ones. What really matters here is the fact that the dialogue goes both ways, that both persons in the dialogue actually speak. The fact that a person has to organise his/her thoughts in order to also share them makes a substantial difference in how much a person's thinking changes.

An employee of a company who listens to a CEO explaining what will change, is unlikely to think differently about the change afterwards. For an employee who witnesses a group discussion about the change, there is only a small chance that their thinking will change even if they do not actually participate in the discussion. What does have a high chance of causing a change in thinking, is that the person involved effectively participates and formulates their own thoughts about the change during the discussion.

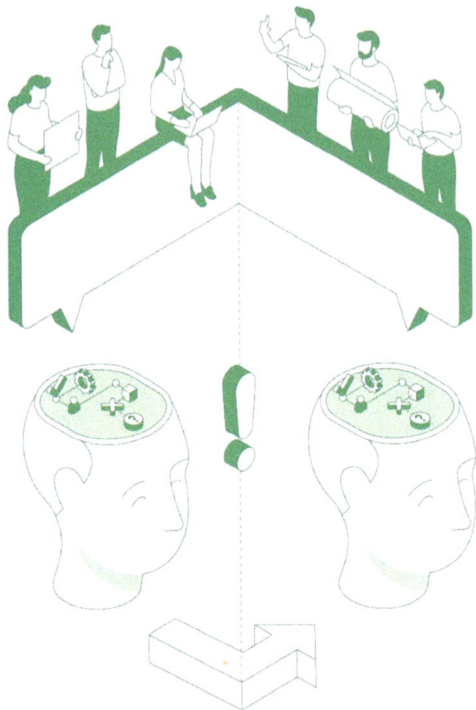

Figure 44. Inhibiting shared mental models block transformation

A real-life example from a project for a large retail company (with over 80 stores) will make the concept of mental models clearer. In this project we transformed the recruitment and selection process from a local paper-based system to a centralised digital process. A significant change for store managers was that candidates applying for their local store could also be hired by a manager from another store across town. The existing habit of retaining a good candidate's CV in their own drawer – thereby preventing other managers from accessing it – was one of the reasons for resistance against the new system.

They were focusing on the fact that with the new system, colleagues from a nearby store – seen as competitors in recruiting a good employee – could steal their candidate. It took a while to teach them to shift thinking from a loss to a gain – being able to hire a candidate that first applied in another store. Once the store managers embraced this new shared mental model, sharing candidates within the digital tool became seamless.

The example shows that the resistance that arises is not always causally linked to the actual change taking place. It can be something that is based on a deeper level and on a conviction that is not necessarily related to the actual change. What is really important is that, for genuine transformation, it is essential to identify shared mental models that may obstruct change, recognising the potential for resistance to reverse progress. Only by understanding and addressing these models can enterprises implement changes that are both meaningful and sustainable.

Culture is a bundle of shared mental models

Enterprise culture is essentially a collection of 'ways of thinking' – or shared mental models – that have over time become institutionalised within an organisation. From the moment an enterprise is created, a continuous process of interaction occurs between individual and shared mental models. In most organisations, this process is unstructured, as few enterprises are deliberately engineered from the outset.

Figure 45. Know why, know how, know who, know what

As a result, organisational routines and the enterprise's perception of its environment are shaped by its history and gradually become institutionalised. Some of these are formally articulated in company vision and mission statements, while others are documented in ISO procedures. However, the majority persist as tacit knowledge within shared mental models. A part of these models is visible on the organisation's commercial website or intranet and can easily be shared with new employees during onboarding activities. Another part only surfaces when specific decisions require explanation.

All of this tacit and explicit know-how and know-why forms the culture of the enterprise. When viewed in its entirety, this culture can seem like a powerful force that drives actions, often unconsciously. However, when examined through the lens of a specific shared mental model, it becomes more manageable, allowing for the description of how existing models can be transformed into new insights. This approach also highlights the best path to challenge current models and identifies which colleagues are necessary to implement these changes.

Deep structures and organisational principles

In systemic organisational coaching, this collection of shared mental models is referred to as the deeper structure of the organisation. To help management and employees better understand their organisation, coaches aim to reveal the underlying organisational principle (Ardui, 2023). Often, management and employees are partially blind to this principle and, despite efforts to avoid repeating past mistakes, they tend to fall into the same traps.

Raising management's awareness of their organisational principle frequently leads to an 'aha!' moment, as they suddenly understand the source of recurring pitfalls. One prevalent shared mental model in this coaching practice is that once management becomes aware of their organising principle, they know how to act accordingly.

In the domain of systemic organisational coaching, there is also a lot of emphasis on consultants showing respect for the organising principle of an enterprise. It is not appropriate to lash out at the organising principle or to condescend to the enterprise. It is thanks to the organising principle of a company that this enterprise is where it is. We couldn't agree more.

However, it is possible that a shared mental model that was once a strength became a weakness, threatening the organisation's future. In such cases, management may be partly unaware of the problem, and it becomes the external consultant's duty to alert them and assist if they wish to address the issue.

Transformational change requires fundamental change in way of thinking.

When we take all the elements together, Daniel Kim's (1993) and Bushe and Kassam's (2005) research, our own findings from case studies, ... we can only state that transformational change in companies will only be possible if there is a substantial change in the way of thinking of the employees of this company. We can operationalise what Bushe refers to as 'ground' in his research by talking about a clear change in the shared mental models.

This change in the way of thinking not only has an effect in the short term, but works through into new changes in the longer term. Similarly, we can explain what Bushe (Bushe & Marshak, 2005) means by 'figure' in his research. If the intervention did not lead to a profound change in the shared mental models, no transformational change occurs.

Figure 46. Transformation requires fundamental change of shared mental models

In other words, if the ideas are not really new but rather a rearrangement of what already existed, then the change will only lead to a few superficial and non-sustainable changes in the way of working.

Again, this is consistent with our findings in the field. Just after Covid19, we were asked by a Belgian government organisation to supervise a day when the middle management of this organisation came back together physically for the first time after several periods of lockdown. During this session, we used the methodology of an AI summit on the topic of the future way of working together.

During the feedback on the results, it turned out that the members of the organising group had a 'déjà-vu' moment. Apparently, the same comments emerged every two to three years from similar interventions. These results were also discussed with the organisation's management team in the past, but beyond some superficial adjustments, they never looked at the root cause of the problem. Again, the organisation missed this opportunity and nothing was done to address the real reasons in the organisation's undercurrent. Maybe more luck in two years...

Transformational change is not always without risks. When a company starts an introspective research process to try to become a better version of itself, it starts a far-reaching process that has an impact not only on the organisation, but also on its employees. Inherent in the organisational process is the fact that each employee also undergoes a reflection. Regardless of the changes this process has on the organisation, there will also always be a change in the employee's own way of thinking.

Figure 47. No real transformation if shared mental models are not fundamentally changed

Some employees will have new ideas about themselves, about the organisation and certainly about their position in the organisation. When it then turns out that the organisation does not then change substantially after all, there will be employees who, by participating in the process, did change their idea. Some of these employees might leave the organisation, which is a pity. Some of these employees might stay in the organisation but are not at all pleased anymore with the direction the organisation goes forward, which is a problem for the organisation as well as for the employee.

Oliver Wendell Holmes Sr. said, *"Every now and then a man's mind is stretched by a new idea or sensation, and never shrinks back to its former dimensions"* (Holmes 1858).

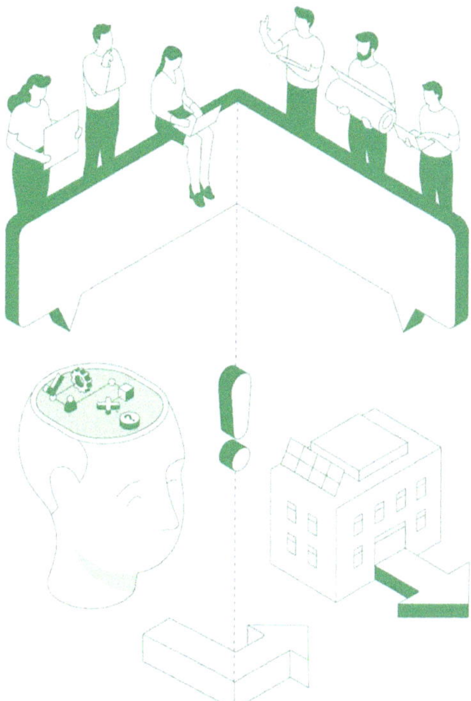

Figure 48. If change does not take place, people might leave the organisation

Dialogical Organisational Development in Enterprise Transformation

In 2009, Gervase Bushe and Bob Marshak (Bushe & Marshak, 2009) introduced the concept of Dialogical Organisational Development to distinguish it from the traditional 'Diagnostic Organisational Development' that had dominated until the mid-1980s. The two approaches are based on fundamentally different belief systems, as illustrated in the following table.

Diagnostic OD focuses on changing behaviour – what people do – while **Dialogical OD** emphasises changing mindsets – how people think.

Since the 1980s, new forms of organisational development based on dialogical principles have emerged. Appreciative Inquiry is one example, alongside Future Search, World Café, and Open Space, among others (Bushe & Marshak, 2013).

Three key mindsets underpin all dialogical OD methods. The first being emergence, encourages disruption and the development of new organising patterns that are better suited to current conditions. The second being narrative, focuses on transforming the core stories that shape organisational thinking and actions. The third being generativity, refers to creating conversations that spark new ideas, enabling people to think and act in ways they had not previously considered.

Diagnostic Organisational Development	**Dialogical Organisational Development**
Reality is an objective fact.	Reality is socially constructed.
There is a single reality.	There are multiple realities.
Truth is transcendent and discoverable.	Truth is immanent and emerges from the situation.
Reality can be uncovered through rational and analytical processes.	Reality is negotiated and may involve power dynamics.

Figure 49. Diagnostic versus Dialogical Organisational Development

In today's complex world, we are increasingly aware that the knowledge needed to find solutions can no longer be encompassed by one person alone. Only when people with the required knowledge are brought together we can achieve results. Bringing people together only makes sense if they actually share knowledge. This is where the importance and value of the dialogical approach lies.

The dialogical mindset is characterised by the following assumptions (Bushe & Marshak, 2016):

- Reality and relationships are socially constructed.
  People's views about what is real, important or true arise from ongoing conversations and social interactions. Therefore, leadership should be less about dictating facts and more about understanding and influencing how people interpret their world.
- Organisations are social networks that give meaning.
  An organisation can best be understood as a network in which people give meaning to what is happening through conversations and shared stories. That is why leaders must pay attention to the informal conversations and meaning-making processes that shape behaviour and organisational culture.
- Transformational leadership shapes how meaning is created – particularly stories that guide experiences.
  Meaning does not arise in a vacuum. It is shaped by the stories and storylines that circulate within an organisation. That is why leadership is narrative work: the

stories people tell about what the organisation is and could become have a fundamental influence on actions.

- Organisations are constantly changing, consciously and unconsciously, with different changes taking place at different speeds.
  There is no stable state to which organisations return – everything is always in flux. Stability is merely a slow change. That is why leaders must see change as something constant and inevitable, making flexibility and responsiveness core competencies of leadership.
- Groups and organisations are inherently self-organising, but disruption is necessary for transformational adaptation and change.
  People and groups naturally organise themselves – they create routines, patterns and cultures. To radically change these patterns, disruption must occur. Therefore, leaders must create conditions that disrupt old habits and support new, adaptive patterns.
- Adaptive challenges are too complex to know all the variables and the right answer in advance, so emergent change processes are needed.
  When problems are complex and uncertain, no single leader or expert has enough information to determine the best solution in advance. Instead, the organisation must discover solutions through iterative, emergent processes involving many stakeholders. Therefore, the leader must no longer come up with top-down problem solving for complex issues — leadership becomes a process of facilitating collective experimentation and learning.
- Leading emergent change requires mobilising stakeholders to take action themselves, and then monitoring and embedding the most promising initiatives.
  Effective leadership in complexity is about enabling others to act — creating conditions in which stakeholders can take initiative, observe results, and reinforce what works. Therefore, leaders must follow and support promising actions, shifting from directing to facilitating.

Taken together, this means that leadership shifts from a performance-oriented mindset (predicting, planning, controlling) to a dialogical mindset (participating, listening, interpreting, cultivating emergence). Leaders become facilitators of meaning, conversation and co-created change rather than architects of predetermined futures.

In this book, we describe our approach using Appreciative Inquiry (AI), but are convinced that similar outcomes can be achieved using other methods grounded in dialogical principles.

In the following sections, we will describe for each of the interventions in our approach how they contribute to this dialogical mindset. Each of these methods have a value on their own, but together they form a systemic approach to enterprise transformation:

- Discover the core strengths of the enterprise
- Dream of the potential the enterprise can achieve
- Define the domains and subdomains that require design
- Model the essence of the desired future enterprise
- Identify the areas of concern on the path from current to future state
- Develop guiding principles for the enterprise's architecture
- Conceptualise the projects required to realise the envisioned future

Discover the core strengths of the enterprise

The AI summit, which marks the beginning of the enterprise transformation, commences with a discovery phase. During this phase, we gather all stakeholders together (the whole system in the room) and encourage them to rediscover positive moments in their professional experience that align with the chosen affirmative topic. We conduct this in small groups to foster an intimate setting, enabling participants to share their knowledge openly.

As previously discussed, selecting the affirmative topic is a pivotal choice. By focusing on this topic, we help it gain prominence. Conducting the discovery exercise on an unrelated or non-affirmative theme could undermine the entire preparatory phase of the enterprise transformation. Crafting an appropriately affirmative and engaging topic is crucial.

The outcome of the discovery phase is a collection of positive stories, one from each participant. From these stories, we extract the positive core – the strengths of the enterprise expressed affirmatively. This positive core will also be used in defining the areas of concern later in the process.

Another significant outcome is the positive mindset that emerges, influencing the entire preparatory phase. Practical experience shows that individuals who first meet during the discovery phase seek each other out during subsequent project phases. This strengthened bond results from sharing positive stories in the intimate discovery setting.

The discovery phase also fosters openness, allowing participants to discuss underlying mechanisms. In traditional problem-solving approaches (diagnostic OD), participants often hesitate to reveal the true causes of issues. However, using positive stories during the discovery phase encourages more direct responses. This openness is facilitated by the trust built through the intimate setting.

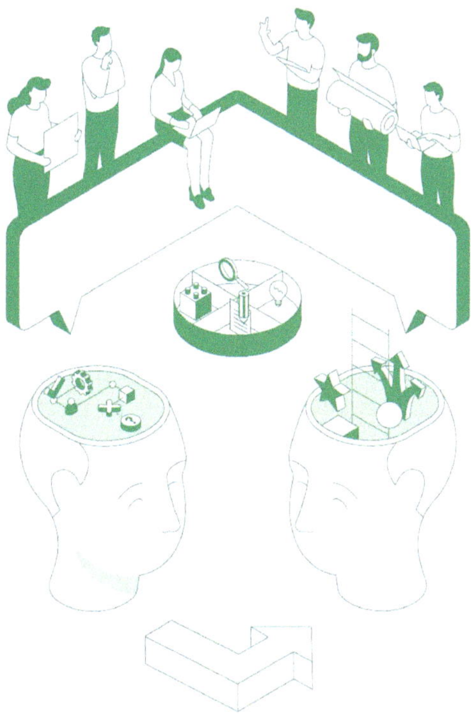

Figure 50. Appreciative Inquiry as a dialogical OD approach

Ultimately, the discovery phase creates an environment that enables participants to challenge existing shared mental models. The importance of this cannot be overstated. Creating the opportunity to think differently is instrumental to the success of the transformation of the enterprise.

Dream of the potential the enterprise can achieve

In the second phase of the AI summit, participants are invited to envision what the enterprise could become after the transformation is complete. A commonly used technique in this phase is the 'miracle question,' borrowed from Solution-Focused Therapy. This question asks participants to imagine a world where all problems are resolved, encouraging them to share their visions for the future without constraints.

Similar to the discovery phase, we initially work in small groups of three, maintaining the intimate atmosphere that encourages participants to share their ideas of a bright future for the enterprise. In the next step, groups of three merge into larger groups of nine to distil individual stories into a shared vision.

The tangible result of the dream phase is a set of stories representing the vision from each group. Equally important is the intangible result – a shift in participants' thinking, with new ideas and mental models triggered by the discussions. Some existing mental models are challenged through this process, facilitated by the positive, future-oriented approach.

Define the domains and subdomains for design

The dream phase helps identify the design domains that require attention during the subsequent design phase of Appreciative Inquiry. Understanding the current situation and having an initial vision of the future state enables us to determine which areas require transformation. In the final part of the AI summit, we establish design taskforces to model the future responsibilities using the DEMO construction model.

Transformation projects are inherently complex, requiring detailed analysis from specialists while maintaining a broad understanding for all stakeholders, even those outside the specialised areas. This dual requirement often leads to challenges in structuring meetings.

One approach is to conduct large, inclusive meetings that ensure stakeholder involvement but limit detailed exploration due to the diversity of participants. Alternatively, more specialised taskforces can focus on specific domains, but they risk becoming disconnected from the broader project, leading to conflicts between different areas.

To address these challenges, we adopt an iterative meeting approach (Extended AI-design), alternating between whole-group meetings and smaller, specialised taskforces. These taskforces have overlapping membership to ensure knowledge transfer across groups, maintaining a shared vision. This iterative process begins at the AI summit and continues as taskforces develop and refine their designs. Once their results reach a presentable level, a second whole-system meeting is held to consolidate and align the outcomes.

The Extended AI-design meeting structure, grounded in social constructionism, ensures that knowledge and insights are developed collectively. Large-group discussions often suffer from limited engagement, with only a few active participants. By switching between large group meetings for consolidation and smaller groups for detailed elaboration, we maintain focus and ensure that key decisions are made inclusively.

This iterative meeting structure, with built-in overlap between groups, provides an efficient, goal-oriented method for involving stakeholders while ensuring that transformation projects remain cohesive and well-coordinated.

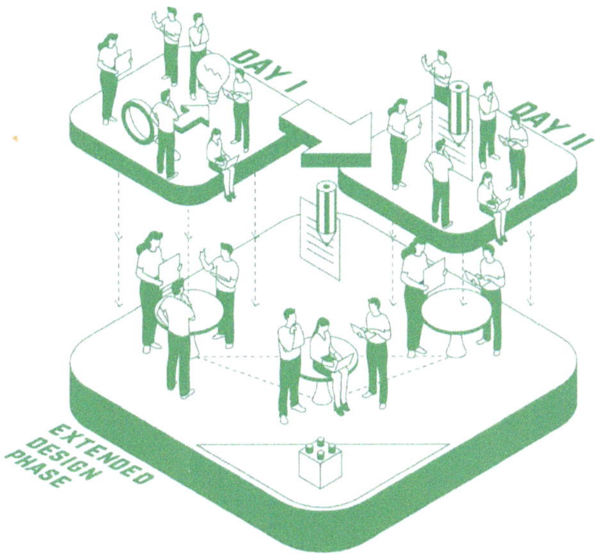

Figure 51. The extended AI-design meeting structure

Model the essence of the desired future enterprise

Transformation projects are inherently complex, bringing together vast amounts of information. Compounding this complexity is the ambiguity that arises between the existing situation and the intended future state, which is a constant feature in such projects. This ambiguity can confuse participants, making these projects intellectually overwhelming. When individuals struggle to fully grasp the situation, it can lead to anxiety and resistance to change.

Participants in transformation projects often come from diverse backgrounds, each with its own specialised vocabulary. Although people may use similar terminology, the meanings attributed to these words can vary significantly, depending on their background. This can lead to misunderstandings, where discussions thought to be resolved are reopened due to differences in interpretation. These setbacks can severely undermine participants' confidence in the process.

In the initial phase of preparation, it is crucial to reduce complexity and focus on core elements. This helps participants develop a shared understanding and reach consensus at a higher level. It is important to avoid delving into too much detail at the outset.

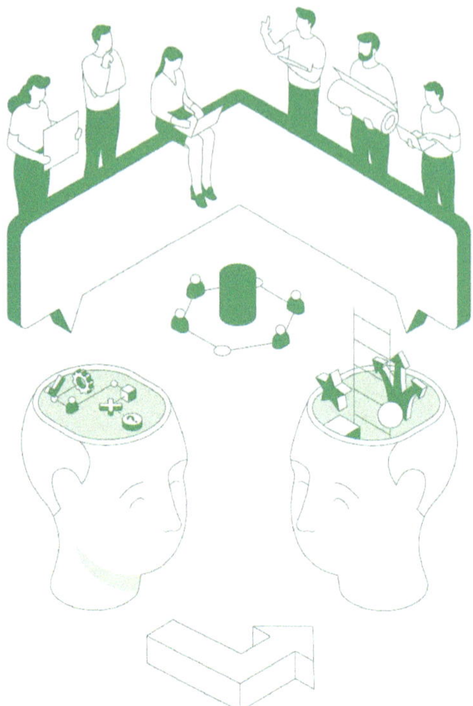

Figure 52. Conceptual modelling as a dialogical OD approach

To achieve this, 'essential models' of the desired scenario are created, compelling participants to align on what the future state truly entails. Depending on the scope of the project, several key design domains are typically modelled:

- **Business domain**: Illustrating the various actors and their interactions, using methods such as DEMO or 'Board of Innovation'.
- **Organisational domain**: Outlining the internal responsibilities necessary to meet the external commitments of the future organisation, employing, for example, the DEMO construction model.
- **Information domain**: Defining the information objects that must be managed to support the commitments identified in the business model, potentially using the 'Existence Dependency Model of Merode' (Snoeck & Dedene, 1998).

Modelling is a challenging activity for many participants as it requires expressing ideas formally using a specific modelling language and naming activities accurately. Group modelling demands that participants share their thoughts and terminology with others and, ultimately, reach consensus, as only one final model is accepted.

The collaborative dialogue initiated through group modelling encourages participants to re-evaluate their current thinking (mental models) and develop new ways of thinking about the desired scenario. Both functional and constructional models are created, ensuring that discussions cover not only functionality but also how the change will be realised.

The essential models serve as reference points for the transformation project and are the foundation for further detailed work. As they represent only the essential aspects of the desired future state, they are more likely to be intellectually manageable for all participants.

Defining areas of concern from A to B

Using the insights gained from discovery, visioning, and conceptual models of the future state, we define key areas of concern crucial for achieving the transformation. Following the appreciative inquiry approach, these areas are framed positively, focusing on what should be achieved rather than avoided.

Typically, the consultant leading the workshops provides examples of Areas of Concern (AOCs) to guide participants. During the workshop, participants work together to develop additional AOCs, limiting them to a maximum of ten to maintain focus on the most critical concerns.

As with previous workshops, this exercise results in a set of tailored AOCs validated by the client and fosters a structured dialogue that challenges shared mental models, advancing the process of organisational development through dialogue.

Crafting Guiding Principles for the Enterprise's Architecture

Crafting guiding principles is one of the most challenging aspects of the design process. Many participants may be unfamiliar with the concept of guiding principles and the discipline of architecture, necessitating substantial guidance from the workshop leader.

The purpose of guiding principles is to provide direction during the implementation of the change and throughout the initial period of its operation. Even with a shared vision and essential models in place, there remains a significant risk of failure if incorrect decisions are made during implementation or early operation. This might occur due to lack of clear commitments on how the change should be implemented and managed once in place.

Alongside the development of the essential models, a taskforce should work on creating two sets of guiding principles:

- **Implementation rules**: These principles guide decision-making during the implementation phase.
- **Coordination rules**: These principles guide decision-making during the operational phase following implementation.

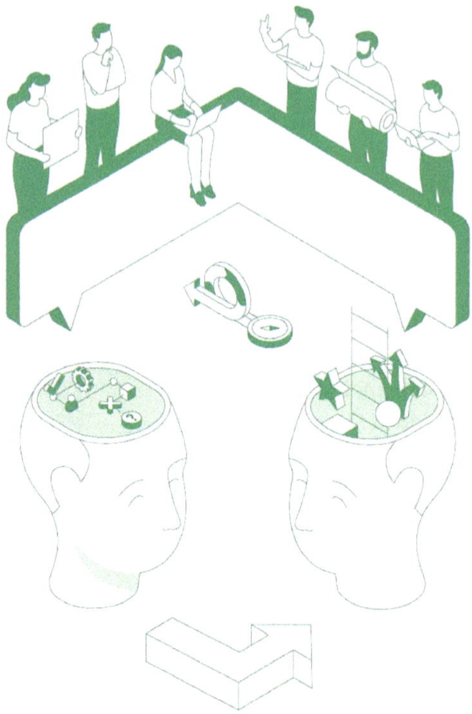

Figure 53. Architecturing as a dialogical OD approach

The development of these guiding principles, also referred to as 'architecturing', acts as a validation of the modelling process. Participants must consider the practicalities of future decisions and anticipate potential challenges during implementation. This reflection leads to the formulation of rules that ensure sound decision-making in various scenarios.

Similarly, participants must anticipate challenges that may arise once the change is complete, developing coordination rules to guide managerial actions in specific situations. This process encourages participants to move beyond conceptual thinking and consider the practical aspects of implementation and management, which may lead to revisiting and revising earlier modelling decisions.

Architecturing fosters dialogue among participants, helping to establish new ways of thinking necessary for realising organisational change.

Write the concept note of the projects needed to realise the dream

During the iterations of the design phase, future implementation projects often emerge from discussions. To make informed decisions regarding these projects, it is essential to gather and consolidate the necessary information. To structure the initial collection of ideas, we propose the use of a standardised template, referred to as a 'concept note'. As will be explained in the purchasing phase, these concept notes will serve as input for the Request for Information (RFI) process.

The following elements must be outlined in the initial high-level draft of the concept note:

- **Concept Description:**
    - Goals and objectives
    - Preconditions
    - Constraints
- **Concept Origin:**
    - Why is this project necessary (current state)?
- **Potential Benefits:**
    - Short-term deliverables
    - Long-term deliverables
- **Context (Dependencies / Constraints):**
    - Alignment with other areas of concern (AOCs)
- **Key Risks:**
    - Potential factors that may hinder project success

The concept note must be reviewed and approved by the Project Management Office (PMO), which will validate the content and present it to the steering committee for further evaluation.

These structured dialogues foster an open mindset among enterprise colleagues, helping them embrace new shared mental models and narratives regarding the enterprise's transformation towards its new identity.

From experience, we observe that while team members may express frustration over frequent meetings, they tend to gain greater confidence in the transformation's success as they begin to see tangible results and understand the rationale behind the approach.

Chapter V: Preparing and Realising Successful Projects

Transformation programmes typically consist of a multitude of projects in the various design domains of an enterprise. For example, projects may be running simultaneously to develop new products and services, implement changes in business processes, and support these new ways of working with new technologies. All these projects stem from the new vision that the enterprise developed. To make this vision a reality, it is essential that these projects are successful. However, Standish Group's research shows that a significant percentage of projects are unsuccessful and that project success rate has shown little improvement over the last 30 years. As discussed in detail in Chapter II, the key success factors can be summarised in the expression, good sponsor, good team and good place (The Standish Group, 2022). In this chapter, we mainly focus on improvements during the preparation of projects.

For a large percentage of transformation initiatives, it is essential to execute information technology projects. Customers and employees expect new initiatives to be supported from the outset by well-functioning, user-friendly software. Hence, it is not surprising that new information technology systems need to be purchased and implemented to provide this support. Purchase of information technology solutions and related services is therefore often an important part of the roadmap to achieve the broader transformation objective.

Procurement of information technology systems can be challenging for several reasons. One possible reason might be the fact that employees lack in-depth knowledge of the tools they need or the tools that are available on the market. Another problem might be the difficulty to integrate the new information technology solution(s) in the existing landscape of the enterprise. A third challenge might be the difficulty in evaluating whether the functionality of the new solution covers the functional requirements the users have been asking for; if a validated list of functional requirements exists at all.

As you can see, there are multiple reasons why the success of a project might already be jeopardised before it has even started. Based on our experience, which also includes crisis management on projects at risk, we dare to state that an important percentage of the projects that are not delivering as expected, have been poorly prepared. The approach that we propose in this book helps prepare projects better. Developing a shared understanding of the project's objectives will lead to the purchase of more appropriate information technology solutions. These solutions have a higher chance of effectively supporting the new way of working. In the cases we present in this chapter, we will show that it is possible to significantly improve this preparation.

Project preparation and procurement go hand in hand. The project preparation activities deliver the content we need to rule options in or out during the procurement. The opposite is equally true: the project preparation is not possible without the information that comes

© DWT Consulting bv 2026
J. De Winter, *Concise Guide to Enterprise Transformation*,
The Enterprise Engineering Series, https://doi.org/10.1007/978-3-032-29931-4_5

to us through the procurement activities. This interdependence between procurement and project preparation is the main topic of the second part of this chapter.

In the first part of this chapter, we will discuss the importance of 'shared understanding'. In order to be able to make the right choices during both the preparation and the implementation of a project, it is important that all parties involved have the same shared understanding of the project. This applies not only to the project's objectives, but also to the way in which the project will achieve these objectives.

We will argue that this shared understanding starts at the very beginning of the project preparation, which serves as a learning process. By building the necessary understanding and trust, the project team will become able to make an informed choice for the best solution and supplier. The same shared understanding is needed during the execution of the project.

In the last part of the chapter we will discuss the topic of organisational change and innovation. In our book we explore a new concept, the transitional organisation. If this responsibility is defined in your organisation, it would be most logical that this transitional organisation takes the lead in innovation and change. On this behalf, also competencies in procurement and project management can be included in the approach. Next to this we will also emphasise on the importance of governance in the final phase of the transformation.

Building Shared Understanding is Key for Successful Transformation

When people ask me what is the most important lever for successful transformation, my immediate response is 'shared understanding'.

In 2001, we worked as consultants in knowledge management and for one of the clients we created a presentation to explain the importance of shared understanding. We showed little circles representing the individual understanding of the project members regarding the existing situation; then we did the same for the individual understanding regarding the desired future state. Obviously, the circles around the future situation had a wider spread than the ones around the existing state. But both groups of circles showed that there was no shared understanding among the project members involved. The final question we asked, was... "If we – all of us together – don't know where we are now and we don't know where we are going... How on earth can we define the way to go then from A to B?"

All the years of practice in between then and now; all the study on how to become more effective in projects and in transformation; all the discussions with participants in the projects. All of these have strengthened my belief that 'shared understanding' is still the key lever to success. These experiences have also allowed to deepen and widen the comprehension of shared understanding as a concept. They have also allowed me to find different approaches to achieve shared understanding.

Throughout the transformation process, there are many different concepts about which we want to achieve shared understanding. In addition, there are many forms that the concept of "shared understanding" can have.

In terms of content, we can already distinguish between the shared understanding of the existing and future state. Equally important is the shared understanding of the transition from today to tomorrow and the competencies needed to achieve this transition. The success of the transformation depends on whether we succeed in getting to know these important components, naming them correctly, and also applying them in practice.

From the paragraphs above, we have also learned that the way to acquire knowledge is completely different in the design phase compared to the implementation phase. At the beginning of the design phase, we do not know yet what the outcome of the design will be; remember the emergent way in which knowledge develops. So, we only really know what the meaning of the desired future situation is at the end of the design process. Once everyone has acquired the knowledge developed throughout the design process (by participating directly or by following a separate learning programme about the design process), there is a chance of achieving shared understanding about the desired future design.

In the coming paragraphs we will look at different forms of 'shared understanding' and 'group learning' that help us to become more successful in enterprise transformation. An important element will always be the appreciative way in which we conduct our inquiry towards a better understanding. Appreciative as in the openness to ideas of other participants in the process, even if they are suppliers. But also appreciative in the comprehension that shared understanding does not mean that each individual needs to understand everything at the same level. It means that together we need to understand everything that is needed to be successful and that we share the knowledge in order to achieve a result together. This open attitude towards knowledge is a prerequisite for knowledge development, since we are convinced that most knowledge is created in relationships.
This is one of the basic elements of the whole philosophy of social constructionism. The knowledge is created in the relationship between the participants in the endeavour that is enterprise transformation. The shared understanding that the team is building up in the preparation of the transformation, accepting also the knowledge delivered by the suppliers during the procurement process, forms the basis of the information and communication sessions during the roll-out so many months later.

When we speak of relationships we immediately arrive at dialogue, the primary mechanism to communicate with others. In one of the final paragraphs of his article, Daniel Kim says that the only way the shared mental models can be changed is through dialogue (Kim, 1993). It feels almost like he doesn't dare to say it out loud, because it is so simple, so back to basics, certainly not something to mention in an article at PhD-level.

But the word 'dialogue' has a very specific meaning and goal. The aim of dialogue is to arrive at new insights together with those involved. This distinguishes dialogue from debate, which is about persuading the other person. Engaging in dialogue requires specific skills, particularly listening, empathy and suspending judgement. In this way 'dialogue' has also connotations of appreciation.

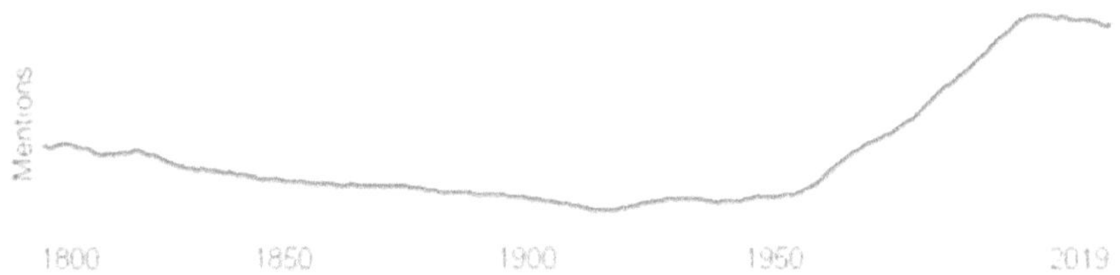

Figure 54. Frequency of the mentions of 'dialogue'

Two more things about dialogue... First, it is interesting to see the history of the usage of the word dialogue. On the website of Oxford Languages one can find the frequency of mentions of the word dialogue (Oxford Languages 2025). It has tripled between 1950 and 2000. The same period in which social constructionism, appreciative inquiry, and dialogical organisational development were developed. Between 1950 and 1970 Taylorism was still the talk of the town, which also explains the lower number of mentions of the word dialogue in that period.

Second, about Dialogical Organisational Development: its most important aspect is the social construction of reality, through language and dialogue. It shifts the shared understanding and conversations in an organisation and that is the trigger for transformative change.

When a group of employees listens to their CEO announce that they will have to work differently, most employees will nod as they listen. But this will not change their behaviour. Only when they are asked to engage in dialogue about the change and they have to argue for themselves why it is necessary and what it means, will their way of thinking change and, ultimately, adapted behaviour will follow. In the next paragraphs we will show different forms of shared understanding.

Between dreaming and realising: the design phase

As we have explained in chapter III, we use the AI Summit for building a shared vision of the future. The discovery and dream phases ensure that the participants develop a shared understanding of the following aspects of their enterprise (for the activities in scope of the inquiry):

- the existing core strengths of the enterprise
- the future developments in the environment in which the enterprise operates
- the future products and services that the enterprise will provide

- the markets the enterprise will be active in and the customers it will serve
- the nature of the relationship the new enterprise will develop with its customers and suppliers.

After the discovery and the dream phase the AI Summit continues with the design phase. This phase is about the shift from 'What do we want to achieve?' towards 'How do we think we can achieve it?'. It is a difficult step for most participants.

From engineering theory and through feedback from engineering practitioners we know that the activity of designing needs an iterative reflection approach. This need is the reason why we introduced the idea of an extended design phase. We start the design phase during the AI summit, but we will continue the design activities in smaller taskforces over a larger period, allowing the iterations to take place.

Building further on all the material that emerged during the discovery and dream phases, the participants can start the design, the last phase of the AI summit. The end goal of the design discussions during the summit covers two elements.

First, the participants at the various tables start working on the question 'how can we actually realise the dreamt enterprise?' From this guided brainstorming, we extract, without too much filtering, all possible ideas that could help us realise the dream. The results of each discussion group are shared with all attendees at the AI summit and are clustered into several themes.

Secondly, for each theme, we ask participants to define the next steps on the road to realising the dreams. These intermediate results will serve to guide the taskforces on the next steps in the 'extended design phase'. The name 'extended design phase' is used to mark the difference in approach with the classic AI summit in which the design phase is ended during the AI summit.

For each theme that requires further and deeper reflection on the question 'how?', we define a taskforce including participants who have in-depth knowledge in the domain. This way we set up a series of taskforces that will work out the theme. One of the products the taskforce must deliver is a conceptual model of the responsibilities that have to be organised to enable the future way of working and to achieve the products and services of the future.

To ensure that the ideas that are created in a smaller taskforce remain aligned with the direction given during the AI summit we introduced two mechanisms in this extended design phase. First, we make sure that there is some overlap in the participants of the different taskforces. So, some collaborators are present in two taskforces, which is no problem since in every organisation there are collaborators that are requested by different taskforces. This overlap ensures that ideas that are emerging in one taskforce and that are relevant for other taskforces get spread in a natural way.

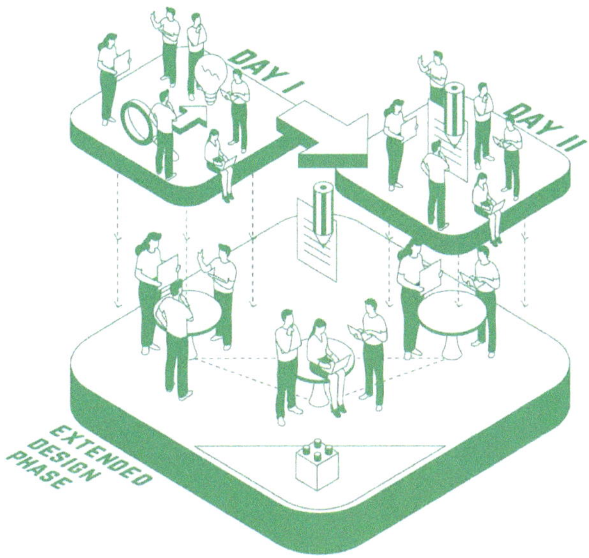

Figure 55. Improving AI: the extended design phase

The second method to keep all taskforces aligned with each other and with the directions given during the AI summit is by organising a new 'whole system meeting' after every three taskforce meetings. During this 'whole system meeting' each taskforce presents its work in progress to all other taskforces. This allows all participants to get acquainted with the work already created by their colleagues and to respond to it based on their own progress.

The 'whole system meetings' are imperative in our approach. They make sure that all involved parties are updated with parallel discussions in the transformation process. They also help keep each of the task forces focused. Plus, they help keep the transformation internally consistent. And finally, they fuel the teams with motivation.

In addition to the conceptual models, each taskforce has to prepare a concept note for each possible project they see emerging from their discussions. This extra task starts after the first 'whole system meeting'. In the final 'whole system meeting', taskforces showcase their concept notes, clearly illustrating how their projects bridge the gap between the current situation and the future state. This meeting is the moment for alignment, where everyone in the room reaches a shared understanding of the projects, their interconnections, and how they collectively steer the enterprise toward its vision.

Shared understanding within the procurement committee

The concept notes that have been presented during the last 'whole system meeting' are the starting point of the next phase in the enterprise transformation, which is the preparation of projects that are necessary to realise the transformation. The concept notes have been presented to the board of the transitional organisation. From this board, they receive approval to start the preparation. One can see every single project preparation as a pre-project that is part of larger programme. These pre-projects are steered by the transitional organisation and deliver a PID for the transformation project at hand. It is the board of the transitional organisation that follows-up on these pre-projects.

Today, in 2025, there are not many companies left that build their own information technology solutions. Most companies will buy existing solutions and will ask to configure them so that they fit the specific needs of the enterprise. Many companies have gone so far in downsizing their operational staff that they are barely able to deliver their operational services. Anything beyond that, such as preparing a strategic project, can only be achieved with external support. Due to the focus on purely operational tasks, internal employees often do not have the opportunity to develop beyond their own operational duties.

The result is obvious. When the question is asked who can represent the enterprise, or more specifically a particular department, in the strategic project, there is a long silence on that side of the table. It is therefore not surprising that we are increasingly seeing strategic projects being populated largely by external personnel.

The procurement of information technology solutions (licences) is therefore increasingly accompanied by the procurement of services for the implementation and integration of the software into the overall information technology architecture, and for guiding the customer through the transition.

Purchasing new information technology solutions to support changing business processes requires a considerable financial investment and is not without risks. In many cases, a specially assembled work group prepares this decision and reports to the transitional organisation board, which ratifies the decision. Today, we usually see that final approval is given by the management board.

The members of the management board do not participate in the preparatory activities, such as workshops, supplier presentations or reference visits to existing customers of the suppliers. Through all the activities organised by the taskforce to formulate a better and more substantiated proposal, we see that the members of the taskforce develop new insights. The people in the management board are not participating in the procurement activities and do not develop these insights. Therefore, they often base their knowledge on past experiences.

This discrepancy poses a risk in the purchasing process that can lead to delays in the best-case scenario or wrong decisions in the worst-case scenario. The members of the management board are only informed on the basis of a brief summary of the entire process. Will they accept the taskforce's proposal or will they play it safe and opt for a solution they know from the past or from publicity materials? Based on our experience, this risk should not be underestimated, as it occurs regularly, especially when the process the company wants to support is more challenging (because it is non-standard), it is important that all decision-makers are involved in the procurement process. If this is not the case, it can lead to the choice of expensive solutions instead of more suitable alternatives that may be less expensive but also less familiar.

Another challenge we see in practice is the rapid evolution of the market for information technology solutions. Continuous innovations can reveal new opportunities that offer cost-effective support for certain processes. Even as a management consultant specialising in a specific market, it is almost impossible to keep abreast of these developments. That is why it is essential to explore these opportunities whenever a company starts a project.

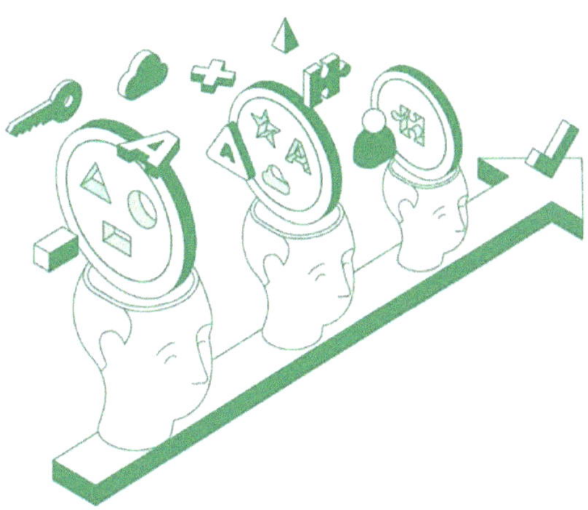

Figure 56. The funnel approach: Aligning mental models on the future solution

Next to savings in maintenance after go-live, the biggest savings on the total cost of ownership of an information technology implementation are realised before the implementation. They are based on the choices made during the design and the procurement of the solution and associated services. The funnel approach brings two aspects of procurement closer together at each stage of the process, namely the options available within the solutions market and the actual needs of the company.

At the outset of this process, we utilise an RFI to invite potential suppliers. It is primarily based on the concept note developed by the taskforce after the AI summit. To maintain a broad range of options, we distribute the RFI to a wide array of prospective suppliers. Our first objective in doing so is to identify emerging innovations in the market and determine how they might assist the enterprise in addressing its challenges. Our second objective, which may initially seem counterintuitive, is to clarify the genuine needs that the new tool must fulfil. Often, users and decision-makers in a specific business domain are unaware of alternative methods to organise and support their work beyond those currently in practice. When asked to delineate requirements, they tend to replicate existing criteria rather than consider innovative approaches. This funnel approach facilitates their exposure to alternative working methods. This is the reason why we propose the RFI as a learning moment in the selection process.

To be clear, this observation has nothing to do with the abilities of these employees but has everything to do with the fact that they do not encounter a fundamentally different approach during their work. It is therefore not enough to show such a different solution to these employees just once. No, it is important that they become truly involved in a structured dialogue so that their way of thinking about possible solutions changes. As long as their know-how and their know-why regarding a different way of working has not evolved, they cannot choose a solution that supports a totally new way of working.

Integrating Procurement into Project Preparation

Purchasing information technology is a delicate process that enterprises find challenging. Objectifying the choice for a particular solution is a challenge in itself. In the following paragraphs, we will explain the following aspects. Firstly, there is the need for the purchasing organisation to remain in control. A second point of attention is the quality of the selection process itself. The third challenge is to ensure that the purchasing process and the preparation of the subsequent project to implement the purchased solution fit together correctly.

Maintaining control throughout the procurement process

Nothing is more inefficient than an uncontrolled procurement process. Vendors have sales organisations focused on courting you as a potential buyer, if possible, without comparing alternatives fairly. They aim to persuade you to select their product, which is their goal. However, this approach can lead to complications for the buyer.

You may find yourself presenting only one solution at a high price to your management, lacking insight into what other vendors offer. It makes comparison difficult due to non-standardised proposals. Furthermore, if you have not involved the information technology and procurement departments, all your efforts may be rendered futile. Even if you limit your search to only a single vendor you must consider aspects like security, compliance with privacy regulations, and integration into existing information technology architecture.

Maintaining control of the procurement process is crucial for making sound decisions. Key moments at the beginning of the procurement process where control is essential, include:

1. Collaborating with management to determine the needs for a solution. What is the reason why the enterprise wants to buy or build? What are the business objectives? This definition of the needs also delineates the scope of the business processes for which you seek a solution.
2. Collaborating with management to identify who should be involved in the procurement committee. Key participants typically include the purchasing department, the information technology department, the legal department, and relevant users or middle managers.
3. Working with the procurement committee to develop a request for information (RFI) that will invite vendors to participate in the procurement process. The RFI, informed by one or more concept notes must contain clear instructions (including questions, content requirements, structure, timing, etc.) for vendors on how to respond. It is imperative that all potential vendors are evaluated against the same criteria as they enter the procurement funnel.
4. Managing the procurement process alongside your committee without permitting ad hoc deviations.

Once you establish control over the procurement process, you will find that suppliers are eager to engage in it. They recognise that chances of securing a sale improve when enterprises prepare for procurement in a structured manner.

Given that the technical solution you wish to acquire and implement is a pivotal element of the enterprise transformation, the next challenge is to ensure that the information technology solution project remains aligned with the broader enterprise transformation programme.

The procurement funnel approach

There is a widely accepted set of best practices for purchasing information technology solutions and related implementation services (van Haren Publishing, 2010; World Bank, 2018). We are therefore surprised that in our experience, we regularly encounter organisations that are in active procurement discussions with information technology suppliers without following these best practices.

For the sake of clarity, we will outline the various steps of this approach here, with a brief explanation of each step. In the following sections, we will explain how we give concrete form and substance to these best practices.

The best practice is called a procurement funnel since it is intended to start the selection process with a large group of possible solutions for the business need(s) at hand. The goal is to make sure that the enterprise is capable to identify the best solution from the initial set of solutions.

So we start with a large set of solutions, and in each step of the process we rule out solutions that do not fit the selection criteria on which we focus in that step. The remaining solutions flow into the next step where we repeat the same process focussing on other selection criteria. Finally, after several steps, we remain with a shortlist of contenders from which we choose the best solution.

As explained here, it looks very simple. But it is important to emphasise that the funnel approach will only be effective under a few conditions: (1) the selection criteria to define the starting group of solutions must be sufficiently open to include unexpected but interesting participants; (2) the selection criteria in each step have to be very clear, measurable, and, above all, aligned with the ultimate goal which is remaining with the best solution; (3) the participants in the funnel and in the selection process need to be capable of evaluating the solutions on the selection criterion at hand; (4) the people involved in the selection need to be capable to reach consensus on the choices made in each step of the funnel; (5) suppliers that have been ruled out in a former step cannot be reconsidered. This is to prevent the entire selection process from being undermined for non-objective reasons.

These are the typical steps in the procurement funnel. We will explain in more detail how we use them in our approach in the next paragraphs. For now, we provide only a brief description.

- **Request for Information (RFI)**
  This is a call for information about possible solutions that suppliers can offer in response to the questions we, the future client, sent out. The request of the client explains a vision for the future way of working and remains open for different solution options. Responses from potential suppliers are not legally binding but allow the client to learn what actual possibilities exist in the solution market.
- **Request for Proposal (RFP)** also called Request for Quotation (RFQ)
  This is a formal request of the client, containing the necessary detailed information, to allow the supplier to make a binding offer based on a solution they are capable of delivering. The information in the offer needs to allow the client to analyse the solution, the implementation effort, and the associated costs.
- **Proof of Concept (POC)**
  This is an incomplete realisation of the solution offered by a supplier in response to an RFI or RFP. Incomplete can be interpreted in different ways depending on

the agreement between the customer and the supplier. The purpose of the POC is to demonstrate that a particular method of delivering the solution is feasible.

- **Team presentation**.
  In this step, the various suppliers can introduce the customer to the key people who will be involved in the implementation. In a service proposal, the quality of the team responsible for carrying out the assignment is crucial. For this reason, the participation of the key figures will be mentioned in the contract with the supplier. Also, the way they will be replaced in case this is needed, will be part of the contract.
- **RACI table**
  This is a clear description of the key activities of the services that must be realised during the implementation. For each of these key-activities an agreement is made between supplier and client on the responsibilities based on the RACI principle, where RACI stands for Responsible, Accountable, Consulted, and Informed. The list of the key activities and the corresponding responsibilities will be part of the contract.
- **Best and Final Offer (BAFO)**
  This is a negotiated version of the RFP or RFQ. It is the result of final negotiations with the various parties still in the running for the sale of the products or services the customer wishes to purchase. If the BAFO is based on a modified scope, all parties involved must be informed of the relevant change so that comparable pricing is maintained.
- **Contracting**
  These are the set of contracts that are negotiated and signed by both supplier and client setting out the mutual agreements between both parties. Separate from other legal aspects, the following parts are necessary in most cases: (1) software licence agreements; (2) general services agreements; (3) data privacy agreements; (4) information technology security clauses; (5) other specific agreements.

Project management and project preparation

In the world of project management, there are many organisations that have set themselves the goal of gathering, developing and disseminating the knowledge and skills needed to carry out effective project management. The importance of these knowledge databases, training courses and methods for increasing the quality and success rate of projects is beyond dispute. The figures published year after year by the Standish group on the number of projects that do not achieve their set goals remain unacceptably high. In the context of the discussion we wish to continue, we briefly mention here the most well-known and internationally renowned initiatives alongside a more locally oriented training initiative.

The Project Management Knowledge Base (PMBOK), which is managed by the Project Management Institute (PMI), deliberately does not refer to itself as a methodology but rather as a collection of guidelines, terminology and best practices for project management (Project Management Institute, 2024). It is a guide that creates a universal language for project management with a focus on processes, knowledge areas and the phases of a project (initiation, planning, execution, monitoring, and closure).

Projects IN Controlled Environments (PRINCE2), on the other hand, is a methodology. The methodology was developed by the British semi-governmental organisation OGC, the Office of Government Commerce, in 1996 as an extension and improvement of the earlier PRINCE methodology from 1989 (Axelos, 2025). The method is intended to standardise projects and provide a common language and approach, thereby increasing the likelihood of success. The method is based on principles, themes and processes that help organise and manage projects, and divide them into manageable phases, with a focus on continuous business justification and learning from experience.

In addition to the PMBOK knowledge base and the PRINCE2 method, there are also numerous training institutes that have specialised in project management and aim to support individuals and companies in their development in the field of project management. One of these institutes is the Dutch organisation NIMO Project Management Institute, to which we will refer in the following paragraphs (NIMO Project Management Institute, n.d.).

In the approach we propose in this book, we place an important focus on the preparation of transformation initiatives and therefore also on the projects related to these initiatives. What do we see when we compare PMBOK, PRINCE2, and the NIMO approach in terms of project preparation?

PMBOK

PMBOK describes five process groups, namely initiating, planning, executing, monitoring and controlling, and closing. With some goodwill, we could say that initiating and planning still be part of the preparation. Planning concerns the following processes: planning scope, time, costs, quality, resources, communication, risk, procurement, and stakeholders. We can make the following observation: to be able to start these processes, all the knowledge required to execute the project must already be available.

The initiation of a project in PMBOK does contain a number of processes that we can classify as preparation:

- Defining the initial project requirement:
  The phase starts with an idea, which is further developed to investigate whether the project is feasible and whether it is worth pursuing.

- Conducting a feasibility study:
  During this phase, a feasibility study can be conducted to assess the viability, potential Return on Investment (ROI) and risks of the project.
- Identifying the stakeholders:
  This involves identifying all relevant stakeholders and recording their interests and potential influence on the project.

In addition, two other processes in the initiation phase that presuppose preparation is complete are as follows:

- Developing a project charter:
  This is a formal authorisation for the project, in which the project manager is appointed and the project objectives, scope, and key stakeholders are defined.
- Obtaining stakeholder approval:
  This is the ultimate goal of the initiation phase, namely to obtain stakeholder approval for the project so that the project charter can be approved and the end result serves the organisation's objectives.

PRINCE2

According to PRINCE2, the activities involved in preparing a project are grouped together in the "Initiating a Project (IP)" process. In this process, the project manager and the client examine the purpose and viability of the project, draw up a project proposal and develop the Business Case. In PRINCE2, this process, called "Starting up a Project (SU)" is seen as a pre-project phase that determines whether a project is worthwhile.

The important activities in the process of starting a project are:

- Investigating the project requirements:
  Determining what the intended project entails and what resources are needed.
- Viability test:
  Assessing whether the project is worth the time, effort, and cost.
- Project proposal:
  Drawing up a document that summarises the project and forms the basis for decision-making.
- Business Case:
  Developing the business justification for the project, which indicates why the project should be carried out.
- Appointing the Project Manager and Project Team:
  Defining who is responsible for what and appointing the team members.
- Drafting the Project Initiation Documentation (PID):
  The most important steering product of the initiation phase, which records the results, plans, and responsibilities.

According to PRINCE2, these activities in the preparation phase will provide a solid foundation for the project, so that the next phases can be started with a clear plan and all the necessary information.

NIMO

According to the NIMO organisation, the preparation of a project involves defining the objective, delimiting the assignment, formulating results, and drawing up a complete project plan with attention to risks and necessary resources. The phase is complete when all ambiguities have been removed and a clear implementation plan is in place.

According to NIMO, the core activities in the preparation phase are as follows:

- Problem to Solution:
  Formulate a concrete result from an idea or problem.
- Clear Communication:
  Communicate effectively about the assignment with all parties involved, such as the client.
- Creating a Project Plan:
  Draw up a complete project plan with details about the reason, goal, results, scope, quality requirements, time and cost.
- Risk Analysis:
  Identify risks in the project and devise measures to control them.
- Planning:
  Plan and budget the activities, necessary resources and finances.
- Phasing:
  Dividing the project into logical phases and determining go/no-go moments.

PMBOK, PRINCE2, and NIMO all mention a number of phases in their project approach that we can categorise as preparatory phases (Jamali, 2016; Matos, 2016). We define ‘preparatory’ as phases in which the upcoming project is considered and its exact content is defined. Opinions differ among specialists on how this should be done, but they do agree that you cannot start a project without prior careful consideration.

Not all scholars agree that the preparatory phase of a project should form an integral part of the project itself. This does not mean that a project should not be well prepared; quite the contrary. The different phases of a project require each another way of thinking and another type of activities. Especially between preparation and implementation the approach is so different that certain scholars advocate a clearer separation of the two parts.
To clarify this, it is important to (1) return to the essence of project-based working and (2) reflect on the position of projects as part of an enterprise transformation.

Why project preparation matters?

Project-based working is used in situations where there is limited knowledge about the topic, where the path to the result is uncertain, or where even the result to be achieved is not yet entirely clear. The start of each project is accompanied by a great deal of uncertainty and ambiguity. The goal of the project preparation phase is to create more clarity in terms of project objectives, activities, workload, risks, timing, and planning. Creating more clarity goes hand in hand with reducing freedom of choice, as some options are retained and other rejected in each phase of the project preparation. While the project itself is accompanied by uncertainty and ambiguity, the approach of the project preparation itself is highly structured . We do not know the answers, but we certainly know what questions need to be asked.

Figure 57 shows what happens during project preparation. The graph is somewhat atypical because the Y-axis on the left has a different meaning than the Y-axis on the right. On the left, we have the degree of clarity, with low clarity at the bottom. On the right, we have freedom of choice, with a high degree of freedom at the bottom.

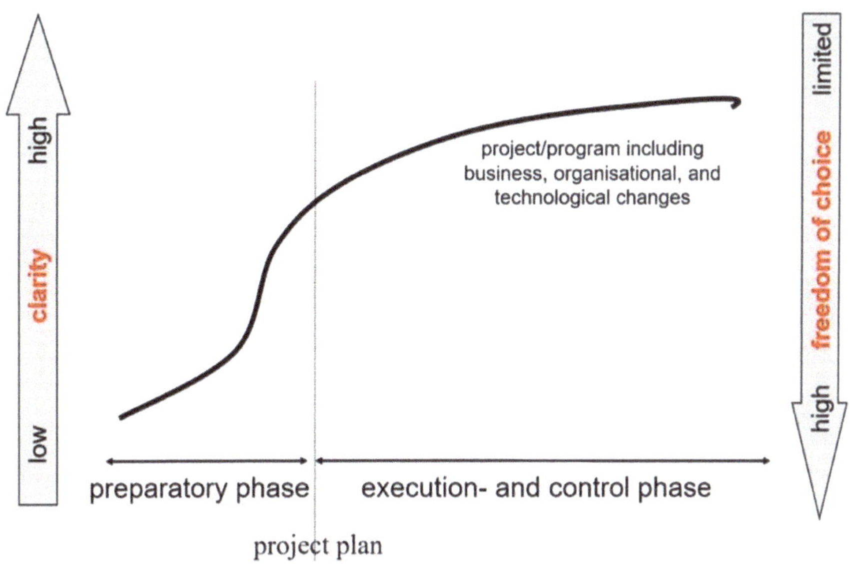

Figure 57. 'Clarity' and 'freedom of choice' during project phases

During the preparation phase, the line on the graph shifts from a position at the bottom, i.e. low clarity, to a higher position, meaning more clarity. At the end of the project preparation, we have made great strides in terms of the clarity about the project. We have a better idea of what to achieve, how to do it, who is needed to do it, and we also have a plan. This also means that we have made choices along the way and that the possibility of changing those choices has narrowed considerably.

The key to successful project preparation therefore lies in gathering the right information and making the right choices based on that information. Because there is so much uncertainty at the beginning, we will repeat this process of gathering and interpreting information several times until we reach a level that makes us confident enough to actually start the project. That moment is visualised with the vertical line marked as 'project plan'.

In project management best practices, three iterations are identified within the preparatory phase of a project. The first is the 'concept phase', where we outline the project at a high level. The second is the 'feasibility phase', during which we explore various solutions to the identified problem. The third iteration is the 'initiation phase', where we detail the project comprehensively.

As a general guideline, we can assert that each of the three phases must address the following questions, with increasing levels of detail at each stage. The 7 W's provide a comprehensive framework for what we seek:

Introduction to the 7 W's (NIMO – Project Management Institute, n.d.)

- **Why?** What is the rationale and necessity of the project?
- **What?** What outcomes does the sponsor aim to achieve?
- **Which way?** In what sequence should activities be executed?
- **When?** When should these sequences be carried out? What is the throughput time, and what are the estimated number of hours required?
- **Who?** Who is required to successfully achieve the project objectives? What qualities should your project collaborators possess?
- **With what?** What resources are necessary to attain your project goals?
- **Where?** At what location will the project be executed?

By the end of the initiation phase, after the third iteration, we will have developed a well-structured Project Initiation Document (PID), also referred to as the project plan, which will serve as the foundation for a go/no-go decision by the project sponsor.

Projects as part of enterprise transformation

In this book, we are looking for an effective approach to achieve successful enterprise transformation. In most cases this transformation requires realisation of several projects that are interdependent. As we stated earlier in this book, designing the desired new state of the enterprise is a crucial aspect. The result of the design is the conceptual realisation of the new desired state. During the design process, we discover in an emergent manner how to translate "what" we want to achieve into "how" we want to achieve it.

The design process results in a number of concrete changes that we want to implement. The implementation concerns the physical realisation of the new desired state. In order to implement these changes successfully, we will split them up into a number of projects. We might decide to group these projects in a programme if the interdependencies of the projects are important.

The reason we want to distinguish between design phase and implementation phase of the transformation is because they have fundamentally different characteristics: (1) the design phase is a creative, non-plannable process, while (2) the implementation phase is a plannable, algorithmic process. Since a project is characterised by a clear project triangle (result – time – resources) and a clear plan for the necessary activities, only the plannable part of the transformation can be called a project.

There is another important reason for making this distinction between the design and implementation. It is the fact that a single design activity might lead to multiple implementation trajectories, i.e. projects. Especially in enterprise transformation we can expect that the changes that we have decided on during design will need physical realisation in more than one domain, and thus in more than one project. It goes without saying that these different projects need to deliver a result that is consistent over these domains. It is typically in the design process that this consistency will receive the necessary attention, since at that moment the transformation is looked at as a whole. That means that the interdependencies between the different projects are also detected during the design. So, separate preparation per project increases the risk that the results of these projects would not deliver a coherent and integrated whole.

A final reflection on how to organise project preparation and implementation in the context of enterprise transformation relates to the transitional organisation. Earlier in this book, we pointed out the importance of the transitional organisation in successfully realising enterprise transformation.

The role of the transitional organisation actually begins long before a business transformation is initiated. It is the task of the transitional organisation to pick up on signals that indicate the need to consider a possible transformation, to offer platforms on which ideas for change can be reported and discussed, and to create space for employees to further explore and develop nascent ideas.

It is difficult to know whether an idea can lead to a transformation programme. In many organisations, this difficulty is one of the reasons they do not take initiatives. Additionally, innovation is an integral part of operations and there are usually channels in place where employees can bring ideas.

If an organisation really wants to work on organisational development and give ideas that exist internally a chance, it is necessary for the transitional organisation to recognise the ideas that arise within itself. An organisation can also choose to focus the transitional attention primarily on the environment. In that case, ideas for transformation are dynamic and will mainly be responses to changes in the environment.

It is the responsibility of the transitional organisation to prepare transformations and any projects in that context, regardless of where a transformation comes from. To start this preparation, the transitional organisation may need to draw on internal experts, possibly supplemented by external specialists. It is important that the team carrying out this preparation has the necessary expertise, both in terms of content expertise and process facilitation expertise.

In recent decades, we have noticed that many organisations no longer have the in-house expertise to initiate these preparatory processes. Teams formed in this context often require more external members than internal employees. As a direct consequence more organisations today need to procure not only tools to support a new way of working, but also consultancy services to help them redesign the existing business processes. I am convinced that this evolution weakens companies and also increases the risk of failure. This can manifest itself in three areas: firstly, due to a lack of internal expertise, there is a greater chance that the preliminary study of a project will be less accurate; secondly, decisions made during the project are validated by external employees with less knowledge of internal operations; and thirdly, knowledge regarding decisions made before and during the project disappears from the organisation when the external expert leaves.

Aligning the purchasing activities in the project preparation approach

In cases where the transformation involves implementation projects of new information technology solutions, it is important that the purchasing activities are aligned with those in the project preparation. A go/no-go decision to start executing a transformation project will include both the purchasing of the involved information technology solution and the start of the implementation services. It is thus important that both decisions, the purchase of the information technology solutions and the start of the project, can be taken at the same moment.

This reflection makes it clear that the purchasing funnel approach and the project preparation phases are intertwined. It is not possible to start a project – decide 'go' in the 'go-no go' moment – if the negotiation of the contracts with the implementation partner is not finalised or if the purchase of the information technology solution is not ready. How we approach the combination of procurement and project preparation is the topic of this section.

It is essential for the procurement process of an information technology tool and the preparatory process of the corresponding information technology project to run concurrently, as we require information from suppliers to form the PID. Conversely, input from project preparation is also vital for the procurement process.

Milestones in the project preparation must be aligned with the activities in the procurement track, as we need information from external partners to make informed decisions at various stages of the project preparation. In the different parts of the project preparation, we will make observations on the necessary status of the purchasing approach.

The concept phase

The first milestone is the approval of the concept note by the project sponsor. This document provides a high-level overview of the current situation and the desired state at project completion. The concept document intentionally avoids detailed specifications for two reasons: first, we aim to keep all options open at this stage to allow for supplier input; second, we may lack sufficient information to describe a solution in detail.

The information contained in the concept note will serve as the primary source for drafting the Request for Information (RFI). The responses to the RFI will form the basis for the analyses conducted during the feasibility phase.

The feasibility phase

The responses to the RFI will help to define a range of potential solution approaches, which we will explore further during the feasibility phase. In line with our earlier discussion regarding the importance of maintaining control, we must emphasise that it should not be the supplier who dictates the course of this phase or its duration. Deciding on the activities and timeline of the feasibility phase remains the prerogative of the procurement committee.

It is crucial to identify the benefits and challenges associated with each solution approach. These benefits and challenges may be technical, such as how to integrate the solution into the existing information technology architecture, or organisational, due to the significant changes required in business processes. During the feasibility phase, support from various experts is essential, including those with expertise in privacy legislation, information technology security, information technology architecture, legal matters, purchasing, and business operations. Regular alignment with members of the purchasing committee is also vital, so that they are not taken by surprise when asked to approve decisions later in the feasibility phase.

Do not hesitate to invite one or more suppliers for additional demonstrations or explanations if you believe it will aid in the decision-making process. The advantage of the feasibility phase is that the buyer is not obliged to follow a uniform process with all vendors. This phase allows for the exploration of innovative approaches that may offer substantial benefits. As these approaches are often novel, it is imperative to have a clear understanding of how they differ from others, as well as the associated risks and implementation challenges.

At the conclusion of the feasibility phase, it is imperative that the project team, internal experts, and the purchasing committee reach a consensus on the decision to proceed with only one solution approach (although with multiple suppliers) in the Request for Proposal (RFP) phase. Once this alignment is secured, the RFP document can be prepared. The purchasing or legal department will have a template that can serve as a foundation. To mitigate potential disputes later in the process, it is advisable to distribute certain documents that will be required later. These may include:

- a standard contract template for services
- a standard contract template for software licences
- a contract for suppliers handling enterprise data (data processing agreement)
- a standard questionnaire on information technology security

Based on the responses from the remaining vendors, their presentations, and the verification of their references, a decision grid can be populated with both quantitative and qualitative scores. The project team will then recommend a preferred supplier to the procurement committee. Should the procurement committee endorse this recommendation, final negotiations can begin.

The initiation phase

During the initiation phase of the project, the following areas require attention:

- Proof of Concept (POC)
- Best and Final Offer (BAFO)
- Project Initiation Document (PID)
- Team presentation
- RACI-tables
- Contracts

The workload associated with these tasks often exceeds initial expectations. Therefore, it is prudent not to announce a start date until at least the RACI tables for the contract have been finalised.

Proof of Concept (POC)

Throughout the feasibility phase, it may become evident that there are one or more significant challenges to address. If these technical challenges are also unfamiliar to the supplier, it may be advisable to conduct a POC. If the supplier can demonstrate, after an assessment that their use case applies to the situation at hand, then a POC may not be necessary.

In a POC, the supplier is required to demonstrate the feasibility of addressing these complex aspects and to show that they possess the necessary capability (resources and competencies) to do so. If the POC is successful, there will be no technical justification for not engaging with this supplier.

A POC is not just a test to see whether a supplier has the necessary technical capabilities to solve a problem. It is also a test to assess whether the collaboration with the supplier is going well. This may involve collaboration between the supplier and your own technical services, but it may just as well involve collaboration between two suppliers who need to work together to make the project a success. It is a unique opportunity to see the technical people at work before the contract is signed.

Only the preferred supplier(s) will be asked to conduct a POC. In most instances, the client covers the cost for the POC. Given that the knowledge gained during the POC can be leveraged during implementation, this is an investment that will ultimately pay off.

Best and Final Offer (BAFO)

During the initiation phase, one may request a BAFO from the suppliers. This may be necessary due to changes in assumptions or scope that have occurred during the initiation phase. Changes could include shifts in responsibilities from the client to the supplier, adjustments in the RACI that result in additional or reduced work for the supplier, and other similar modifications.

A BAFO request may result in an unchanged offer if the supplier is confident that their proposal is already optimal or competitively low. Conversely, it may lead to a genuine reduction in price, particularly if the supplier anticipated a BAFO and had factored in a margin for price adjustment. However, BAFOs often do not yield significant benefits, as the offers may already have been negotiated extensively.

A BAFO that focuses solely on reducing implementation costs is generally counterproductive, as it may prompt the vendor to later submit claims for unforeseen additional work or, worse still, assign less qualified consultants to the project, thereby compromising the quality of execution and maintaining their profit margins. Engaging less qualified consultants is rarely conducive to the successful delivery of a project.

Project Initiation Document (PID)

The term PID originates from the PRINCE2 body of knowledge, although various project management methodologies also necessitate a similar document at the conclusion of the initiating phase. The PID serves as a reference point throughout the project for the business owner, the project team, and the suppliers involved.

A PID typically includes the following components:

- Project goals
- Scope (including a 'not in scope' section)
- Project organisation and governance
- Business Case
- RACI tables
- Constraints
- Stakeholders
- Risks and mitigation strategies
- Project controls
- Reporting framework
- Summary

It is imperative that the PID fully aligns with the content of the contracts.

Team Presentation and Project Governance

The expertise, quality and strength of the individual members of the project teams are vital for achieving successful project outcomes. It is therefore important to pay due attention to selecting the project staff. Having the right individuals with the necessary skills is one thing, making sure that they will work together as a team is another challenge. The first step is for team members to get to know each other, so it is considered best practice to convene a meeting with all project members, alongside those who will play a role in the project governance. The individuals occupying the important roles in the projects should be explicitly named in the contracts with the suppliers and also in the PID.

The following roles should be represented:

- Project Sponsor (executive manager on the client side)
- Business Owner (client side)
- Delivery Manager (Supplier A)
- Delivery Manager (Supplier B)
- Project Manager (client side)
- Project Manager (Supplier A)
- Project Manager (Supplier B)
- Lead Consultant (client side)
- Lead Consultant (Supplier A)

- Lead Consultant (Supplier B)
- Lead Architect (client side)

This meeting can also serve as the project kick-off, provided there is sufficient time to foster familiarity among the team members.

Matrix of Responsibility – Accountability – Consulted – Informed (RACI)

RACI is an acronym that delineates the various types of responsibilities within a project: Responsible, Accountable, Consulted, and Informed (Wikipedia, 2025). The RACI matrix clarifies the tasks assigned to individuals or groups in the successful delivery of the project. An accurately constructed RACI matrix can significantly enhance the likelihood of a project' success before it even commences.

Figure 58. RACI Table

Effective project management relies on a collective understanding of roles and responsibilities. Employing a RACI matrix to designate and define each role is an excellent approach to maintaining project alignment and positioning it for success.

- **Responsible**: The individual(s) tasked with the responsibility for a deliverable are generally responsible for developing and completing the project outputs. These parties are typically hands-on team members who contribute directly to the project's completion. The responsible team comprises the project's "doers", actively ensuring that each deliverable is achieved. Examples of responsible parties include project managers, business analysts, and developers.

- **Accountable**: Accountable parties ensure adherence to project deadlines and, ultimately, the successful completion of the project. This group frequently overlaps with those informed of project progress. Examples of accountable parties include product owners, business owners, sponsors, and key stakeholders.
- **Consulted**: The opinions of consulted individuals are essential, and their feedback must be considered at every stage of the project. These individuals provide critical guidance that often serves as a prerequisite for other project tasks. For instance, they may offer legal advice throughout the project lifecycle. In cases of new product development or expansion, this could encompass the entire organisation. Examples of consulted parties include legal experts, information security specialists, and compliance consultants.
- **Informed**: Informed parties must remain updated throughout the project. While they are not required to be consulted or participate in decision-making, they should be kept informed of all project developments. Typically, this group consists of business owners or stakeholders who prefer a high-level view of the project. Keeping this group in the communication loop – such as including them in the initial project kick-off and project demonstrations as optional attendees – is essential. This group often also overlaps with the accountable category. Examples of informed parties include project committee members, external stakeholders, and business owners.

An essential component of the contracts includes the RACI tables, which clarify roles and responsibilities for specific activities or modules of the contract. The RACI matrix acts as a vital reference point, ensuring a shared understanding of project tasks and accountability.

Contracts

Following the procurement process, we progress to contract negotiations. The specific contracts required will depend on the deliverables associated with the project. Different contracts may be necessary for software licences than for the implementation services needed to integrate the software within the existing information technology infrastructure. If change management services are provided by a separate entity, a contract for those services will also be required. Additionally, liabilities may need to be insured, and a separate contract addressing data privacy compliance and information technology security may be necessary.

To prevent potential setbacks during the contracting phase, it is prudent to provide standard contract templates alongside the RFP documents and request each supplier to indicate whether they agree to the standard contract terms. If a supplier disagrees, their counterproposal can be solicited for legal review.

Given that our PID is based on the RFP responses and the BAFO from the selected supplier, discrepancies between the parties concerning content and pricing should be minimal. Therefore, most contract negotiations typically revolve around legal aspects and financial claims for potential issues.

It is crucial to refrain from commencing the project before the contracts are signed. First, there exists the risk that negotiations may falter. More importantly, initiating the project prematurely sends a detrimental message to executive management, implying that their approval is not regarded as significant.

How a learning experience influences the decision-making during procurement?

In the next two cases we highlight the significance of incorporating a learning moment into the purchasing process. These examples show that innovative solutions will only be chosen if everyone involved in the procurement process recognises and acknowledges the benefits of the solution. This is a challenge in itself, but it becomes particularly difficult if certain decision-makers only participate in procurement activities on an occasional basis.

European retail company (2015–2016)

Over 30 years this European retail company has grown rapidly to a total of over 330 stores in seven European countries. You can find them in most capitals and major cities of the Netherlands, France, Sweden, the United Kingdom, Belgium, Germany and Denmark. Due to their size and geographic spread, we might say that they are stuck in the middle. The are way too big on a European scale to continue their personnel administration and planning without technical support, but too small per country to find a good yet affordable solution. In the past, various attempts were made to select an appropriate HR information system, but all of those attempts failed. Finding an affordable solution was extremely difficult, at least when the overall price per employee is used as the main criterion.

The objective of the intervention was to help the European HR department find a solution that could support the employee planning process, which was standardised at a European level. At the "input-side" of the planning solution an integration was needed with a solution for personnel administration, while the output of the planning had to be integrated with a time and attendance solution and a payroll solution. In other words, we needed to reconcile the headquarters' requirement for a unified HR information system capable of supporting personnel planning with the local HR need for a solution supporting time and attendance and payroll calculations.

The complexity arises from the differing regulations and requirements pertaining to time management and salary calculation in each country. Consequently, a single solution capable of supporting time management and salary calculations across all eight countries is non-existent in the price segment a smaller company can afford. Of course, solutions exist that can cover payroll legislation in eight European countries, but one should not forget that for each country the solution needs to be configured separately. This would become as expensive as buying eight local systems. Let alone the cost of maintenance and upgrading eight local configurations to keep up with local legal changes. One other potential avenue to achieve this objective is to implement a central HR information system and interface the necessary data with the local payroll systems. While technically feasible, this solution would also incur such high costs per employee – given the small workforce in each country – that it would become unacceptably expensive.

An alternative approach would be to establish a central HR information system and extract the necessary data from the local payroll systems. This option, too, is technically viable but would similarly result in high expenses.

So, we knew, or at least expected, that the solution would be expensive if calculated per capita. Because of this we could also expect that it would be a difficult decision to take. Therefore, it was important that the decision-makers could see that all possible scenarios were evaluated during the procurement process. This way we could at least argue that the price per capita is high, but that all other options would lead to a similar price. So, at the onset of the project, two major challenges needed to be addressed. First, it was essential to identify a technical solution that remained financially viable. Second, it was crucial to ensure that the final decision-makers could make informed decisions based on a collective understanding of the proposed solution and its alternatives. The latter was of equal importance to the former; if any decision-maker continued to believe that a more cost-effective solution could be found, it would impede the decision-making process.

To navigate these challenges, we established a highly structured purchasing approach and formed a purchasing committee that included all decision-makers. We employed a three-tiered framework similar to that used in project management: (1) a steering level consisting of all decision-makers, (2) a management level involving the project manager and the business owner, and (3) an execution level with representatives from each country.

An agreement was reached with the decision-makers stipulating their obligation to attend steering committee meetings, although they could appoint a delegate to attend supplier demonstrations and presentations.

The purchasing strategy was based on best practices in procurement, commencing with an RFI, followed by an internal feasibility study. Based on the findings from the feasibility study, we would issue an RFP, culminating in a request for BAFO.

At the outset of the procurement process, it was essential to determine the types of suppliers to invite into the purchasing funnel. We opted for a broad approach to explore the market thoroughly and ensure that no potential solutions were overlooked. This learning phase involved all participants in the procurement process, including decision-makers, fostering a shared understanding of the realistic solutions available in the market. Such mutual comprehension was crucial to facilitate informed decision-making at the conclusion of the purchasing process.

During the initial round of presentations following the RFI, it became apparent that certain setups were excessively complex and costly, while others lacked credibility due to insufficient geographic coverage by the presenting companies. However, some promising solutions emerged that genuinely aligned with our requirements. Notably, one of these solutions was so innovative that it had not yet garnered widespread awareness. Had we not broadened the scope of the RFI to encompass all possible solutions, we would have remained oblivious to its existence.

Equally important was the participation of decision-makers in the procurement process. Their involvement enabled them to recognise the benefits of this novel solution, thus increasing their willingness to consider it, provided we could address the inherent risks associated with a first implementation of a new information technology solution.

In the subsequent RFP, we invited two solutions: the innovative option and another well-established solution with numerous positive references, albeit less innovative. Throughout the RFP and BAFO phases, both solutions were rigorously scrutinised. Simultaneously, we engaged in discussions with the supplier of the innovative solution to explore risk mitigation strategies.

Ultimately, the client selected the innovative solution. This decision would not have been possible without the structured procurement process we implemented. First, the innovative solution would not have been included in the purchasing funnel; secondly, the decision-makers would likely not have embraced such a risky choice had they not understood the market's possibilities and the potential value of alternatives for the company. The selected solution was successfully implemented at a lower cost.

Belgian distribution company (2017–2023)

Between 2017 and 2023, this Belgian distribution company, which we will call ‘retailer’, completely overhauled its information technology solutions for human resources. With an average employee base of approximately 12,500 individuals, the HR information system serves as a vital technology at the heart of the retail business and its applications. All changes in the employee demographic – such as new hires, departures, and personal modifications – are automatically integrated into other information technology solutions, including the identity and access management system.

The first part of the programme, running from 2017 to 2020, involved the implementation of soft HR modules alongside applications for personnel administration and recruitment. A procurement approach was utilised to select both an implementation partner and a suitable methodology for the project; the choice of software solution had already been predetermined.

The subsequent programme, conducted between 2020 and 2023, focused on implementing a new system for time management and payroll calculations. Annually, approximately 17,000 employees and students are remunerated based on the calculations produced by this new system. Given the strong presence of unions within the retailer organisation, along with the potential for strikes in the event of issues, the transition to the new payroll and time management systems imposed significant additional pressure on both the HR department and the program team.

A key consideration during the procurement process was whether to opt for a cloud-based application – a requirement set forth by the information technology department – or to continue using on-premises solutions, which appeared to be the safer alternative. At the time of procurement, little to no Belgian organisations had adopted the cloud-based payroll application from this vendor, and the ones who did, were small entities making it an inadequate comparison to our retailer.

Based on our positive experiences with the use of a learning phase in the procurement process, we decided to start with an RFI. The RFI invited providers to respond to one or more lots, with suppliers also given the option to submit a combined offer.

For the time management component, we identified potential implementation partners across three tiers: (1) companies operating at a Belgian level, (2) companies with a European presence, and (3) companies functioning on a global scale. In the context of payroll, we sought a partner adept in implementing a Belgian payroll system, thus narrowing our list of candidates to those with expertise in Belgian payroll implementations and local social secretaries for payroll services.

Upon receiving responses to the RFI, we encountered an unexpected situation. For the implementation, we received several price estimates, one of which was significantly lower – less than 50% of the average quote from other suppliers. A common reaction in procurement is to avoid selecting both the most and the least expensive options. However, as we framed the RFI phase as a learning opportunity to assess the offerings in the solution market, we were keen to understand how they could deliver results at such a reduced cost.

We learned that this vendor, a subsidiary of a South African company, had developed an entirely different approach and had successfully implemented it in numerous projects worldwide, albeit never in Belgium, where the payroll market is predominantly controlled by social secretaries to whom payroll processing, including all statutory matters, has been outsourced.

This solution certainly had the potential to significantly reduce implementation costs. Knowing that getting the programme's return validated at the level of the retailer's HQ would be a significant challenge, we took the decision to investigate this possibility further.

Additional challenges associated with this solution were: (1) it could only be implemented using a cloud-based system, and (2) we would be obliged to work with a small, relatively unknown company based in Belgium. These factors could complicate our chances of convincing the business owners to consider this new and unfamiliar solution.

To address these challenges constructively, we introduced an intermediary step between the RFI and the RFP, termed the 'Payroll Motor Assessment'. This assessment aimed to verify whether the innovative solution would indeed deliver the anticipated benefits. The assessment could only be conducted by the small Belgian company itself. To ensure that all suppliers had equal opportunity during the RFP process, we decided to share the assessment results with all participants at the outset of the RFP.

The assessment, particularly the presentations surrounding it, provided the project team with an opportunity to engage the business owners fully, educating them about the intricacies of this innovative solution. Initially, we received very negative feedback from the business owners. However, as they gained insight into the reasons behind the differences in solutions, their scepticism began to diminish, and they started to embrace the concept. Ultimately, the business owners agreed to modify the RFP to accommodate this solution as a viable alternative.

When we received the RFP responses, it was notable that only one supplier proposed the innovative solution, while all other suppliers maintained their original pricing despite having access to the same information and assessment results. This streamlined our decision-making process, as the price for the innovative solution was only half of the one for the alternative solutions.

This serves as an example of how it is often easier to achieve cost savings during the preparation phase of a project than during execution, provided that the RFI and feasibility stages are genuinely utilised as learning opportunities. Given the rapid evolution of market solutions, even specialists find it challenging to stay abreast of recent innovations. A well-organised RFI phase is an effective response to this challenge.

Both cases also show the importance of achieving shared understanding (1) about the innovations that have been developed in the solutions market, and (2) about the determining factors of the proposed solutions.

Governance and Change

At first glance, the concepts of governance and change seem to be contradictory. Governance is used to ensure that the enterprise deals with identical questions from the environment in a similar way. That sounds more conservative than change-oriented. Nevertheless, in the next section we will indicate how governance has a place in change management. Before we delve into this, we will first look at the activities of the transitional organisation.

Activities of the transitional organisation

In Chapter III we introduced the transitional organisation. Conceptually, we distinguish between the operational organisation and the transitional organisation. The former is responsible for organising, managing and executing the known operational activities. The transitional organisation is responsible for organising, managing and executing the transformation.

When reading the text on the transitional organisation, you might well wonder why this should be a 'different organisation'. Why isn't it simply the C-level management that oversees these activities and makes these decisions?

We are not saying that this isn't possible, nor that it cannot be successful. What we are saying, however, is that leading the transition and managing traditional operations are two distinct matters. They have different starting points and require different actions. And, not least, they can be contradictory. Resources allocated to the transition cannot simultaneously be allocated to traditional operations. Assessing the return on investment for both will also need to be done differently.

In the following section, we will therefore discuss the concept of the transitional organisation. We do not, however, take a stance on whether this concept should be implemented as a completely separate organisation. It is, however, important to ensure during implementation that the transformation can be managed. It does not seem sufficient to simply give all managers an additional objective alongside their operational objectives, namely leading the transition.

Because the responsibility of leading the transition is not explicitly stated in many companies, it seems that it does not exist or that it is not necessary. Organisations that have made the strategic choice not to change at all, do not need a transitional organisation. However, most companies do want to allow or even encourage change. To enable this process and capture change initiatives, it is necessary to recognise and investigate them. The responsibility for doing so must therefore be organised, hence the transitional organisation.

Since the transition requires the organisation to change, the transitional organisation will also be responsible for deciding how the organisation will achieve this. It has one extra responsibility compared with the operational organisation: the design of the desired future organisation.

Building further on the above, we must recognise that the transitional organisation will have a different responsibility, workload, and structure in times of transition than in times of stability. The main responsibility of the transitional organisation in times of stability is to scan the operational organisation and the environment of the enterprise for all kinds of input that might be interesting to investigate. The transitional organisation organises the investigation of these inputs and delivers advice to act on them or not.

The transitional organisation will undergo a real metamorphosis in the event that transition is imminent. The board of the transitional organisation will appoint a steering committee for all the activities related to the transition. Reporting to this board, the steering committee will appoint individuals to start inquiring into the need for transition. For the sake of the clarity, we will call these individuals transition managers, and depending on the magnitude of the transition there can be more than one. The first activity of the transition manager is to translate the request received from the board and the input delivered to the transitional organisation into an affirmative topic. This affirmative topic will be the agenda of an AI summit. As foreseen in the AI methodology, the transition manager needs to make sure that the whole system is invited to participate.

Once the AI summit has started all persons invited will participate in the discovery and the dream sessions first. Secondly, the extended design phase will start. In the first part of the design the taskforces are nominated and are given their task. Then they start working separately on their topic and they present their intermediate results in the 'whole system meeting'. After the 'whole system meeting' they finalise the design of their topic and they reflect on the projects that they envision from their perspective. Finally, each taskforce delivers a concept note for each of their projects.

The project notes are presented to the board of the transitional organisation. The board then decides in which domains a thorough preparation of the transformation is needed. It is at that moment that the board of the existing transitional organisation needs to install the new transitional organisation that needs to be capable to lead the whole transformation. In the preparation of the different projects, other roles will need to be populated, like procurement specialists, enterprise architects, domain specialists. During the preparation the different teams will report regularly to the board to ensure that the board can steer this whole transformation preparation. It is also the board that will decide which of the projects needs to start and at what time.

Let us take the example of project x. After the feasibility phase of project x, it starts becoming clear what the objectives will be and what needs to be put in place to make it a success. At that moment, while the person responsible for the further preparation of project x continues to work on the initiation phase, it is the right time to start looking for the future members of the core team. The outline of the project is becoming clearer, as is the expected start date and the main positions to fill. In the ideal world, the future project manager can constitute the core team one or two months before the actual start date of the project. This period is ideal to build the foundation, which is the core project x team.

One of the key success factors for project x is the core team. It isn't just about having talented individuals on board – it's about fostering accountability that flows not only between team members and the programme manager but also among the team members themselves.

Success lies in integrating the responsibilities into a unified framework that fits project x and the total transformation. Every core team member must grasp not just their role but also the intricate web of interdependencies linking their work to the broader transformation. Decisions need to reflect the transformation priorities, not just individual project x goals.

This calls for two shifts:

1. A deep understanding of project interdependencies.
2. A shared commitment to the overarching vision of the transformation.

Core team members must see themselves as part of **'one transformation team'**, unified by shared mental models – conceptual and operational – crafted collaboratively throughout the transformation's preparation.

A cohesive transformation culture doesn't arise by chance – it requires active cultivation. A project manager is one of the gardeners of this culture. Early in the transformation, key questions must be addressed:

- How do we work together to achieve our goals?
- What decisions should be made at the transformation level versus within individual projects?
- How will we communicate, and what topics belong in which meetings?

These discussions form the operational shared mental models that guide the team. It's the project manager's responsibility to reinforce these practices in the early stages, embedding them until they become second nature.

Most programmes involve external suppliers, each laser-focused on delivering their slice of the pie. Supplier collaborators, while part of your project, often prioritise their internal deliverables, juggling expectations from their management with yours. Tensions spike when their success depends on outcomes from other projects, adding stress to an already complex dynamic.

How do we inspire a sense of shared purpose across such a diverse group? From the very start it is critical to build a shared understanding of the future solution. This isn't just about the information technology systems or new business processes. It's about cultivating the right mindset across the team to construct a shared vision.

Asking the right questions is pivotal. We are not solving a pre-defined technical problem but navigating an adaptive challenge. Unlike technical solutions, which usually come with clear paths and best practices, adaptive challenges require exploration, dialogue, and co-creation. The solution unfolds in iterations. This iterative dialogue is the bedrock of the shared mental models needed for a successful transformation. These shared mental models do not only work for the people working in the transformed organisation, but they also help the members of the projects to align on the right mindset.

Governance: steering the transformation ship

Why do we need to talk about governance? Did we not say in the above commentary on Dialogical Organisational Development that changing the way of thinking is a sufficient condition to bring about the change? Gervase Bushe's study (Bushe & Kassam, 2005) even posits that change happens better when governance practices are not employed.

There are two main reasons why we nevertheless believe that governance plays an important role in achieving change.

The first reason concerns the complexity of the overall transition and the interdependence of the different actions; preparation of projects and projects themselves being initiated. Some parts of the overall change process can only be successful if other parts are realised correctly. It is therefore important to keep a close eye on the status of these projects and to adjust when certain contingent projects are delayed. It is equally important to check that projects will indeed deliver what was foreseen because this result is, for instance, a condition for enabling another project. Interdependent projects therefore need to be steered at the level of the board in terms of results and timing.

The second reason is more at the legal and financial level. As mentioned above, companies undergoing transformation often use external suppliers for the implementation of supporting infrastructure elements. For a dredging company, this may be ships that operate in a totally different way. For a retail chain this may be the software that allows automatic picking of goods in a 'dark store'. In other words, these projects can be extensive, complex, and very expensive. They also might have a big impact on making this change happen. These kinds of projects require clear contractual and financial agreements that must also be closely monitored.

For every project, a steering committee is appointed and approved by the board of the transitional organisation. The steering committee guides the project in stormy seas. It provides oversight, approves adjustments, and ensures alignment between the transformation's goals and its execution. Monthly meetings keep them informed, and in times of crisis, these gatherings become critical decision-making forums.

In the steering committee; every party that is actively working on the project is represented. A supplier can be represented by a service delivery manager, the internal information technology department by your own CIO, and the business for whom the project is executed by the business owner. Together with the project sponsor and the project manager, these representatives gather on a regularly basis.

In large programmes it is difficult to gather all the different parties that are involved in one large steering committee. In these cases, it is wise to make a distinction between a programme steerco and different project steerco's. This way of splitting governance into supplier steering committees and a strategic steering committee can streamline decision-making and maintain confidentiality.

It is important to align the structure of governance with the interdependencies of the projects that need to be driven. In a project where several information technology solutions are being built to form one overall solution, there is a lot of interdependence at the technical level. Given the importance of integrating the different systems, it is necessary to take the architecture of the overall solution all the way up to the steering level of the programme. Especially when the different solutions are realised by different suppliers.

In another programme, technical integration may be less of an issue, but there might be an important question in terms of organisation and change. At that moment, it is not necessary to discuss architecture at steering group level but perhaps change management.

When things are running smoothly, governance meetings at the project level might feel redundant. But when challenges arise, they prove invaluable. Effective governance doesn't just address problems – it prevents them, ensuring that everyone from suppliers to stakeholders is aligned and accountable.

Transformation doesn't end when projects are completed – it continues as the organisation learns to live its new reality. The governance structures, taskforces, and shared vision established during the programme lay the groundwork for a future where change isn't just managed – it's embraced.

By aligning projects, empowering teams, and instituting governance frameworks, one does not just implement change; instead, an enterprise capable of thriving in an ever-evolving world is created.

Rolling Out the New Way of Working: Managing Change

The rollout phase is where the rubber meets the road. The preparatory and implementation phases of the projects give you the knowledge to define what is changing and why. Once it is clear what exactly is changing for which roles, it is important to guide and support the necessary change in activities and behaviour.

The first step in the change process involves a business impact analysis (BIA). This BIA identifies the specific changes that will affect each role. We document the differences between how employees currently work and how they will work in the future. For each of these differences, we assess what the employee needs to cope with this change. For some changes, this simply involves communication and a new description of the process. For other changes, this may involve training on a new system or comprehensive skills training.

Once the BIA has been carried out and the necessary communications and training are in place, the change phase can begin. A powerful framework for this is PROSCI's ADKAR model (Hiatt, 2006, 2012), which breaks change down into five stages:

1. **Awareness**: Employees must first understand what is changing.
2. **Desire**: They need the motivation to engage with the change.
3. **Knowledge**: They require training to grasp the broader context and implications.
4. **Ability**: They must develop the skills to apply the change effectively.
5. **Reinforcement**: New behaviours must be sustained, preventing a slide back to old habits.

Breaking down the ADKAR Stages

- Awareness: Change begins with understanding. Employees may not adopt new practices if they are unaware of what is expected. Yet, many organisations falter here, with training sessions becoming the first ocassion where employees hear of the change. This oversight can be rectified through thoughtful communication, led by either the communications officer or direct managers.
- Desire: Awareness alone does not spark engagement. Employees must see the value of the change and want to participate. If resistance emerges, direct managers play a pivotal role in fostering alignment through one-to-one conversations.
- Knowledge: Once employees are on board, they need training that goes beyond mechanics. They must understand why the change matters – how it benefits the organisation and what their role is within it.

Figure 59. The ADKAR change approach

- **A**bility: Knowing why is not enough. Employees must master the how – the specific skills required to thrive in the new way of working. Tailored training is essential here, ensuring each role has the tools it needs.
- **R**einforcement: Change is not one-and-done. Old habits die hard, and without reinforcement, employees may revert. Regular check ins, feedback, and re-training ensure the transformation sticks.

The beauty of the ADKAR model is its clarity and measurability. It provides a roadmap for identifying areas where the organisation is thriving and where more support is needed. But ADKAR is not a silver bullet – it works best when the new ways of working are clearly defined. The preparatory phase must lay this groundwork, aligning the team's mental models with the future vision.

At its core, enterprise transformation is not just about systems or processes – it is about people. It's about creating a culture where individuals see themselves as part of something bigger, where shared mental models guide decisions, and where trust and accountability enable collaboration.

By cultivating a 'one transformation team' culture, aligning shared visions, and supporting employees through change, an organisation does not merely deliver a programme; it builds itself to be ready for the future.

Chapter VI: Transformation in Action

The road to transformation is rarely straightforward, and no two organisations experience it in exactly the same way. At DWT Consulting, we have had the privilege of working with diverse enterprises since 2008, using methodologies such as Appreciative Inquiry (AI) and the Design and Engineering Methodology of Organizations (DEMO) to help them navigate their transformation journeys.

These methods did not come to us by chance; they became cornerstones of our work through study and practice – beginning with Appreciative Inquiry in 2007, shortly after meeting Professor Ronald Fry in Leuven, Belgium in 2006. Later, we developed our knowledge in Enterprise Information Technology Architecture at the Antwerp Management School, Belgium in 2009. Between 2011-2012, we deepened our expertise in Appreciative Inquiry through an intensive immersion at Case Western Reserve University (CWRU, Cleveland USA).

In this chapter, we will focus on one case where we applied our transformation approach in its fullest form, namely the intervention we led at the National Geographic Institute (NGI, Brussels Belgium). This intervention began in 2010 and was completed in 2011. The intervention was led by two senior consultants: Wim Ploegaerts, a seasoned business and information technology consultant with a large engineering and information technology architecture background; and Jan De Winter, a seasoned business consultant with a extensive background in organisational design and change management. Both consultants have expert knowledge of business analysis using DEMO and other conceptual modelling tools that have been mentioned previously in this book.

What makes this case description particularly interesting is the fact that the management team that initiated this intervention in 2010, still holds overall responsibility for the organisation in 2026. This makes the members of the management team privileged witnesses to both the intervention itself and the changes that took place after the intervention. Building further on research into dialogical organisational development, we claim that our approach also leads to longer-term changes. The fact that the same people can testify to these changes fifteen years after the intervention makes this case even more special. Their contribution to this case description adds additional value to this book.

The name of the case is based on the affirmative topic that we used during the AI summit, "Delivering Strategy in Turbulent Times". At the time of the intervention, the NGI was facing a number of internal and external challenges. On the one hand, there was a strategic project within the NGI that, despite a major financial investment, did not deliver the expected results. On the other hand, there was accelerated evolution in the market due to the availability of cheap and even free digital maps. On top of that, there was a political and social evolution in Belgium that undermined the importance of the organisation. You will be able to discover these reasons in more detail as you study this

J. De Winter, *Concise Guide to Enterprise Transformation*,
The Enterprise Engineering Series, https://doi.org/10.1007/978-3-032-29931-4_6

case further. As with any case, it is important to understand the context in which the intervention took place.

We will first briefly outline the history of the NGI. We will then discuss developments in products and services up to 2010 and the way in which the NGI was organised.

Next, we will focus on the intervention itself, discussing its objectives and the approach we chose.

When discussing the results, we will first zoom in on the short term and discuss both the visible and invisible results between 2011-2014. The longer-term results cover the period 2015–2025 and illustrates what the NGI evolved into.

Some History about the National Geographic Institute

Before we start explaining the intervention that we guided in the National Geographic Institute (NGI), it is important to enable you to become acquainted with this well-established Belgian organisation.

The NGI is one of the oldest Belgian institutes and was created in 1831, almost immediately after the establishment of the Kingdom of Belgium. Although under different names, the Military and Topographical Depot (1831-1878), the Military Cartographic Institute (1878-1947) and the Military Geographic Institute (1947-1976), the NGI has been responsible for drawing up topographical maps of Belgium for more than 194 years.

In 1970, discussions started to demilitarise the Military Geographic Institute and turn it into an institution serving the Belgian state, which led to the establishment of the National Geographic Institute (NGI) in 1976.

What had been military staff maps became topographical maps. The NGI remains under the responsibility of the Ministry of Defence, which is still the case today. Although the NGI receives an annual budget, they are also encouraged to generate income from the sale of their products to third parties.

More recently, an additional responsibility was added to the mission of the NGI. From 2020 onwards, the NGI is also responsible for making all federal geographic data available to the world, and for supporting other government agencies to use geospatial information for better decision-making. This is called the geo-broker role. The evolution from 'producer' through 'integrator' to 'geo-broker' of the NGI is one of the long-term outcomes of our intervention in 2010-2011.

The Evolution of the NGI's Products and Services until 2010

The NGI's mission has remained largely the same since the establishment of the NGI in 1976 (National Geographic Institute (Belgium), 2025). The following tasks are considered the most important:

1. Carry out the work necessary to establish and maintain a geodetic network and a precision levelling network, aerial photographic coverage and the production and updating of basic maps on the national territory;
2. Publish basic and derived maps;
3. Undertake work, studies and experiments that are of general interest within its field of activity;
4. Set up and manage a national documentation centre for aerial and satellite imagery coverage of the country;
5. Provide theoretical and practical training for the staff of ministerial departments, public utility institutions, private companies and third countries in the fields falling within the remit of the NGI. Contribute to the training of technicians called upon to carry out assignments in third countries;
6. Collect and disseminate information in a national database to coordinate the activities undertaken by public and private services in relation to the topographical and cartographical management of land and subsoil.

Where the mission of the NGI and the objectives remained the same for a very long period, this was not at all the case when it comes to the practical way the mission needed to be fulfilled. As an organisation specialised in information gathering and distribution, the NGI has been affected by similar changes to those affecting other information-processing organisations.

In response to these changes, in 2003 the NGI had decided to start a series of business process re-engineering projects (BPR), aiming at the modernisation of its operations. At the beginning of 2004, the NGI started three BPR exercises, the first one focused on strategy, the second one on finance and the third one on the topographic inventory, called ITGI (Inventaire TopoGéographique/TopoGeografische Inventaris).

A fourth BPR exercise, dealing with the creation and commercialisation of digital maps, was planned after the finalisation of the BPR ITGI. The future digital maps were going to use the information in the ITGI database, so this reorganisation could only start after finishing the ITGI project.

The objective of the ITGI was a new way of storing and managing digital geographic information to allow the NGI to abandon the cartographic information storage on a sheet-by-sheet basis, and to replace it with a seamless object-oriented information storage. An important difference between the two approaches is the fact that one can start making maps without being limited by map sheet boundaries.

From a functional point of view, this difference does not seem to be very large, but technically it had important consequences. First, it meant that all data had to be reloaded into a new database, and second, that the generation process for deciding what needs to be put on a specific map had to be redesigned.

The strategy and finance related BPR-projects delivered the expected results within the expected timeframe. The BPR-ITGI started in 2004 with a planned completion in 2010, but did not advance as expected for several reasons.

As planned, the NGI started the fourth BPR-project in 2010. This project was focused on the front-office. The idea was to start the development of new maps based on the information in the new ITGI database. This initiative, still based on the strategy in 2003, was faced with a substantially changed situation from the outset.

In 2010 it became clear that the evolution of the geographic information systems (GIS) market was evolving much faster than initially estimated. New competitors arrived with 'good enough and free of charge' maps of the Belgian territory. Google Maps and OpenStreetMap, a crowd-based map, emerged and GIS products evolved rapidly, with a strong focus on open-source standards. The impact of these developments was becoming increasingly clear, and it was expected that it would continue to grow. An urgent and radical change within the NGI was needed.

The initiatives that the NGI had already taken were, despite the significant investment that accompanied them, insufficient to compete with the new geographic initiatives in the market. The institute therefore faced major challenges because considerable time and financial resources had been invested in the refactoring of the back-office database, without yielding the necessary results in products and services. With limited financial resources and little time, it was necessary to develop a new, more cost-effective and faster method for making topographical maps.

The Intervention: Delivering Strategy in Turbulent Times

In the following section, we describe the intervention in detail, starting with the objectives of the intervention as agreed in the agreement and the adjustments we made after the intake interviews.

We will then zoom in on the activities of the intervention itself and the products we delivered.

Overall objectives and approach as planned in the agreement with the NGI

The overall objective of the intervention as mentioned in the agreement is to "optimise the front-office organisation of the National Geographic Institute". The meaning of this optimisation is further clarified as follows:

- Optimising cooperation between the departments responsible for creating products and services on the one hand and the departments responsible for distributing products and services on the other.

- Standardising work processes involved in the realisation and distribution of products and services.
- Collecting the necessary requirements and architecture constraints to be able to choose the information technology tools that will support these activities.

Based on this brief description of the objective, it is clear that this assignment requires an integrated approach taking into account the following aspects. First, the human component when looking for new forms of cooperation between individuals. Second, the organisational component when defining new roles and responsibilities in the new business processes. Third, the information component in analysing what information is managed in these new business processes.

With our approach, we aimed to make a significant contribution to the design and implementation of a renewed front-office organisation for the NGI. In our view, this renewed front-office organisation would be responsible for the marketing, sales, and realisation of new and existing geographic products and services.

This front-office organisation would operate in an effective and integrated manner with clear responsibilities and authorities. Close cooperation with NGI's customers will be linked to structured product development processes in order to offer both tailor-made services and new standardised products.

The scientifically based approach we were taking in this intervention would first and foremost lead to a clear description of how NGI can realise this renewed front-office. Based on our recommendations, the Administrator-General can proceed with the implementation of the preparatory actions.

Thanks to the participatory approach adopted during this intervention, changes will also be initiated in terms of cooperation between people and in employee motivation. Increasing the willingness to cooperate in the realisation of the new front-office is an important additional objective. These intangible achievements cannot be captured in the process descriptions and models but nevertheless are of great importance.

These initial manifestations of behavioural change combined with our recommendations will serve as a basis for the Administrator-General to further develop the set-up of the new front-office. It goes without saying that these initial signs of change can only be reinforced if actions are taken within the NGI to support, encourage and further develop the changes.

In this intervention, we propose a comprehensive approach consisting of four major phases. We start with an inventory phase based on intake interviews (Scoping), followed by a two-day vision workshop using Appreciative Inquiry (Kick-off). After the vision workshop, we will provide intensive support to the employees involved in developing and describing the new approach in detail using DEMO (Content development). Finally, we will formulate our recommendations, describing how the NGI can implement these changes in practice (Delivery).

We see the role of a consultant during this project as more of a facilitator. In concrete terms, this means that we will use the knowledge and skills of the organisation itself, which will lead to a high degree of participation and involvement.

A catalyst also introduces a new element that causes the existing elements in the mix to behave differently. By contributing expertise based on external “best practices”, we will provide leverage that will raise existing knowledge and skills to a higher level.

In addition, we will also influence the necessary behavioural change among the participants involved. It is very important that the management of the NGI actively supports this behavioural change.

Adaptations to objectives and approach after the inventory phase

Based on the results of the inventory phase, we discussed some important adaptations to the scope of the intervention.

During the inventory phase, we found that the BPR project concerning the ITGI had not achieved the expected results. This made it very difficult to properly develop the informational models. It was therefore decided to focus the intervention primarily on organisational optimisations and the necessary changes in this area.

The delay in the previous projects was also a sign that the organisational changes had a greater impact than anticipated. Therefore, a second adaptation to the intervention was needed. Instead of focussing on the front-office of the NGI we decided to involve the back-office as well.

These changes in the objectives and the approach led to three practical changes in the set-up of the intervention:

- The group of participants in the workshops changed because we invited not only representatives of the front-office, but also collaborators in the back-office.
- The scope of the discussion shifted from ‘commercialising geographic information products’ to ‘producing and commercialising geographic information products’.
- The nature of the content shifted from a hybrid content consisting of organising work and geographic information to a more focused content related to organising work and work processes.

The goal of the project has shifted from a more internal focus initially towards a more external focus with impact on the internal processes. The project aims to improve and strengthen the operations of the NGI in relation with its customers. The objective is to be able to deliver products and services in a more effective way.

The appreciative inquiry towards a renewed NGI – discovery and dream.

We based the start of the intervention with the NGI on the approach proposed by Appreciative Inquiry. We decided to start with an AI summit where we brought in representatives of all organisational domains of the NGI. We chose the participants, and we crafted the affirmative topic in close collaboration with the Administrator-General. During the first two-day workshop, we planned to have at least a session for discovery, a session for dreaming and the start of a session on design.

Based on the research we were doing at the time, we knew that the design session needed to be extended to allow in-depth design activities. Therefore, we proposed to organise the intervention as follows:

- **AI summit** – La Foresta – Oud-Heverlee, Belgium
    - All participants are two days on site
    - Five workshop sessions
        - Two Discovery sessions
        - Two Dream sessions
        - One Design session (kick-off)
- **Four design domains** – Office – Brussels, Belgium
    - For each design domain: workshop 1
    - For each design domain: workshop 2
    - For each design domain: workshop 3
- **'Whole system meeting'** – Oude Abdij – Kortenberg, Belgium
    - All participants are one day on site
    - AI-speed-dating
    - Four domain presentations
- **Four design domains** – Office – Brussels, Belgium
    - For each design domain: workshop 4
    - For each design domain: workshop 5
    - Design Domain 1 to 4 → workshop 6
- **'Whole system meeting'** – Terkameren Abbey – Brussels, Belgium
    - All participants are one day on site
    - Four domain presentations
    - Project proposals based on concept-notes

The AI summit in La Foresta

The first step in our intervention utilised the AI methodology. Given the institute's recent challenges and notable friction within the management team, we decided to commence the intervention by (1) identifying the organisation's positive core and (2) fostering a willingness among participants to go the extra mile in redesigning the institute for renewed success.

The affirmative topic for the AI workshop was titled "Delivering Strategy Together in Turbulent Times," emphasising the necessity for collaboration among participants during these challenging circumstances to safeguard their organisation.

The discovery exercise employed the STARS approach, inviting each participant to reflect on a moment of success within the institute using the following framework:

- **S**ituation: What was the context?
- **T**ask: What was their role?
- **A**pproach: What steps did they take?
- **R**esult: What was achieved?
- **S**uccess: Why did it work?

Success stories were initially shared in groups of three, where each participant alternated between being the storyteller, the active listener, and the reporter. Following the sharing of all stories, participants elicited the essence of each narrative, which collectively constituted the positive core of their organisation. This essence was then communicated to the entire workshop group.

With the positive core established, we moved into the dream phase, asking, *"What could NGI look like in five years?"* Participants envisioned a future where the institute thrived in a competitive market. To sharpen this vision, we guided them through questions about:

- **Market**: Who are our customers?
- **Products**: What do we offer them?
- **Formula**: How do we engage with them – supplier, partner, or distributor?
- **Orientation**: Are we production-oriented or market-driven?

The result of this discussion led to a clear distinction between two markets, a primary market and a secondary market. In the primary market, the NGI wanted to establish a partner relationship with a limited number of customers. An important characteristic of this partner view is the fact that the NGI envisioned co-creating geographic data in its core systems with the customers in the primary market. This means that the requests of a partner client can impact the way geographic data is managed in the core systems of the NGI.
For a client in the secondary market, the NGI will create derived products that will use the core geographic data of the NGI. This implies that the relationship with clients from the secondary market is a transactional relationship between supplier and client rather than a partner relationship.

The open discussions about the NGI's future ambitions during the dream phase created a shared understanding among the participants in the discussion. The fact that the participants share a common view of the organisation's current situation is as least as important as that view itself.

During the discovery and dream phase of the AI summit, we not only defined the positive core and the future ambition of the NGI, but we also worked out a set of areas of concern. These areas of concern represented challenges the NGI had to overcome to evolve from the current situation towards the desired future organisation. We expressed these concerns in a positive way so that they can be understood as aspirations or characteristics of the organisation it wants to become.

In the case of the NGI, we defined nine areas of concern. To make clear what we mean with positively framed areas of concern, we share five out of nine as examples.

- Constructive collaboration
  Constructive collaboration means that NGI collaborators work together during their project or production activities on the basis of shared knowledge and with a view to achieving a clearly defined result.
- Focused NGI
  A focused organisation has a clear and shared (communicated, discussed and accepted) picture of its priorities, and a flexible coordination mechanism ensures that the front, middle, and back offices are aligned with customer demand.
- Targeted workforce
  NGI works with flexible collaborators who possess the necessary skills and expertise and who are willing to evolve in the rapidly changing environment of the geographic information market.
- Market-oriented NGI
  A market-oriented government institute makes use of the opportunities that arise in the market by responding to them in a timely manner (time-to-market). To do this, the organisation must also have the necessary insights into and knowledge of the markets in which it operates (market knowledge). The evolution of the market is twofold. The potential of the geographic information market has increased, but the emergence of other players means that customers and partners are free to choose whether or not to work with the NGI (competition).
- Open and positive NGI
  NGI collaborators are an essential part of achieving the objectives of its customers (the public, partners, and the secondary market). A value-driven HR policy aims to foster open and positive relationships between all those involved, both inside and outside the organisation.

For many participants, this was their first experience with a workshop centred on Appreciative Inquiry. Given the existing hierarchical organisation and the difficult situation the NGI was facing, some participants showed apprehension about attending a two-day workshop, with fears of not being able to openly speak or discussions devolving into arguments.
From the start of the first workshop, participants were informed that in these sessions

hierarchy and seniority were suspended and that everyone's opinion would be treated equally. These remarks, together with the AI-based approach, enabled us to maintain a positive and solution-oriented discourse throughout the workshop. At the conclusion, numerous participants expressed their satisfaction with the collaborative atmosphere achieved over the two days.

The appreciative inquiry towards a renewed NGI – extended design phase.

Based on the discovery- and dream-sessions during day one of the AI summit, we proposed the Administrator-General to work with four design domains. This decision was made before the start of day two during the AI summit.

1. **Distribution Cycle**: Market analysis, pricing, and sales follow-up.
2. **Product Development**: Creating offerings for primary and secondary markets.
3. **Project Management**: Managing uncertainty and risks, clear communication and timely delivery.
4. **Prioritisation**: Selecting projects that align with the institute's limited resources.

Taskforces were formed for each domain, tasked with developing actionable strategies over three meetings. Their findings would feed into a whole-system workshop, ensuring alignment and clarity across teams.

The NGI-case was the first where we introduced an important change in the design phase compared to the traditional AI approach. We have named this change the 'extended design phase'. The literature on Appreciative Inquiry does not literally state that the design phase must take place according to a fixed paradigm. But almost all the cases that have been described show that the design phase is part of the AI summit. This means that the design phase is completed by the end of the AI summit. This does not allow for an iterative approach to design.

In our approach to the design phase, the iterative approach is a crucial component. Designing requires iteration. Designing also requires in-depth knowledge of the domain being designed. And designing in a group requires that real experts are able to discuss these highly technical aspects with each other. This is virtually impossible in a large group that includes both technical experts and non-experts.

To allow for good design, it is therefore necessary to bring experts together in smaller groups to discuss one particular component. What we do need to ensure is that these small, specialised groups remain close enough to the fundamental idea that emerged in the dream phase during the AI summit.

We realised this through two controlling/stimulating constructions in the extended design phase. The first is the fact that after three meetings of the small, specialised design teams, we organise another 'whole system meeting'. At this meeting, all the small design teams explain their ideas to the entire group and receive feedback.

The second has to do with the composition of the specialised design teams. We ensure a small overlap in participants so that ideas from one team also become known to another team.

Using conceptual modelling during the extended design phase

As mentioned above, four work groups were set up to translate the vision formulated in the dream phase into a concrete design for each design domain. A known risk with this approach is that the work groups get bogged down in discussions about concepts or lose themselves in the details. To avoid this kind of talk, we required the work groups to create a conceptual model based on the Design and Engineering Methodology for Organisations (DEMO).

This approach helps the work group to focus on the essence and to leave out the details in an initial phase. A second important advantage lies in the fact that the models use the language that the business is accustomed to. This approach also helps to achieve a shared meaning of the terms used in the model. Finally, an important advantage of this approach is that the documentation of each work group consists of a conceptual model that is concise, understandable, and clear.

Because the four work groups used the same method, it was also easy for participants in one work group to 'read' the models of another work group. The models can be drawn up by workshop participants provided they are sufficiently familiar with the method. Participants can learn how to interpret the models within a few hours. During the intervention at the NGI, the models were drawn by the consultants.

The first model from the NGI-case that we show here as an example describes the essential transactions of project-based work. On the left-hand side, we have the steering committee and on the right-hand side the project organisation in the three most important phases of a project, namely the concept, the feasibility and the implementation phase. In this version, both the steering committee and the three project phases are drawn as a black box. In this model, we do not look at the way in which the steering committee or each project phase work internally, but only at the responsibilities between the two. In a subsequent model, we will look at the internal workings of both constituents.

Because project-based working was a significant step for the traditional hierarchical organisation the NGI had at that time, developing this model was of great importance. To make the required change in this case, it was vital that a shift in authority was realised from individual responsibilities as a director of one department to group responsibility as a member of a steering committee for multiple projects.

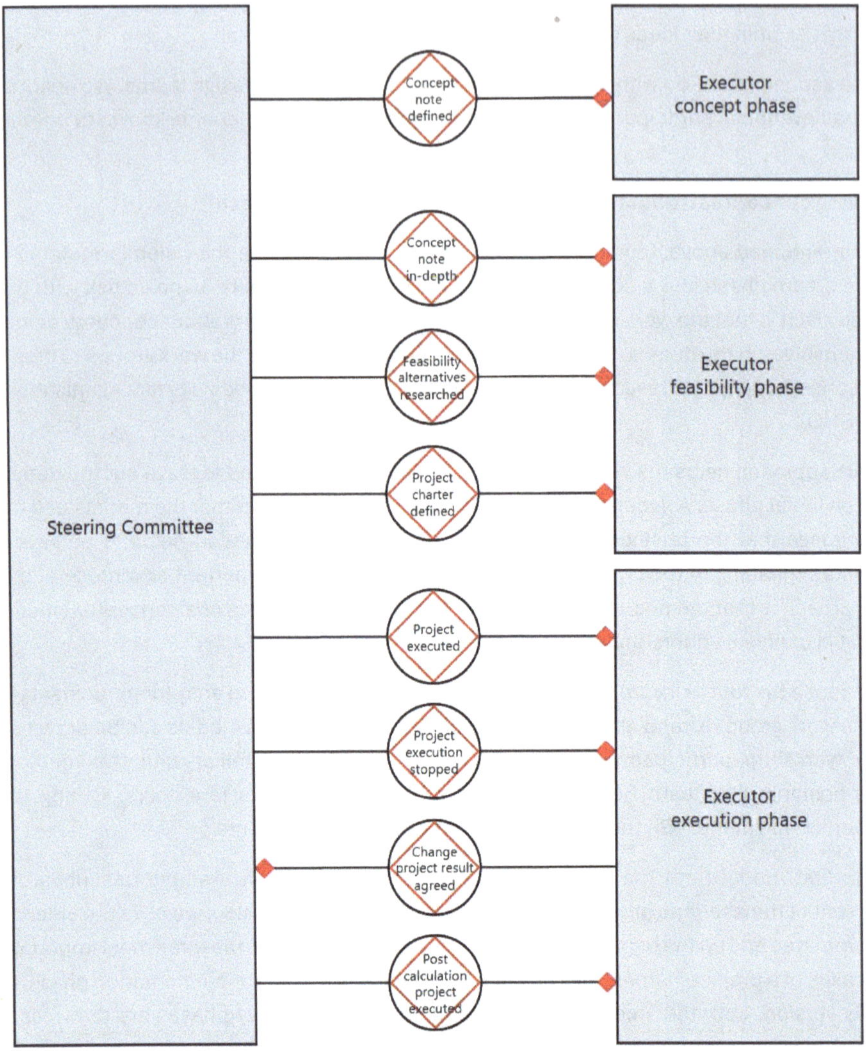

Figure 60. NGI-case: conceptual model project management

DEMO related illustrations can be viewed via the QR-code and the related url: https://enterprise-transformation.com/book-cgtet/version-1/image-60/

The fact that the directors of the NGI were involved in developing these conceptual models was important in the acceptance of this shift in responsibilities, even though these were not laid down in a decree.

As mentioned, the following model shows the internal organisation of both the steering committee and the project team in the different phases. The model we show here explains the responsibilities that must be organised during the feasibility phase. Similar models were made regarding the concept phase and the execution phase. The three transactions between the steering committee and the project team during the feasibility phase of a project lead to responsibilities that must be included in the project team. Each time these underlying responsibilities have been carried out in the project group, it can be communicated to the steering committee that a phase has been completed.

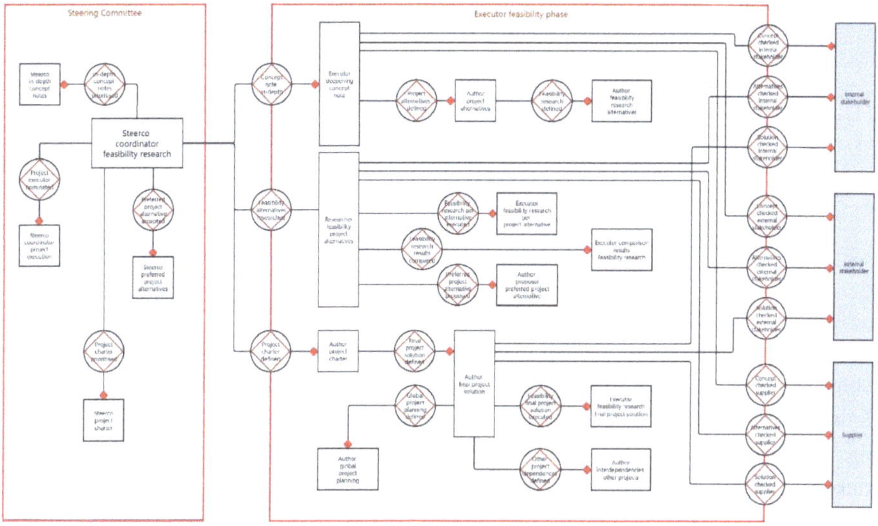

Figure 61. NGI-case project responsibilities feasibility phase

DEMO related illustrations can be viewed via the QR-code and the related url: https://enterprise-transformation.com/book-cgtet/version-1/image-61/

An important advantage of the detailed construction model is that it makes clear which competencies are necessary to achieve a good result. The project group must have the technical skills to be able to elaborate the concept and to come up with different scenarios that can be tested for feasibility. The people in the project group will then have a very clear idea of what is expected of them. The NGI has also decided to develop a template for each step in this new project approach that clearly indicates what is expected as the output in that particular step.

The 'whole system meetings'

As mentioned above, we have introduced the 'whole system meetings' as a means of ensuring the necessary consistency and direction in all change activities. During the AI summit, a shared vision of the future of the organisation is developed in the dream phase. The intention is that all work groups keep this vision in mind throughout the entire design process. Three points are particularly important in this regard:

- Due to its iterative nature, the "extended design phase" is inherently quite long. Given the time between the AI summit and the delivery of the results of the design process, it is likely that some ideas will become diluted. In addition, there will inevitably be an influx of new, different or even earlier ideas.
- The "extended design phase" often involves people who did not participate in the AI summit themselves. These people are usually added because their expertise enables them to make an important contribution. It is important that these people are well briefed on the output of the AI summit.
- In the work groups, specialists are asked to further develop ideas, but also to test their feasibility. It is not unusual for these groups to question what was proposed at the AI summit.

By asking the various work groups to review their ideas and progress, we ensure that the whole remains on track towards the dream. In any case, it remains a balancing act between dream and feasibility. A dream solution that cannot be realised does not help anyone move forward. The opposite is also true, rigidly clinging to the existing situation makes it impossible to evolve.

Using speed-dating to pick up the energy of the AI summit.

Appreciative Inquiry has the great advantage that it generates a lot of positive energy, especially during the discovery and the dream phase. If you want to see this energy, we advise you to look at the video on Appreciative Inquiry that was created during one of the AI summits related to another case (https://vimeo.com/62253142) (in Dutch). It helps a lot if you can recapture that energy during the 'whole system meetings'. That is the reason why we entered the speed-dating moment in the first 'whole system meeting'. A second advantage of the speed-dating moment is that it allows you to recognise little changes that have been made between the AI summit and the 'whole system meeting'. How does it work? First, you invite every participant to think about something (small or big) that has changed in the working environment after the AI summit. Ask the participants to choose something that they relate to the changed way of thinking that has been initiated during the AI summit.

Then you ask all participants to sit or stand in a long double row in a way that they can have a conversation with the person standing in front of them. You ask them to explain in two minutes what it is that they have noticed changing. After two minutes, they switch talking so the other person gets to tell his or her observation. After four minutes, one person goes to the next person and they start over.

In forty minutes, twenty participants have shared twenty different observations of changes that are related to the AI summit. Not only it opens the eyes of the participants, saying, "Wow, I didn't know all this." Also, it brings back the energy in the group. Therefore, it is a perfect exercise to start the 'whole system meeting' with. In the NGI-case it worked very effectively.

Set-up of the transitional organisation.

As we have explained in the theoretical part of this book, the installation of the transitional organisation is of great importance in enabling enterprise transformation to be successful. It is perfectly logical that it is, but so often it is forgotten. Putting the responsibility of the transformation in the hands of the existing management of the organisation is not the right solution either.

In the NGI-case this was of crucial importance for the success of the transformation. The NGI in 2010 had three important objectives, related to three external organisations or clients.
The first objective was related to the needs of Belgian citizens and businesses and was represented by the federal government. They were mainly interested in the first mission of the NGI, updating the maps of the Belgian territory.

The second objective was related to the military needs and was represented by the Ministry of Defence. They were asking to perform specific geographic tasks to comply with NATO obligations and for the Belgian soldiers active abroad in peace-keeping missions. The third objective was related to the needs of the International/European community. They were represented by the European Commission and EuroGeographics, asking to perform specific geographic tasks for European new products and services.

At the moment of the intervention, the NGI had three senior directors – each taking up one of the three responsibilities and defending their objective in case of priority discussions. As a consequence, the collaborators that were working in more than one domain were regularly confronted with different viewpoints when they asked the question: "What should I do first?" Since collaborators had escalated these priority discussions in the past without really seeing a lasting improvement, they did not expect a change. Unless a real tangible change would be installed in the way priorities would be discussed by the senior management, the problem related to priorities would remain.

In a governmental organisation where powers are laid down by decree and formal responsibilities are included in job descriptions, it is not easy to make changes at short notice. At the same time, it became clear during the AI summit that this was a material issue for the NGI. For this reason, a work group was set up to take responsibility for the design domain named as “prioritisation”. This work group naturally included representatives from the NGI's senior management but was not limited to them.

We found the solution to this problem by combining two things. First, we acknowledged the need for this enterprise transformation to set up a transitional organisation alongside the operational organisation. As mentioned earlier, this transitional organisation was responsible for initiating and managing the transformation, while the operational organisation was responsible for managing the day-to-day running of the organisation.

Second, it was also crucial for the NGI to set up a project-based organisational structure alongside the departmental organisational structure. Given the complexity of digitising the NGI's production process and the associated degree of uncertainty, only a tightly managed project-based approach has a chance of success. The existing departmental organisation does not allow for such a complex change in the way production is carried out.

During the first ‘whole system meeting’, the design team working on “prioritisation” proposed to manage the change by working with various steering committees, each of which would be responsible for a number of projects.

In these steering committees, decisions will in future be taken by a team of managers. This is in contrast to the decisions that are currently taken within a single department by a single manager. As a result, the decision on priorities will no longer be left to the individual employee level, but will be taken collegially by the directors who are members of the relevant steering group. In addition, it was also proposed that the stakeholder or in other words, the customer of a project should also serve on this steering group.

Three steering committees were put in place shortly after the first ‘whole system meeting’. A first one focused on the primary market. The second coordinated the projects of the secondary market. A third steering committee was set up for technological projects. The steering committees can decide autonomously on the projects within their allocated budgets. If these are insufficient or in the event of major shifts in resources, budget, or time, the general management will be involved. Coordination between the various steering committees also takes place at general management level, as does the setting of priorities and initial budgets.

The steering committees translate their objectives into plans (activities and projects) and appoint project managers. The project managers are also allocated a budget for this purpose and can therefore make decisions within the objectives and resources allocated to them. By installing this new approach on such short notice, the NGI was capable of preparing the new budget cycle using projects instead of departments, which was an important step in the transformation.

Short-term Impact of the Intervention Itself (2011 – 2015).

The results of the intervention can be divided into short-term results, visible in the years immediately following the intervention, and longer-term results.

First, we will discuss the visible or tangible short-term results. Then we will zoom in on the changes that are not tangible, but are visible in the behaviour of the employees.

Visible results of the intervention.

In an internal presentation to NGI employees – dated 31 January 2011 – the results of the BPR-project "Optimisation of Mid & Front-office" were summarised as follows:

- **Focus areas**
  these provide insight into the environment in which this BPR will take place
- **Strategic Product Market Matrix**
  the definition of the primary market and the secondary market
- **Ambition**
  definition of the NGI's ambition per market
- **Construction models**
  define the actors and their responsibilities, the relationships and the information needed to realise the ambitions
- **Guiding principles**
  these principles translate the ambitions into concrete recommendations
- **New project management method**
  which will increase the chance of success of our projects
- **New organisation**
  which will help the NGI to realise its ambition
- **New decision-making chain**
  which ensures that everyone is steering in the same direction
- **Objectives for 2011**
  the translation of the new vision into achievable goals

Looking back on this presentation, it seems unlikely that we achieved all these results with a single intervention. Viewed from another perspective, however, it is plausible that these results were achieved. Why?

The intervention covered a total period of approximately seven months. A total of about thirty-five people participated. In terms of numbers, that is about 15% of the entire organisation. However, the two most important reasons why this was possible are (1) the fact that everyone involved was aware of the importance of the change that was needed, and (2) that all activities during the intervention were output-oriented. There was indeed a lot of dialogue between colleagues, but always with a specific goal in mind... to achieve a clear result at the end of each dialogue.

An interesting question is which output was delivered in which part of the intervention. The two-day gathering at the start, containing the discovery and dream phase, delivered the focus areas (= areas of concern), the strategic product market matrix and the ambition.

The construction models, the guiding principles, the new project management method, the new organisation and the new decision-making chain are products of the extended design phase. They are the product of the translation from the question 'what?' – the main focus during discovery and dream phase – and the question 'how?' on which we focus during the design.

The objectives for 2011 are not really a product of the intervention itself. It is a product of applying what was agreed upon during the intervention. Towards the end of the intervention, the management of the NGI was required to prepare the next year's budget. As we already explained, the financial situation of the NGI was not easy. Setting the objectives for 2011 in the way they did, the management showed all employees that they were committed to the decisions that they had made during the intervention.

All the results were important for the success of the intervention, but three have proved to be very important. They are also closely related to each other. As already explained, the individual directors used to focus strongly on their personal responsibilities and less on the common responsibilities of the overall organisation. If this behaviour were to remain the same after the intervention it would certainly lead to the impression that nothing had really changed. Employees would still encounter the problem of priority discussions between higher management of the NGI. It would also negatively impact the positive spirit that was developing after the first two-day workshop. Therefore, it was important to find a durable and visible construction to help the management decide together.

The new project management method delivered a possible breakthrough. Project governance typically has a three-layer structure with a steering committee at the top. In this steering committee, all participant parties are represented, namely the project sponsor, the business owner of the project, and the delivery managers of the suppliers.

After the BPR-project 'Mid and Front-office' a number of commercialisation projects would start. These projects would require collaboration between almost all departments, and they would deliver results for the primary or the secondary market. Therefore, it was logical to create one steering committee for the primary market and a second one for the secondary market. Given the fact that almost all activities would be organised in projects that would fall under one or the other steering committee, it was also logical that the steering committees would be responsible to tackle priority problems of the collaborators. This way, the department heads would not decide on their own, but together with their colleagues in the relevant steering committee. A third steering committee would be responsible for the strategic technological projects.

In this steering committee, the information technology director of the NGI could chair and the directors of finance and of production could represent the business owner.

During the first 'whole system meeting', the various work groups presented the progress of their design activities. The work group responsible for the new project management method presented the three layers in the governance structure. This was accompanied by the question of who would ideally sit on the steering committee. The 'prioritisation work group' then presented their initial ideas for ensuring that the NGI would be managed more effectively.

At that point, the idea of linking the two propositions grew. One suggestion was that the directors would relinquish their powers as department heads to the steering groups, but that they would also serve on the steering groups. The idea was not welcomed by everyone, but the seed had been planted. In the three subsequent sessions, the idea was further developed and refined. Finally, a clear distinction was made between the powers of the steering committee and those of the department heads, making the initial idea acceptable to all involved.

This led to what was called a "new decision-making chain". The projects were grouped into three blocks: (1) business development for the primary market, (2) product development for the secondary market, and (3) information technology projects. All these blocks run transversely through the entire NGI organisation and are managed by three steering committees. The steering committee decide on topics that fall within their scope and budget. If it is not possible to decide within one steering committee, the matter is escalated to the general management.

A department head remains responsible for their department and can also escalate to the same general management in case of emergency. By correctly identifying both decision-making chains and defining which powers had to be assumed where, it became clear that this could work. However, there were two very important conditions. The projects had to be much better prepared than had been the case up to that point, and the follow-up of the projects also had to be much tighter. These concerns were expressed with two slogans... "hocus pocus focus" and "to measure is to know".

Non-visible results of the intervention.

When we look at this change process through a systemic lens, we do not just look at visible changes in the workplace. Sustainable change comes about through changes in the undercurrent of the organisation. Only when the organisation's way of thinking changes will there be lasting changes in the organisation's behaviour. In our approach, we talk about changes in the shared mental models of the organisation. Sometimes these changes in thinking are due to serious moments of crisis. But that is certainly not always the case.

Let us examine the changes in mindset that have taken place among NGI employees during the intervention period. In order to identify these changes, we will attempt to summarise them in a single slogan.

Hocus, pocus, focus

The changes we have seen in other areas of information management over the last half-century have also had an impact on the world of the NGI. Since demilitarisation in 1976, the organisation has undergone a continuous stream of significant changes. The techniques used to map the terrain, the way in which the map is presented to the user, the production processes, the sales processes. Just about everything the NGI did had changed.

Throughout this period of change, there was one constant: the availability of the necessary financial resources to implement these changes. Innovative methods were developed and funds were allocated to digitalisation initiatives. Even though there may have been long periods during that time when the NGI was asked to make savings, there was never any doubt that the NGI had a responsibility to map Belgium and that this fact justified its existence. This was also because there was no real competition during that entire long period.

But around the turn of the century this situation changed drastically. Two important developments contributed to this. Firstly, after the fall of the Berlin Wall, the Belgian government attached less importance to defence. From the mid-1990s onwards, there were continuous cuts in defence spending. An important consequence of this was that the NGI's resources also declined. The state reforms also impacted the NGI as a lot of its institutional clients shifted to the regional level and started developing their own capacity to answer their specific mapping needs.

In February 2005, Google Maps became available online for the first time and shortly afterwards we also saw cars driving around Belgium with cameras mapping the entire area. The rapid availability of free maps with sufficient accuracy for the majority of users also had a major impact on the NGI. Suddenly, it seemed as if map-making was taking care of itself. This idea was naturally picked up by policymakers who determined the NGI's budgets.

At that very moment, the NGI had invested a great deal of its resources in the ITGI project. A project that had not yet achieved all desired results in 2010, implying that the production of digital maps based on this ITGI database could not be started.

These three elements – reduced budget + Google Maps + ITGI delay – coming together at the same time forced the NGI to spend every euro cent even more wisely. Focus is suddenly a necessity for the organisation to survive. During the intervention the actual changes in the environment and their future evolution were discussed in a structured way during the dream exercises. These structured reflections created a shared understanding among all participants of the changed position the NGI was in.

To measure is to know

In two of the workstreams during the extended design phase, those involved increasingly came to the conclusion that it is necessary to have a clear picture of the current status of a task in order to be able to accurately estimate how much work is still needed to complete it. Both the "prioritisation" work group and the "project management" work group concluded that the current way of working within the NGI did not provide sufficient insight into this area.

These insights were reinforced by the negative experience with the ITGI project. The problem was not only that the project suffered significant delays, but also that it was virtually impossible to estimate when it would be completed.

Both work groups were therefore convinced that the change would only have a chance of success if there was strict reporting on how much time an employee had really spent on a particular task.

In addition to reporting on the work performed, it was also necessary to be able to estimate a particular task before its execution could begin. Estimates had, of course, been made in the past, but these were not really checked. This was partly because the execution was not measured, but also because management did not really care about it.

Immediately after the intervention, "measuring is knowing" became important and there were real discussions regarding whether estimates or reports were correct or not. Management's attention to "measuring is knowing" was, of course, further reinforced by limited resources and the need for focus.

Everything we do involves projects.

In the project management work group, we discussed why organisations work with projects. Projects are used when there is a great deal of uncertainty, when the way to arrive at a solution is not yet clear, when people with different areas of expertise have to work together to find the solution, when we are doing something for the first time.

It was soon pointed out that everything they do at the NGI is new, requires the knowledge of various experts, and involves searching for a solution. It also became increasingly clear that many of the difficulties encountered by employees today could be more easily resolved if a good project management method would have been put in place.

Provided, of course, that the discussions about priorities would actually lead to supported decisions and that the progress of the work would be reported correctly.

At the end of the intervention (January 2011), three steering committees were set up, each managing a number of projects. Priority was given to those projects that were necessary to achieve the 2011 objectives. The NGI therefore started working with this project-based approach from day one after the intervention.

From producer to integrator

During the intake interviews, we asked one of the NGI directors a question about Google Maps. The answer was very enlightening. Google Maps could never provide the precision required for topographic maps, he said. That was also the main reason why the NGI was the only organisation capable of mapping the Belgian territory.

Of course, that was what the NGI had been doing for more than 190 years. The method used by the NGI to map Belgium had changed, of course, but until then, the NGI had always been the producer of the base mapping material used to make the maps. This mental model of the NGI's role was very much present within the NGI at the start of our intervention in 2010. It was probably also one of the reasons why Google Maps was not really seen as a competitor by some NGI collaborators. Google Maps could not replace the NGI as a supplier of topographic maps.

During the dream phase in the first workshop, there were already some statements that the NGI might not remain the sole producer of base material for maps. This was also expressed in the ambition for the primary market. But the main discussions on this topic were in the work group on business development for the primary market. In that setting, concrete examples were given of how map material from partners, such as the NMBS (Belgian rail company) or Elia (company responsible for electrical power infrastructure), could be reused by the NGI in a real partnership. An important remark during these discussions dealt with the quality control of the required data that would remain the responsibility of the NGI, as issuers of the geographic data.

It is therefore very striking that, as early as 2011/2012, one year after the intervention, the NGI published a strategy document declaring the start of integrating map material from other sources in addition to producing its own data. This shift was only made possible because the shared mental model of the NGI's role in this area changed during and after the intervention.

From inside-out to outside-in

The whole idea of collaborating with partners and working with them to find affordable services and tailor-made map material was completely new to NGI employees. Until then, they had not had much experience in this area, apart from a number of services provided to the Ministry of Defence.

In the initial phase, the discussions in the "primary market business development" work group were therefore somewhat sterile. The services remained closely linked to "map-related" products.

Nevertheless, there were also interesting avenues to explore here. The idea of defining a "business development manager" role, who would act as a single point of contact in discussions with a partner (e.g. NMBS (national railway organisation Belgium)) to listen to that partner's needs, was a realistic and achievable first step. Identifying which organisations could be considered as partners for the NGI was already a major added value. It would also make it possible to define potential areas of overlap.

These discussions were the first steps in looking at the specific needs of certain important customers. Until then, each customer had been regarded as a purchaser of map material, more specifically of the material that the NGI had available.

What this exercise also taught those involved was to think in terms of what has value for the other party. If something has value for a partner, it is interesting for the NGI to build and deliver it. Sometimes it is not even a product, but a specialist who performs a certain service for the partner.

The change in the way of looking at a customer started during the intervention. Even though it was probably rather limited at first, it was of great importance in the formulation of the refined strategy a few years later.

NGI must stand on its own two feet

At the start of the intervention, there was a certain sense of fatalism within the NGI. The idea that things would not be as bad as they seemed, that everything would work out in the end. And if it did fail, well... that wouldn't be so bad.

To mark the change in way of thinking on this point, we share the content of the final slide of the presentation already mentioned.

There is no point in waiting for external help. We will have to ensure that NGI stays afloat ourselves. We will do this by setting concrete objectives and giving priority to the most important ones.

We will do this by setting targets for concrete progress and by achieving concrete results in the short term.

Everyone must commit to this, and we will take our future into our own hands with the resources currently at our disposal.

The fact that a large part of the total population, including most management roles, had experienced the activities during the intervention was of great importance in this mind shift. In every meeting after the intervention, one or more references were made to the intervention. "This has definitely been decided there..."; "We did indeed discuss that idea there..."; "No, we do not do that anymore, we have decided to do it differently..." .

Also, the fact that all participants were capable of explaining the 'why' of these decisions is of great importance. Because the shifts in way of thinking come from dialogue amongst participants and not from listening to a guru, it implies that all participants have thought about these reasons themselves. So, when a colleague gives some pushback, the participants have answers ready to counter the pushback.

Long-term Impact of the Intervention Itself (2015–2025)

An important claim of Dialogical Organisational Development concerns the long-term impact of an intervention. Gervase Bushe talks about the difference between superficial changes that, in most cases, do not last long and transformational cases that are based on a changed foundation, called 'ground'.

In an interview, fifteen years after the intervention at the National Geographic Institute, Ingrid Vanden Berghe, Administrator-General, told us that the institute has continued to change over the past fifteen years. After the first wave of changes implemented in the first years after the intervention, there have been new changes that have always built on the ideas developed during and after the intervention. What is also striking is the fact that twelve years after the intervention, it was not necessary to organise a similar exercise to initiate the new changes. Once the company accepted the basic attitude of change, NGI continued to adapt according to the new insights it gained.

In addition to the way of thinking of Dialogical Organisational Development, we want to emphasise on an extra insight that we have gained out of the NGI-case. The concept of 'culture' and 'ground' are difficult to operationalise in practice and therefore less feasible in consulting practices. As we define shared mental models as the building blocks of corporate culture, this fuzzy concept of corporate culture becomes easier to understand and, as a result, easier to grasp in practice. Based on the NGI-case, we try to understand which underlying mental models have made a particular change possible.

If we gain more insight into this, we may be able to better define – in advance – which mental models are preventing a particular change. And we could steer our dialogical actions in that direction.

From 'producer' over 'integrator' to 'geo-broker'

One of the most striking evolutions the NGI went through in the last fifteen years is one related to the production of basic geographic material combined with the role the NGI is assuming in its commercial environment.

In figure 62 you see the evolution of the part of basic material that is produced by the NGI. On the left, the circle called 'Producer A-Z' represents the NGI producing 100% of its basic geographic material, the situation before our intervention. At the start of the ITGI project (2004), the NGI was still convinced that it would maintain its producer share.

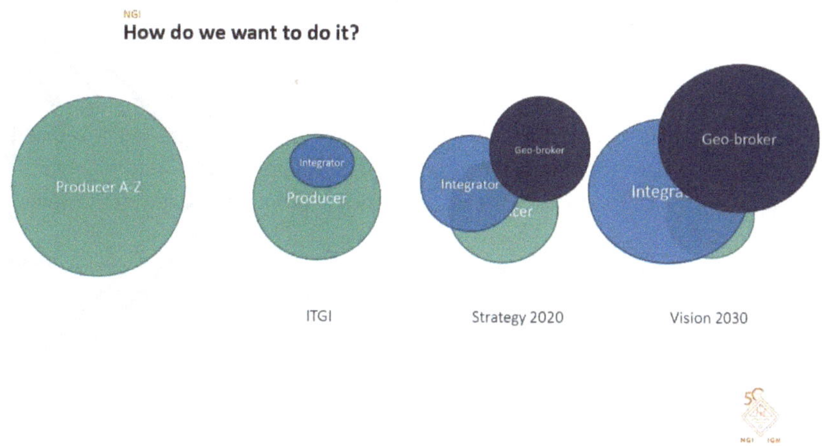

Figure 62. The evolution from producer to Geo-broker

After the intervention, the NGI published a strategic paper stating that external material would be integrated into the ITGI database. The smaller circle represents the fact that the NGI had to reduce costs drastically from 2011 and was therefore no longer able to produce the same amount of basic geographic material.

The integrator role was also associated with a technical evolution. In the older digital systems (before ITGI), it was not possible to load as much data as in the newer systems that supported the ITGI approach. Therefore, in the older systems the data was limited by working on a limited area, called a map. The ITGI allowed the NGI to load much more data, and therefore the limitation was not useful anymore. The whole of Belgium was managed in one area. This made it much easier to integrate external material because one could work on a shared reference structure.

In the vision paper Strategy 2020, the NGI added a new role, the 'Geo-Broker' role. In this new role, the NGI acts as a broker for all governmental institutions that need geographic data. It means that the NGI discusses with other governmental institutions to understand their specific needs for geographic products and services. To be able to deliver the requested solution, the NGI not only looks at what they have at hand, but also to what they still need to integrate from external parties. Once the complete dataset or solution is available, the NGI delivers it in the client-specific format.

Obviously, from an overall government perspective, it is far more advantageous to buy the basic data only once and to integrate it and have it delivered by this 'Geo-Broker'. But the concept will only be successful if the Geo-Broker can deliver the data on time, at the required level of quality, in the right technical format, and at a cheaper price. This requires an entirely different organisation than the one we encountered in 2010.

In 2025, the NGI has become this organisation. And why? There are some shared mental models that began to shift:

- From producer to integrator
  Obviously it was important to normalise the idea of accepting other parties' basic material. At first some technical and procedural difficulties had to be tackled. Difficulties like: referential data that is not corresponding, structures of data, problems with overlapping areas, and very important the quality of the basic material.
  This phase can maybe be best understood as... "*Yes, it is OK, the NGI will integrate your data. Thanks by the way, but there are limits. What the NGI does with it, is the same as for all other data...the NGI defines the output.*"
- From inside-out to outside-in
  Eric Bayers, Adviser General of the NGI, describes the situation prior to the intervention as follows: "*Before the intervention, we produced data and sent it to the market with the message... take it if you want it.*
  One of the most important ideas that emerged during the intervention was that we needed to conduct a needs analyses of our partners. We hadn't done that at all before. After the intervention, we held many discussions within the primary market, with the key partners.
  After the intervention, we also fine-tuned the ITGI project based on these needs analyses. The insight into the needs of our clients has been one of the most important consequences of the intervention."

Over time, the two shared mental models reinforced each other. By acting as an integrator of data from partners, one also begins to recognise what data these partners need and why. By engaging in dialogue with emergency services, specific needs are discussed, such as the shortest route to an incident. This stimulates a creative approach to data analysis for the ITGI data model. How can we respond to this life-saving need and what data do we need to link together to do so? But it also prompts the idea of supplying data from other sources to those priority partners, liberating them from tedious work with this data, including harmonisation, data quality assessment or even public procurement.

By doing it repeatedly, you get better at it and start challenging yourself to simply be the best at it. You project that confidence to your partners, and then they will choose you to support them. The related shared mental model evolves in a similar way. If you were to tell a new NGI employee today that you did not used to talk to partners about their needs, they would not be able to understand that, which is of course understandable.

From 'silo-based production house' to 'project-driven innovator'

Probably the most important characteristic of the NGI that needed to be reversed at the time of the intervention was the silo-based NGI. There is no doubt about the fact that all NGI collaborators were doing their very best and put lots of energy into their jobs. However, it did not always lead to happy employees and good results. Somehow the institute became stuck in its own organisation and was unable to find its way out.

This became particularly clear during the intake interviews that we had at the start of the intervention. The most typical complaint about this phenomenon was that employees were caught in a difficult dilemma as soon as they had cross-departmental work to do. In such situations, they risked getting involved in priority discussions between directors. The siloed structure and the ambition of the directors to realise their department-defined goals paralysed the collaboration of employees, which led to a great deal of their frustration and delayed results.

Combine the above with the fact that the process of making topographical maps is complex and time-consuming while project time was not specifically allocated, we can understand why large projects like the BPR-ITGI fell behind schedule. The NGI did not have an effective system to plan, allocate, and track progress of the work performed and was therefore not able to accurately estimate the remaining work.

Today, fifteen years later, the NGI is one of the best-performing agencies in the Belgian government, even though the production process for which it is responsible remains highly complex. The question is then, what made this transformation possible?

Everything we do involves projects

During the extended design phase, one workstream dealt with project management. As we mentioned earlier, it quickly became clear to the participants that they really needed a workable project-based approach in order to address the challenges they were facing. The following example gives an idea of the scale of complexity involved. They needed to find a solution to design the digital process to create maps as automated as possible. Having digital maps with different scales and using a single set of data in a common object-oriented and continuously updated database. How to come to a single set of rules and symbols to represent the objects on a single spot on the map.

Such a technical challenge requires bringing together all the expertise that the NGI possesses. It also requires an organisational approach that can deal with issues that arise with such a high degree of uncertainty. And it is also necessary to monitor whether the efforts made are effectively leading to a solution. Project-based working is one such approach, but it can only work if it is applied correctly. As we said, the NGI started working in a project-based way immediately after the intervention.

To measure is to know

The difficulty, the scale, the delay on the BPR-ITGI and its impact on the entire organisation set off alarm bells for the NGI's management. This must not happen again. But of course, there is still a long way to go between this statement and the realisation of an effective follow-up system.

A very important part of this is the establishment of a PMO, a department that assumes this responsibility with the support of management. In addition, a great deal of work has gone into analytical accounting and the detailed description of the processes. In the beginning, measuring is knowing was strongly perceived as a means of controlling employees. Gradually, especially among new employees, it is being viewed more positively... *"by reporting my activities, you know what I'm doing"*.

An important part of developing into a project-driven innovator is creating a system for identifying new ideas. Earlier in this book, we discussed the transitional organisation. One of the tasks of this transitional organisation is to capture and assess ideas that arise from within the organisation itself. At the NGI, this is done via the concept note and the steering committees. Jan De Waele, Adviser general at the NGI, explains this as follows... *"Anyone who has an idea can write a concept note about their idea. We take every concept note very seriously because we know that the best ideas emerge from the people who are confronted with the difficulties their ideas aim to solve. There is a template that the contributor must use. The concept note is sent to the project council, which assesses whether the idea should be investigated further or possibly added to an existing project. Once accepted, the further detailing and follow-up are the role of the steering committee. We also always answer the contributor personally, out of respect for the effort he or she has put into the contribution."*

From the start of working with projects, management has adhered very strictly to the detailed processes for deciding and escalating. In the beginning, this was necessary to make it clear to employees that they no longer risked being in a priority discussion. By giving this the necessary attention, the management showed that this new approach really had their support.

During and immediately after the intervention, a lot of attention was paid to the distinction between the powers of the steering committees and the department heads. As a department head, you are responsible for your employees as a hierarchical manager. As a member of a steering group, you are jointly responsible for the success of a project. The cross-functional management of projects across the hierarchical structure was exciting at the time because it was new to the NGI, but above all because it was crucial to achieve the objectives.

In difficult circumstances, with even tighter budgets, the NGI demonstrated to itself and to those around it that it was able to meet complex challenges. In the period immediately following the intervention, the NGI saw a significant reduction in its number of employees. By proving that it was capable of achieving results and by submitting well-prepared innovation dossiers, the NGI obtained additional budgetary resources on two occasions. As a result, the organisation has grown again and has also been considerably rejuvenated, which is an important development for the future.

From 'traditional government institute' to 'modern human-centric organisation'

The NGI has made tangible changes to become a modern organisation that is showing day by day that the collaborators of the NGI are its most valuable assets. At the start of the intervention, the NGI did not feel like the vibrant organisation it has become. Times were difficult and morale was challenged in 2010. But look at the organisation now... Where does this resilience come from? How did the NGI manage to withstand years of pressure and emerge so robust fifteen years after this existential crisis?

In difficult financial times, most organisations can fall back on defence strategies that allow them to survive. This is no different for government organisations. Limited budgets push them to maintain their core activities and weather the storm. The situation at the NGI was similar in one respect, but also fundamentally different.

Long before the intervention, as from 2005 onwards, the NGI was faced in various ways with the fundamental question of whether it still had a reason to exist. Existing customers told the NGI that they would solve their map problems by using Google Maps. The Belgian army questioned the relevance of the NGI's services because at that time their operational focus laid outside the Belgian territory. Citizens did not want to pay for a topographic map in their bicycle GPS because open-source applications contained more recent data. These were just a few of the many examples that confronted the NGI with new forms of competition that appeared much more fashionable and efficient.

During the intervention, NGI employees became increasingly aware that help for the NGI would not come from outside the organisation. This was reflected in the following shared mental model:

- The NGI must be able to stand firmly, on its own two feet.
  During the discovery phase, right at the start of the first workshop, we asked participants to share stories about situations in which they had been personally involved in positive, successful activities within the NGI. All participants shared their own career highlights at the NGI. From these stories, we distilled the strengths of the NGI. A common thread emerged... the NGI had always overcome its difficulties on its own, without outside help. This realisation stuck with the participants and was further reinforced during the remainder of the intervention.

Working together to find solutions in the various workstreams; exploring new approaches to their partner clients; solving internal problems; all these examples led to solutions that the NGI itself had control over.

It also explained the statement at the end of the intervention… 'Everyone must commit to this, and we will take our future into our own hands with the resources currently at our disposal.'

In 2015, the question whether the NGI was still necessary was also reflected in the federal government coalition agreement. It stated that consideration should be given to the future, place and structure of the NGI. The underlying thinking of the negotiators was rather… 'How do we say goodbye to this relic from the past in the right way?'

What the negotiators could not have suspected at the time was that the NGI had meanwhile learned how to deal with such questions. These type of questions were seen as an opportunity to make it clear to the stakeholders what the NGI stood for and where it could stand if it were given the means to do so.

With a robust SWOT analysis and strengthened by the vision of a future "Geo-Broker", the NGI made it clear to the newly elected government that the NGI belonged to the Ministry of Defence, but that it could also offer significant value to all government departments that had needs in the field of GIS products and services. The fact that they had been sitting at the table as discussion partners with many of these government departments in recent years made their case even stronger.

Ingrid Vanden Berghe, the Administrator-General of the NGI, was particularly proud when she explained that the NGI chose to carry out this important analysis itself without external guidance. This was further proof that the NGI had learned to determine its own future.

The NGI is at the heart of the rapidly evolving information technology sector, specifically in the sub-segment of geographic information systems. Alongside artificial intelligence and gaming, the geospatial information sector has seen enormous developments over the past twenty years.

It is therefore absolutely essential for an organisation such as the NGI to keep abreast of these developments. To achieve this, the NGI has a very progressive training policy. Employees are strongly encouraged to continue their education in their field.

The organisation still has departments, but collaboration across these departments is strongly encouraged through projects and tribes. The projects are a formal part of the organisation, while the tribes are informal. Tribes are set up by the employees themselves around all kinds of themes. The use of a very specific GIS tool, the impact of artificial intelligence on GIS, well-being at work, the NGI's circle of friends… these are all examples of tribes in which colleagues can meet. The NGI's management supports the tribes in terms of time and space.

A visual example of the NGI's people-centred vision is also their new organisational chart. Within the NGI, there are also managers and employees who work together in departments and projects, but they present themselves as a circle with their customers, vision and strategy at the centre.

Figure 63. The NGI organisation chart

Another new feature in the organisational chart is the “secondment” section. The NGI provides “GIS experts” to its partners. These are employees who have developed their knowledge and expertise within the NGI and who remain NGI staff members but work on location at the customer's premises. For the time being, this is only available to partners within the government.

Epilogue

In this epilogue, we would like to present the readers some observations that may prove to be useful in the coming years.

First, we would like to zoom in on the wave of change to which we have all been exposed in recent years. The period from 2020 to 2026 has been marked by a number of events of a different order. It has also significantly changed our view of the world. This changed view of the world will also influence decisions within companies.

In addition, we would also like to look ahead to developments in the field of information processing. Not by making yet another prediction about what Artificial Intelligence will mean for our companies, but by building on the ideas of the Standish Group and linking them to the advent of evolvable software systems. On this basis, we also dare to give advice on the choice of future IT solutions, which is also part of our approach.

Finally, we will conclude with some closing thoughts on the approach we have proposed in this book.

Ever-increasing Cycles of Change

The world is not standing still, quite the contrary. Changes are coming thick and fast, one after the other. And with the advent of Artificial Intelligence, there is no sign that this evolution will slow down. We even have difficulties in making it clear to everyone that we have once again found ourselves in a different reality. While many people have never heard of VUCA yet, it is already outdated. As from now we live in a new era, characterised by BANI.

VUCA was first used in 1987 after the fall of the Berlin Wall. The term has been used increasingly in the context of management since 2002 (Bennet, 2014; Sarkar, 2016). VUCA provided a framework for interpreting the challenges faced by organisations in a broad sense. It offered tools for gaining insight into the unpredictability and magnitude of the changes that managers have to address. The letters stand for:

- **V = *Volatility***: characterises the rapid and unpredictable nature of change.
- **U = *Uncertainty***: indicates the unpredictability of events and issues.
- **C = *Complexity***: describes the interconnected forces and problems that obscure cause-and-effect relationships.
- **A = *Ambiguity***: points to unclear realities and possible misunderstandings arising from mixed messages.

VUCA was the first framework of its kind, but clearly not the last. Today, the world is perceived as even more chaotic and unpredictable than it was 20 years ago. This is partly due to a number of recent crises such as the pandemic, wars, and the climate crisis.

J. De Winter, *Concise Guide to Enterprise Transformation*,
The Enterprise Engineering Series, https://doi.org/10.1007/978-3-032-29931-4

The BANI model was conceived by futurist Jamais Cascio in 2018 (Cascio, 2022) and is seen as a more appropriate framework for today's more chaotic world.

- **B = Brittle**: Refers to a world that is fragile and vulnerable.
- **A = Anxious**: A world that causes fear and stress in people due to its high unpredictability.
- **N = Non-linear**: The causes and consequences of events are increasingly difficult to predict and there is no clear logic.
- **I = Incomprehensible**: The complex and chaotic nature of the world makes it difficult to fully understand.

In an article in Forbes on 3 February 2025, Kevin Kruse (Kruse, 2025), an expert in leadership development and emotional intelligence, describes what BANI actually means. His examples are telling:

B is for Brittle

By exaggerating our drive for efficiency, our entire system has become fragile. Small problems on the other side of the world have immense consequences where you least expect them.

An earthquake in Taiwan shuts down a semiconductor chip manufacturer. Suddenly, cars can no longer be assembled in many places around the globe.

A software update goes wrong and millions of Windows computers shut down. Flights are cancelled all over the world and there is a global slowdown in all kinds of production.

We can no longer really count on everything running smoothly, and having buffer stock is probably no longer a luxury.

A is for Anxious

In the VUCA world, we were uncertain, but today there is a raw fear that is always present.

When we listen to the news, we are constantly confronted with the worst facts. It eats away at our confidence, paralyses us and makes it increasingly difficult to make decisions because the risks are so daunting.

As leaders, we cannot really solve this, nor do employees expect us to, but they do seek empathy and a little optimism.

N is for Non-linear

The connections between cause and effect are no longer recognisable today. Linear thinking no longer helps us find answers.

So what can we do? Answers only come by quickly interpreting the outcome of actions, iterating the action and acting in an agile manner.

I is for Incomprehensible

Being smart does not really help when the world is incomprehensible.

We are drowning in data, technology is evolving faster than we can comprehend, and Artificial Intelligence is accelerating this even more.

If we no longer understand everything, we will have to take action without the certainty we had in the past. Taking calculated risks, taking small steps quickly, and relying on our intuition might be the best approach in the future.

It is important to understand the differences between the VUCA era and the BANI period that started recently (Felipe, 2025; Menaria, 2024; Tshetshe, 2025). The biggest change is in the first letters, B and A. The image of a fragile process makes business leaders aware of the immense dependencies that have arisen. High risks of disruption in a company's primary process are dangerous and must be avoided.

The geopolitical situation, the problems of making political decisions in countries that until recently seemed stable (the Netherlands, France, Belgium, the United States of America, to name a few), military conflicts that cannot be resolved within a reasonable time frame, all of this makes people anxious. Widespread fear among the population puts a brake on economic development.

Forward-thinking decision-makers are already starting to change their decisions based on new considerations. As is often the case, these changing decisions become an additional source of fuel for these negative thoughts, creating a self-perpetuating spiral. In the specialised periodicals we see several articles that indicate that companies are thinking of changing strategy, which also influences the information technology strategy. Until a few years ago the choice for cloud was a no-brainer (Cho, 2015). Today we see that several CIOs want to step back from this approach, they want to avoid more vendor- or cloud lock-in, they want to change their strategy regarding core- and non-core applications (Bain & Company, 2020; Spinnaker Support, 2023; Whiting, 2025; Gold, 2025).

The change from VUCA to BANI is fully in line with the concept of fluidity as it is described by Schönfeld (2025). As we mentioned before, fluidity is characterised by the following: (1) the blurring of boundaries or the merging of objects, phenomena and concepts; (2) the technology that acts as a catalyst and enables the change; and (3) the debate, the escalation of conflicts and the fruitless attempts to introduce regulations.

It is the anxiety from BANI that is responsible for the conflicts and the debate that coincide with the examples of fluidity. The same anxiety is the fuel for the disruption in our societal systems we live through in this era. Just as we need leaders for our enterprises capable of showing empathy and optimism, we need them at local, national and international level in our society. Even there we need swift action, reflection and iteration. We need agile governments that can take the right decisions despite the fact that not all risks can be measured. And the moral framework that they should use in the validation process of these decisions needs to be humanism.

What it takes to achieve a state of 'infinite flow'

We use BANI and fluidity to describe the characteristics of the current environment in which companies find themselves. It is a difficult environment that causes a great deal of uncertainty. Accelerated technological changes are also creating additional challenges for these companies. Just when companies could use some stability, important macroeconomic and geopolitical changes are also taking place. It is not clear which change is at the root of all the other changes, but in fact that does not matter. The world is in turmoil and, whether they like it or not, companies will have to find a way out that allows them to consolidate, continue or flourish.

In this complex environment, agile companies will find it easier to find this way out. They are able to make small adjustments more quickly to the way they approach customers and manage suppliers. To enable these rapid adjustments, it is important that they are also able to continuously adapt their underlying information technology systems. The concept of 'Infinite Flow' is in line with this since it claims that enterprises will no longer be working with large projects with long lead times and high overheads (The Standish Group, 2022). Working with pipelines of small adjustments, with continuous integration and delivery on modular systems that are decoupled.

"Infinite flow" is therefore the way forward for organisations in these turbulent times. But, we must not forget that there is a condition attached to this way of working. Fast, agile, pipeline-driven changes are only possible if the technical layer meets the necessary technical conditions.

To support continuous small changes, the technical foundation needs to be modular, decoupled (meaning no combinatorial effects), highly testable and deployable, amongst other requirements. Otherwise, even with the right culture, the technical debt or architecture would create bottlenecks.

We must therefore look at the current status of the information technology foundation of companies to see whether an enterprise can immediately evolve to a state of 'Infinite Flow'. The Standish Group itself does not comment on the number of organisations that have achieved this status. Nor do we believe it is necessary to know these percentages. What is important is that an enterprise can assess for itself, where it currently stands.

To bring structure to the multitude of situations in which companies find themselves, we have developed a quadrant. Without claiming that it is scientifically substantiated, it will nevertheless help to provide insight into the decisions to be made. We focused primarily on two variables: evolvability and control. Evolvability means that the information technology solution in question allows small adjustments to be made quickly. Control means that the customer using the information technology solution also has control over how it should change.

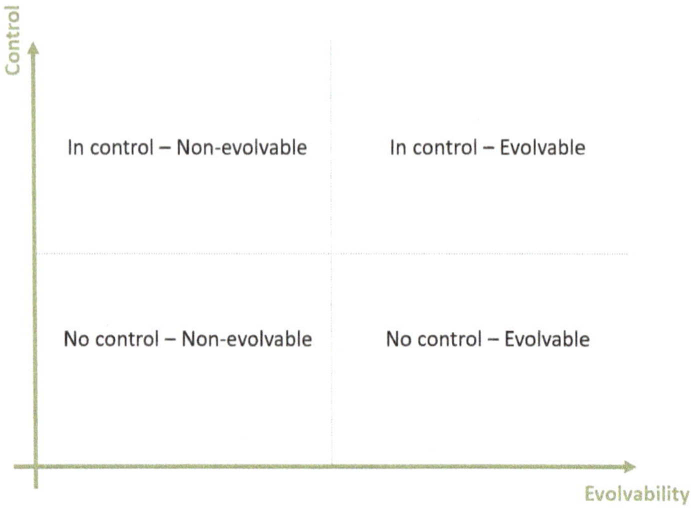

Figure 64. Quadrant of evolvability and control of IT systems

Based on these two parameters, we can then define the following types of profiles of enterprises:

- Evolvable information technology solutions / in control
  - These are enterprises that have flexible information technology solutions over which they themselves have control. They are therefore ready to operate in a form of 'Infinite Flow'.
  - Our advice: Please continue to build on the lead you have already established.
- Evolvable information technology solutions / not in control
  - The vast majority of information technology solutions of this enterprise consist of evolvable systems, but the customer has no control over their evolution, for example because the information technology solutions are owned by a third party and are located in a public cloud.
  - The other part consists of proprietary solutions (evolvable or otherwise) over which they have control.
  - Our advice: Opting for a cloud solution helps you achieve a certain degree of evolvability without having to manage development and maintenance yourself. If maintaining control over the evolution of these solutions is important to you, you can discuss with your cloud provider how to increase evolvability and reduce dependency. In addition, it is a good idea

to convert your own applications into evolvable proprietary applications if necessary.

- Non-evolvable information technology solutions / in control
    - The vast majority of information technology solutions consist of non-evolvable systems that are fully managed by the company itself. This means that the company has control over the evolution of these systems. Changing these systems requires a traditional project-based approach.
    - The other part consists of information technology solutions within evolvable systems, whether managed in-house or in a cloud environment.
    - Our advice: It is important to embrace the concept of evolvability and, where possible, to launch one or more 'traditional projects' to replace your own rigid systems. In doing so, you may opt for a different approach or pace depending on whether the systems in question are back-end or front-end systems.
- Non-evolvable information technology solutions / not in control
    - The vast majority of information technology solutions consist of non-evolvable systems that are not owned by the company itself or over which the company itself has no control when it comes to changing these systems.
    - It is clear that these companies are in an unfavourable position when it comes to increasing their own agility. Since they are completely dependent on the party that manages the systems, they can only evolve in the same direction as the owner of the systems.
    - We assume that there are not many companies in this situation, but we have encountered enterprises in this position in our practice.
    - Our advice: Urgently enter into discussions with the owner of the systems in the hope of convincing them to initiate certain changes.

Even though we do not know the exact distribution of enterprises across these four types of situations, it is immediately clear that achieving a 'Infinite Flow' status remains a major challenge for most enterprises. And that the way to achieve the 'Infinite Flow' status means that you will need projects to replace non-evolvable systems with systems that are modular and decoupled and that allow pipelines of smaller changes.

A number of important questions arise when we want to move towards evolvable systems under our control.

- Question one: does this mean that we are going back to the situation where each enterprise had its own information technology solution built, or are applications in a public cloud also still an option?

- Question two: does the principle of evolvability and control apply to all areas within the enterprise, or can we still distinguish between primary and secondary business processes?
- Question three: do truly evolvable information technology solutions exist, or is this just another hoax?

We will conclude this reasoning with our answers to these three questions, which you will find in the next section.

Choose your Systems Wise

Do truly evolvable information technology solutions exist?

If the answer was 'no', then we would not have suggested looking into them. Let us take a quick look.

Normalised Systems (NS) is a theory and development approach for evolvable software — developed from scientific research at the University of Antwerp, Belgium by Prof. Dr. Herwig Mannaert and Prof. Dr. Jan Verelst (Mannaert & Verelst, 2009; Mannaert, Verelst & De Bruyne, 2016). The concepts were published in papers and conferences from the late 2000s onwards and later consolidated in a comprehensive book in 2016. NS translates this theory into practice through tooling and a development platform (NSX) that generates "skeletons" and code expanders so that changes have a limited impact — with the aim of predictable maintenance costs and lasting evolvability.

There is now real adoption in industrial applications: NSX was founded in 2011 as a spin-off from the University of Antwerp, Belgium, to apply the theory on an industrial scale. According to the organisation itself, more than 60 applications are in production at some forty customers, and the company employs more than fifty permanent staff, including some forty master's in engineering and computer science. These projects cover sectors such as energy, IoT/smart city, integration platforms and administrative systems, such as systems for taxation, property management, HR and eHealth.

These applications are continuously rejuvenated by NSX, in accordance with NS Theory (NS Rejuvenation). This is NSX's achievement over the past ten years: all applications are regenerated every three to six months with the newer version of NS Tooling so that no combinatorial effects occur in the generated software. This is a unique and essential part of the approach, which means that 90% of an application is never older than three to six months.

It is also important to note that NSX facilitates knowledge transfer in a community around NS Tooling that customers can use themselves. There are hundred and fifty certified NS developers in Belgium and the Netherlands, and the learning curve is very short (five to ten days) for a trained software developer.

Quoting the website of NSX: "*NSX believes that software evolvability, being able to cope with changes, is absolutely pivotal to control today's rising maintenance costs. It is also crucial for business agility, as organisations need to rapidly scale up new innovative developments and to respond quickly to changing business needs.*

While most software is prone to so-called combinatorial effects, ripple effects propagating changes through the entire structure, NSX software is based on the Normalized Systems Theory, and guarantees that a bounded set of changes has a bounded impact on the system." (NSX bv, 2025)

Are public cloud solutions a good option?

The principle of infinite flow emphasises that information technology should no longer be developed in large, risky projects, but in a continuous stream of small, manageable steps. This has important implications for the assessment of cloud solutions.

- Are cloud solutions sufficiently flexible and adaptable?
  Large cloud packages offer stability and standardised processes but sometimes limit the granularity with which micro-adjustments can be made. The key question then becomes: does the solution allow sufficient scope for frequent, incremental changes via configurations and APIs (Application Programming Interface), without having to initiate heavy change cycles each time?
- What about release and update management?
  In an infinite flow environment, dependence on sporadic vendor releases is a risk. Organisations need solutions that support frequent updates and allow them to set up their own CI/CD pipelines (Continuous Integration/Continuous Deployment) without having to touch the core of the solution every time.
- How do we create integration with development pipelines?
  Some cloud solutions will allow to connect seamlessly to the organisation's DevOps practices, but many are essentially standalone applications that can only be connected via API's. If the cloud environment does not facilitate easy integration, infinite flow becomes impossible and we return to cumbersome project structures.

In addition to the infinite flow framework, it is also interesting to look at cloud solutions in the light of BANI concerns. This framework offers an additional lens for understanding the limitations and possibilities of cloud solutions.

- Brittleness
  While cloud platforms appear robust, they can be fragile in the event of vendor lock-in or sudden changes in licensing policy. Organisations must therefore assess the resilience of their cloud strategy, especially when core processes become dependent on a single supplier.

- Anxiety
  The constant stream of updates and security issues can create unrest within the organisation. Transparent governance and clear agreements with the supplier are necessary to maintain trust.
- Non-linearity
  Minor incidents in cloud environments – such as a change in API logic – can have disproportionately large consequences. Managing dependencies therefore requires a proactive architectural vision and continuous monitoring.
- Incomprehensibility
  The complexity of multi-cloud landscapes makes it increasingly difficult for managers to maintain a clear overview. This increases the need for strong architectural principles and a governance model that reduces the essence to manageable decisions.

When we bring together infinite flow and the BANI framework, we create a double touchstone for cloud choices. On the one hand, solutions must offer the possibility of continuous, small iterations (infinite flow). On the other hand, they must be sufficiently resilient, transparent and understandable to function in a fragile and non-linear world (BANI).

Cloud solutions are therefore not a foregone conclusion, but a strategic choice that must be thoroughly tested. For secondary processes, standardised cloud solutions can often be efficient and cost-effective. For primary processes, where agility and differentiation are crucial, it may be wiser to invest in more modular systems that are better aligned with the principles of infinite flow and more resilient to the challenges of BANI.

If we bring together all these insights on cloud solutions and normalised systems on the one hand and infinite flow on the other hand, it becomes clear that they both can help us in our search for qualified pathways towards infinite flow, especially if we bring primary and secondary business processes in the equation too.

If we compare the principles of infinite flow with the principles of Normalised Systems (NS) as applied in NSX, and the principles of public cloud solutions we get the following results:

1. Micro-adjustments

   - Cloud: lots of functionalities as standard, but micro-adjustments are often limited to configuration. For real changes, one must wait for vendor releases or complex customisations.
   - NS: the architecture is specifically designed to avoid combinatorial effects, so that small adjustments always remain local and can be implemented predictably. This is exactly in line with infinite flow.

2. Pipelines of change

- Cloud: Continuous Integration/Continuous Delivery is usually limited to extensions or integrations. Core changes go through vendor cycles.
- NS: because the code always remains correct and rebuildable, changes can be incorporated fully automatically into pipelines. This allows one to create true continuous change.

3. Lock-in & agility

- Cloud: vendor lock-in is a structural risk. Functionality and release schedules are largely beyond your control.
- NS: the logic and data remain entirely under your own control. The architecture is vendor-neutral and completely transparent. This provides maximum strategic agility.

4. Complexity & comprehensibility (BANI: incomprehensible)

- Cloud: black box character; difficult to understand exactly how processes work.
- NS: completely transparent, systematically structured, and scientifically substantiated. Complexity remains manageable.

5. Evolution in a BANI world

- Cloud: strong, but vulnerable to unpredictable external changes (e.g. regulations, market, connection). Adaptation often takes longer.
- NS: designed to respond quickly and reliably to unexpected changes through continuous micro-adjustments.

Summarised

Where cloud solutions are strong in secondary processes (standardisation, unburdening), they are less suitable for bringing an organisation to an infinite flow state for its core processes. Normalised Systems, on the other hand, offer exactly that: a scientifically based way to make systems naturally suitable for continuous evolution in small, manageable steps.

In light of achieving a state of 'Infinite Flow' and being capable to smoothly adapt one's information technology solutions with the demands of the business, we strongly recommend using cloud solutions for supporting, non-differentiating processes. Normalised Systems are the best choice for core and primary processes where agility, micro-changes and strategic differentiation are crucial.

The reasoning set out above mainly concerns the limitations and possibilities of a system's technical layer. Two important points should be borne in mind here: (1) Building solutions based on NS still requires a thorough preliminary analysis that yields accurate requirements; (2) Building the solutions requires the availability of developers capable of building normalised systems. The benefits of evolvable core systems must be weighed against the effort required.

Final remarks

Dealing with change in enterprises is timeless and will remain of great importance in the future. We are confronted with change time and time again. Some changes occur in the environment in which our companies operate and are difficult or impossible to control. Some changes penetrate deep into the operational functioning of our organisations and have a major impact on the way we do things. Many people, both employees and entrepreneurs, view these changes with concern. They, and sometimes we too, wonder whether everything will turn out all right.

As a specialist in human resources and organisational development, we have been confronted with major and minor changes in the organisations we have worked for since the start of my professional career 36 years ago. Since 2008, we have been contributing to these changes as a designer and have started to develop the approach we have outlined in this book.

When you are in the midst of change, it seems as if every change is different. When you learn to look at it from a distance, you see that change in organisations contains patterns that recur. This is logical, because all enterprises are different manifestations of the same social system. And such a social system has laws that become apparent when the system has to adapt.

In 2018, on the occasion of DWT Consulting's 10th anniversary, the late Professor Emeritus René Bouwen spoke about the method as follows: "*I think it is a strong point in the method of DWT Consulting that the informational and the relational approach, how people interact with each other, can be combined. The combination of both the informational 'high tech', and the relational 'high touch' is really necessary to create a liveable future for people.*" (DWT Consulting, 2018).

We believe that it is very important to use a combination of methods when dealing with change in organisations. This method should guide people in their relationship to change, whereby it is important to connect with the relational aspect, which is at the core of social systems. In addition, it is important to transcend the purely relational by stabilising new ideas, concepts and ways of thinking so that they can form the basis for the new way of working.

Appreciative Inquiry taps into the relational aspect of the system and DEMO anchors the new ideas in models. Over the past ten years, this combination has demonstrated that in practice one plus one can indeed equal three.

All References in Alphabetical Order

Ardui J. M. (2023) *A Pathway to Humble Authority: Embracing Your Power Without Being Attached to It*. Jan Ardui Publications, Leuven.

Avital M., Boland R. J., Cooperrider D. L. (eds) (2008) *Designing Information and Organizations with a Positive Lens (Advances in Appreciative Inquiry, Vol. 2)*. Elsevier Science, Oxford.

AXELOS (2025) 'What is PRINCE2?'. Available at: https://www.prince2.com/uk/what-is-prince2 (Accessed: 29 October 2025).

Bailleur P. (2013) *Architect van je organisatie: Breng het beste in mensen naar boven*. LannooCampus, Leuven.

Bailleur P. (2015) *20 dingen die je wil lezen voor je organisatie naar een levend systeem transformeert*. E-book, Bailleur & Partners CommV, Sint-Katelijne-Waver.

Bailleur P. (2021) 'De link tussen LEAN en Living Systems', *Living Systems Coaching Blog*. Available at: https://www.philippebailleur.be/post/2015/07/31/de-link-tussen-lean-en-living-systems (Accessed: 29 October 2025).

Bailleur P., Meulmeester A. (2023) *Navigate: Een gids voor leiders in complexe tijden*. LannooCampus, Leuven.

Bain & Company (2020) 'CIOs say they want to avoid vendor lock-in, but most are still with one provider'. *Snap Chart*. (Accessed: 29 Oct 2025). https://www.bain.com/insights/cios-say-they-want-to-avoid-vendor-lock-in-snap-chart

Barrett F. J., Fry R. E. (2005) *Appreciative Inquiry: A Positive Approach to Building Cooperative Capacity*. Taos Institute Publications / Chagrin Falls, OH, in association with Berrett-Koehler Publishers, San Francisco CA.

Barrett F. J., Fry R. E., Wittockx H. (2011) *Appreciative Inquiry: Het Basiswerk*. LannooCampus, Leuven.

Bennett N., Lemoine G. J. (2014) 'What a difference a word makes: Understanding threats to performance in a VUCA world', *Business Horizons*, 57(3), pp. 311–317.

Bloch M., Blumberg S., Laartz J. (2012) 'Delivering large-scale IT projects on time, on budget, and on value', *McKinsey on Finance* 45 (Winter), The McKinsey Group, Boston MA. Available at: https://www.mckinsey.com/~/media/McKinsey/Business%20Functions/McKinsey%20Digital/Our%20Insights/Delivering%20large-scale%20IT-projects-on-time-on-budget-and-on-value/Delivering%20large-scale%20IT-projects-on-time-on-budget-and-on-value.pdf (Accessed: 29 October 2025).

J. De Winter, *Concise Guide to Enterprise Transformation*,
The Enterprise Engineering Series, https://doi.org/10.1007/978-3-032-29931-4

Bouwen G. (2010) *Leiden naar Talent en Bezieling: Energie van mensen verbinden tot Teamkracht*. LannooCampus, Leuven.

Bouwen R., De Witte K., Verboven J. (1996) *Organiseren en Veranderen: Handboek Organisatiepsychologie en -sociologie*. Acco, Leuven.

Bushe G. R., Kassam A. F. (2005) 'When Is Appreciative Inquiry Transformational? A Meta-Case Analysis'. *The Journal of Applied Behavioral Science*, 41(2), pp. 161–181.

Bushe G. R., Marshak R. J. (2009) 'Revisioning Organization Development: Diagnostic and Dialogic Premises and Patterns of Practice', *The Journal of Applied Behavioral Science*, 45 (3), pp. 348–368.

Bushe, G. R. 2013. "Generative Process, Generative Outcome: The Transformational Potential of Appreciative Inquiry." In *Constructive Discourse and Human Organization*, edited by D. L. Cooperrider, D. P. Zandee, L. N. Godwin, M. Avital & B. Boland, *Advances in Appreciative Inquiry*, Vol. 4, pp. 89–113. Bingley: Emerald Group Publishing.

Bushe, G. R. & Marshak, R. J. (2013). Dialogic organization development. In G. R. Bushe & R. J. Marshak (Eds.), *Dialogic Organization Development: The Theory and Practice of Transformational Change* (pp. 1-56). Oakland, CA: Berrett-Koehler Publishers.

Bushe G. R., Marshak R. J. (2015) *Dialogic Organization Development: The Theory and Practice of Transformational Change*. Berrett-Koehler Publishers, San Francisco CA.

Bushe G. R. (2020) *The Dynamics of Generative Change: Exploring the Patterns, Principles, and Practices of Transformational Change*. BMI Publishing, Vancouver BC.

Cascio J. (2022) 'Human responses to a BANI world'. Medium. Available at: https://medium.com/@cascio/human-responses-to-a-bani-world-fb... (Accessed: 29 October 2025).

Cho W. S., Chan A. (2015) 'An integrative framework of comparing SaaS adoption for core and non-core business operations: An empirical study on Hong Kong industries', *Information Systems Frontiers*, 17(3), pp. 629–644.

Cooperrider D. L., Srivastva S. (1987) 'Appreciative Inquiry in Organizational Life', *Research in Organizational Change and Development*, Vol. 1, pp. 129–169. JAI Press, Greenwich CT.

Cooperrider D. L., Whitney D. (2001) *A Positive Revolution in Change: Appreciative Inquiry*. In: Cooperrider D. L., Sorensen P. F. Jr., Whitney D., Yeager T. F. (eds) *Appreciative Inquiry: An Emerging Direction for Organization Development*. Stipes Publishing, Champaign IL, pp. 9–29.

Cooperrider D. L., Whitney D., Stavros J. M. (2003) *The Appreciative Inquiry Handbook: The First in a Series of AI Workbooks for Leaders of Change*. Lakeshore Communications / Berrett-Koehler Publishers, San Francisco CA.

Cooperrider D. L., Whitney D., Stavros J. M. (2008) *The Appreciative Inquiry Handbook: For Leaders of Change*. 2nd edn. Berrett-Koehler Publishers, San Francisco CA.

Creasey T., Taylor T. (2014) *Best Practices in Change Management*. Prosci Learning Center Publications, Loveland CO.

De Haan E., Beerends E. (2012) *Organisatie-ontwikkeling met Theory U: Hoe komen we de bocht door? Werkvormen en cases*. Uitgeverij Boom Nelissen, Amsterdam.

De Winter J. (2015) *Initiating Enterprise Transformation Using Appreciative Inquiry*. Paper presented at the *World Appreciative Inquiry Conference (WAIC 2015)*, Johannesburg, South Africa, 7–10 July 2015.

De Winter J. (2015) *Re-engineering the Design Phase of Appreciative Inquiry*. Paper presented at the *World Appreciative Inquiry Conference (WAIC 2015)*, Johannesburg, South Africa, 7–10 July 2015.

Deloitte (2013) *The Outsourcing Handbook: A Guide to Outsourcing*. Deloitte Touche Tohmatsu Limited, London. Available at: https://www.deloitte.co.uk/makeconnections/assets/pdf/the-outsourcing-handbook-a-guide-to-outsourcing.pdf (Accessed: 29 October 2025).

Dietz J.L.G (2006) *Enterprise Ontology : Theory and Methodology*. Springer, Berlin Heidelberg.

Dietz J. L. G., Mulder H. B. F. (2020) *Enterprise Ontology: A Human-Centric Approach to Understanding the Essence of Organisation*. Springer, Cham.

Dietz J. L. G., Mulder H. B. F. (2024) *Enterprise Ontology: A Human-Centric Approach to Understanding the Essence of Organisation*. Springer, Cham.

Dietz J. L. G., Mulder H. B. F. (2025) *Enterprise Design Fundamentals: Settling an Enterprise Business and Devising the Enterprise Organisation*. Springer, Cham.

DWT Consulting. (2018) 10 years DWT Consulting. Available at: https://www.linkedin.com/in/dwtconsulting/ and https://vimeo.com/257137630. (Accessed: 29 October 2025).

Felipe Jr., R. (2025) *The role of school heads in a Brittle, Anxious, Nonlinear and Incomprehensible (BANI) environment: The case of leadership buoyancy*, (SSRN Working paper)

Geneca (2011) *Doomed from the Start? Why a Majority of Business and IT Teams Anticipate Their Software Development Projects Will Fail*. Geneca, Oakbrook Terrace IL.

Available at: https://www.geneca.com/why-up-to-75-of-software-projects-will-fail/ (Accessed: 29 October 2025).

Gergen K. J. (1994) *Toward Transformation in Social Knowledge*. 2nd edn. Sage Publications, London.

Gergen K. J. (2022) *An Invitation to Social Construction: Co-Creating the Future*. 4th edn. Sage Publications, London.

Gold J. (2025) 'CIOs are rethinking how they use public cloud services—here's why'. *CIO.com*. Available at: cio.com. (Accessed: 29 Oct 2025).

Hayes J. (2007) *The Theory and Practice of Change Management*. 2nd edn. Palgrave Macmillan, Basingstoke.

Hitchins D. K. (2009) *Systems Engineering: A 21st Century Systems Methodology*. John Wiley & Sons, Chichester.

Habermas J. (1981) *Theorie des kommunikativen Handelns*. Suhrkamp Verlag, Frankfurt am Main.

Habermas J. (1995) 'Kommunikatives Handeln und detranszendentalisierte Vernunft'. In: *Nachmetaphysisches Denken II: Aufsätze und Repliken*. Suhrkamp Verlag, Frankfurt am Main, pp. 142–170.

Habermas J. (1995 [2017]) 'Communicative Action and Detranscendentalised Reason'. In: *Post-Metaphysical Thinking II: Essays and Replies*. Polity Press, Cambridge, pp. 142–170.

Hiatt J. M., Creasey T. J. (2012) *Change Management: The People Side of Change*. Prosci Learning Center Publications, Loveland CO.

Hiatt J. M. (2006) *ADKAR: A Model for Change in Business, Government and Our Community*. Prosci Learning Center Publications, Loveland CO.

Holmes, O. W. (1858). *The autocrat of the breakfast-table*. Boston: Phillips, Sampson and Company.

Hoogendijk C. (2015) *Appreciative Inquiries of the 3.0 Kind: How Do We Connect, Share and Co-create for Tomorrow's Human Wholeness*. Center for Appreciative Inquiry / Kessels & Smit, Utrecht.

Hoogervorst J. A. P. (2009) *Enterprise Governance and Enterprise Engineering*. Springer, Berlin Heidelberg.

Hoogervorst J. A. P. (2009) 'Enterprise architecture in enterprise engineering', *EMISA Journal*, 3(2), pp. 4–24.

Hoogervorst, J. A. P. (2012). "On the Realisation of Strategic Success – A Paradigm Shift Needed: Enterprise Governance and Enterprise Engineering as Essential Concepts." In *Proceedings of the 4th Enterprise Engineering Working Conference (EEWC) Industry Track*, Delft, The Netherlands, May 7-8, 2012.

Hoogervorst J. A. P. (2017) *Foundations of Enterprise Governance and Enterprise Engineering*: Presenting the Employee-Centric Theory of Organisation. Springer, Cham.

Hoogervorst J. A. P. (2018) *Practising Enterprise Governance and Enterprise Engineering: Preparing Enterprises for the Digital Age*. Springer, Cham.

Hoogervorst J. A. P. (2025) *Enterprise Engineering: Shortcomings of the Dominant Conceptual Focus*. Unpublished manuscript, Delft University of Technology, Delft.

Hoogervorst J.A.P. (Unpublished) *De tragedie: hoe het onbenul het voor het zeggen kreeg – Over de onbenulisering van organisaties en de overheid*, To be published.

Hovelynck J., De Weerdt S., Dewulf A. (eds) (2006) *Relationeel organiseren: Samen leren en werken in en tussen organisaties*. LannooCampus, Leuven.

ISO/IEC/IEEE (2011). *ISO/IEC/IEEE 42010:2011 Systems and software engineering — Architecture description*. ISO, Geneva.

Jamali G., Oveisi M. (2016) 'A Study on Project Management Based on PMBOK and PRINCE2', *Modern Applied Science*, 10(6), pp. 142–152.

Johnson J., Mulder H. B. F. (2016) *Chaos Chronicles: Focusing on Failures and Possible Improvements in IT Projects*. The Standish Group International, Inc., Boston MA.

Johnson J., Mulder H. B. F. (2020) *Endless Modernization: How Infinite Flow Keeps Software Fresh*. The Standish Group International, Inc., Boston MA. Available at: https://www.rocketsoftware.com/sites/default/files/resource_files/endless-modernization-how-infinite-flow-keeps-software-fresh-report.pdf (Accessed: 29 October 2025).

Kruse K. (2025) 'Forget VUCA. The world is BANI now', *Forbes*, 3 Feb. Available at: https://www.forbes.com/sites/kevinkruse/2025/02/03/forget-vuca-bani-is-the-new-framework-world/?sh=... (Accessed: 29 October 2025).

Kim D. H. (1993) 'The Link between Individual and Organizational Learning', *MIT Sloan Management Review*, 35(1), pp. 37–50.

Kim D. H. (2001) *Organizing for Learning: Strategies for Knowledge Creation and Enduring Change*. Pegasus Communications, Waltham MA.

Kotter J. P. (2012) *Leading Change*. With a new preface by the author. Harvard Business Review Press, Boston MA.

Laloux F. (2014) *Reinventing Organizations: A Guide to Creating Organizations Inspired by the Next Stage of Human Consciousness*. Nelson Parker, Brussels.

Maes G. (2014) *Verborgen krachten in de organisatie: een politiek model van organisatieverandering*. Acco, Leuven / Den Haag.

Maier, M.W., & Rechtin, E. (2009). *The Art of Systems Architecting*, 3rd edn. CRC Press, Boca Raton, FL.

Mannaert H., Verelst J. (2009) *Normalized Systems: Re-creating Information Technology Based on Laws for Software Evolvability*. Koppa, Kermt.

Mannaert H., Verelst J., De Bruyn P. (2016) *Normalized Systems Theory: From Foundations for Evolvable Software Toward a General Theory for Evolvable Design*. Koppa Digitale Media, Kermt.

Mannaert H., Peremans H. (2020) *Grondslagen van de Engineering*. Koppa, Hasselt.

Marshak R. J. (2020) *Dialogic Process Consulting: Generative Meaning-making in Action*. Berrett-Koehler Publishers, San Francisco CA.

Masselink R., de Jong J. C. (2013) *Handboek Appreciative Inquiry: Sociaal Constructionisme in de Dagelijkse Praktijk*. Boom Nelissen, Amsterdam.

Matos S., Lopes E. (2013) 'Prince2 or PMBOK – A Question of Choice', *Procedia Technology*, 9, pp. 787–794.

Menaria, N. (2024) *Comparative analysis of VUCA and BANI frameworks*, *International Journal for Multidisciplinary Research (IJFMR)*, 6(2), pp. 1–10.

Morgan G. (2006) *Images of Organization*. Sage Publications, Thousand Oaks CA.

Mulder H. B. F. (2006) *Eenvoud in Complexiteit: Een Constructivistisch Perspectief op Organisatieontwikkeling*. Lemma, Den Haag.

National Geographic Institute (Belgium). (2025). *Over het NGI*. Available at: https://ngi.be/over-ngi/ (Accessed: 29 October 2025).

NIMO Project Management Instituut (n.d.) 'About us'. Available at: https://www.nimo.nl/en/home-english/ (Accessed: 29 October 2025).

NSX bv. (2025). *Breaking software barriers: Software evolvability and bounded change impacts*. Available at: https://normalizedsystems.org/ (Accessed: 29 October 2025).

Op 't Land M. (2008) *Applying Architecture and Ontology to the Splitting and Allying of Enterprises*. PhD thesis, Delft University of Technology, Delft.

Oxford Languages. 2025. "Dialogue." *Oxford Learner's Dictionaries*. Oxford University Press. Available at:

https://www.oxfordlearnersdictionaries.com/definition/english/dialogue (Accessed 29 October 2025).

Project Management Institute (2024) *2024 Annual Report*. Project Management Institute, New town Square PA. Available at: https://www.flipsnack.com/79D666ED75E/pmi-2024-annual-report/full-view.html (Accessed: 29 October 2025).

Provan K. G., Kenis P. (2008) 'Modes of Network Governance: Structure, Management, and Effectiveness', *Journal of Public Administration Research and Theory*, 18(2), pp. 229–252.

Rozanski, N., & Woods, E. (2012). *Software Systems Architecture: Working with Stakeholders Using Viewpoints and Perspectives*, 2nd edn. Addison-Wesley, Boston, MA.

Sarkar A. (2016) 'We live in a VUCA world: The importance of responsible leadership', *Development and Learning in Organizations*, 30(3), pp. 9–12.

Senge P. M. (1990) *The Fifth Discipline: The Art and Practice of the Learning Organization*. Doubleday/Currency, New York NY.

Schön, D. A. 1993. "Generative Metaphor: A Perspective on Problem-Setting in Social Policy." In *Metaphor and Thought*, 2nd edn, edited by A. Ortony, pp. 137–163. Cambridge University Press, Cambridge.

Schönfeld H. J.J. (2025) *Dancing with Change & Fluidity: From Organization to Organizing*. Inspinity BV, Amsterdam.

Snoeck, M. & Dedene, G. (1998). Existence dependency: The key to semantic integrity between structural and behavioural aspects of object types. *IEEE Transactions on Software Engineering*, 24(4), 278–297.

Snowden D. J., Boone M. E. (2007) 'A leader's framework for decision making', *Harvard Business Review*, 85(11), pp. 68–76.

Snowden D. (2020) *Cynefin – Weaving Sense-Making into the Fabric of Our World*. Cognitive Edge-The Cynefin Co., London.

Spinnaker Support (2023) 'Composable ERP: Break free from vendor lock-ins'. *Blog*. (Accessed: 29 Oct 2025).
https://www.spinnakersupport.com/blog/2023/11/28/composable-erp/

Stroh D. P. (2015) *Systems Thinking for Social Change: A Practical Guide to Solving Complex Problems, Avoiding Unintended Consequences, and Achieving Lasting Results*. Chelsea Green Publishing, White River Junction VT.

The Standish Group International, Inc. (2016) *CHAOS Report 2016: The Winning Hand*. The Standish Group International, Inc., Boston MA. Available at:

https://www.standishgroup.com/sample_research_files/CHAOSReport2015-Final.pdf (Accessed: 29 October 2025).

The Standish Group International, Inc. (2022) *CHAOS Report 2022: Beyond Infinity*. The Standish Group International, Inc., Boston MA. ISBN 978-1-733-59822-4.

Tshetshe Z. (2025) 'Recognising "Being" in the BANI world', *International Journal for Multidisciplinary Research*, 7(1), pp. 1-9.

van Aken J. E. (2013) 'Design Science: Valid Knowledge for Socio-technical System Design', in Helfert M., Donnellan B. (eds) *Design Science: Perspectives from Europe*, Communications in Computer and Information Science, vol. 388. Springer, Cham, pp. 1–13.

Van der Stock E., Verhaert R., Mulder H. (2018) *Heb jij je (beleids)informatie en technologie onder controle? Het spanningsveld tussen IT'ers en niet-IT'ers*. Politeia nv, Brussel.

van Haren Publishing (2010) *IT Outsourcing: RFP Process and Supplier Selection*. van Haren Publishing, 's-Hertogenbosch. (Internal industry guide; statement cited: "The four essential documents in the supplier selection process are the RFI, the RFP, the request for BAFO and the contract".)

Weinberg G. M. (1975) *An Introduction to General Systems Thinking*. John Wiley & Sons, New York.

Whiting R. (2023) 'CIOs weigh the new economics and risks of cloud lock-in'. *CIO.com*. Available at: cio.com. (Accessed: 29 Oct 2025). https://www.cio.com/article/1257417/cios-weigh-the-new-economics-and-risks-of-cloud-lock-in

Whitney D., Trosten-Bloom A. (2003) *The Power of Appreciative Inquiry: A Practical Guide to Positive Change*. Berrett-Koehler Publishers, San Francisco CA.

Wikipedia (2025) *Systems theory*. Available at: https://en.wikipedia.org/wiki/Systems_theory (Accessed: 29 October 2025).

Wikipedia (2025) *Enterprise Engineering*. Available at: https://en.wikipedia.org/wiki/Enterprise_engineering (Accessed: 29 October 2025).

Wikipedia (2025) Appreciative Inquiry. Available at: https://en.wikipedia.org/wiki/Appreciative_inquiry (Accessed: 29 October 2025).

Wikipedia (2025) *Responsibility assignment matrix*. Available at: https://en.wikipedia.org/wiki/Responsibility_assignment_matrix (Accessed: 29 October 2025).

World Bank (2018) *Negotiations and Best and Final Offer (BAFO): Procurement Guidance – First Edition*. The World Bank, Washington DC. Available at: https://thedocs.worldbank.org/.../ProcurementGuidanceNegotiationandBestFinalOffer.pdf (Accessed: 29 October 2025).